The Spirit of Digital Capitalism

For my father, Jean-Pierre, whose love of capitalism and incredible generosity have subsidized a good deal of my existence.

The Spirit of
Digital Capitalism

Jenny Huberman

polity

First published in 2022 by Polity Press

Polity Press
65 Bridge Street
Cambridge CB2 1UR, UK

Polity Press
111 River Street
Hoboken, NJ 07030, USA

ISBN-13: 978-1-5095-5395-2
ISBN-13: 978-1-5095-5396-9(pb)

A catalogue record for this book is available from the British Library.

Library of Congress Control Number: 2022933268

Typeset in 10.5 on 12pt Plantin MT
by Fakenham Prepress Solutions, Fakenham, Norfolk NR21 8NL
Printed and bound in the UK by CPI Group (UK) Ltd, Croydon

The publisher has used its best endeavours to ensure that the URLs for external websites referred to in this book are correct and active at the time of going to press. However, the publisher has no responsibility for the websites and can make no guarantee that a site will remain live or that the content is or will remain appropriate.

Every effort has been made to trace all copyright holders, but if any have been overlooked the publisher will be pleased to include any necessary credits in any subsequent reprint or edition.

For further information on Polity, visit our website:
politybooks.com

Contents

Detailed Contents   vi
Acknowledgments   viii
Prologue: An Occupational Hazard   x

Introduction: The Digital Age and the Spirits of Capitalism   1

1 The Spirit of Competition: Crowdsourcing through Incentive Competitions   20
2 The Spirit of Collaboration: Crowdsourcing through Communities   43
3 The Spirit of the Game: Smartphone Apps and the Digital Extraction of Surplus Value   65
4 In the Spirit of Convenience: Amazon Go and Surveillance Capitalism   81
5 The Spirit of the Gift: The Work of Techno-philanthropy   100

Conclusion: The Spirit and Contradictions of Digital Capitalism   127

Notes   147
References   174
Index   186

Detailed Contents

Acknowledgments   viii
Prologue: An Occupational Hazard   x

Introduction: The Digital Age and the Spirits of Capitalism   1
 Digital capitalism   4
 The spirits of capitalism   7
 Silicon Valley and the spirit of digital capitalism   11
 Overview of the chapters   16
 A note on ideology   18

1 The Spirit of Competition: Crowdsourcing through
  Incentive Competitions   20
 Unleashing the spirit of competition, saving the world, and
  celebrating smartness   22
 Leveling the playing field and accelerating progress   27
 You pay only the winner!   29
 HeroX and platform capitalism   34
 Protecting competition and nurturing networks   37
 Conclusion: democratizing innovation or exacerbating inequality?   41

2 The Spirit of Collaboration: Crowdsourcing through
  Communities   43
 The community in society   44
 Wired to collaborate   47
 Putting community crowdsourcing to work   50
 "The accidental business"   50
 Community crowdsourcing goes corporate   55
 Conclusion: the wealth of networks or corporations?   59

3   The Spirit of the Game: Smartphone Apps and the Digital
     Extraction of Surplus Value   65
     Earning with apps   67
     Blurring the boundaries and gaming the tasks   70
     Multiplying moments and multiplying millions   73
     Conclusion: free time or free labor?   77

4   In the Spirit of Convenience: Amazon Go and Surveillance
     Capitalism   81
     Amazon Go   82
     Surveillance capitalism   83
     The ideology of convenience   87
     Conclusion: Ideology, extraction, and the convenience economy   95

5   The Spirit of the Gift: The Work of Techno-philanthropy 100
     Hyper-agents   102
     MarketWorld   104
     Techno-solutionism can save the world   106
     The business of giving   110
     Teaching the techno-elite how to give: The Silicon Valley Social
         Venture Fund   113
     Blurring the lines between purpose and profit: impact investing
         and social enterprise   117
     The Giving Pledge: making moral agents   120
     Conclusion: the power of the gift   124

Conclusion: The Spirit and Contradictions of Digital Capitalism   127
     The spirit of digital capitalism   128
     Competition and collaboration   132
     Creativity and automation, liberation and surveillance   135
     Techno-solutionism and social salvation   137
     Charity and avarice   138
     The consequences of the cultural contradictions of digital
         capitalism   139
     Glimmers of hope   145

Notes   147
References   174
Index   186

Acknowledgments

I'm often amazed and admittedly envious when I read the acknowledgment sections of other authors' books. They frequently span pages of thanks, and I find myself marveling at how these authors managed to get so many people to read and engage with their work. I live in a lonelier intellectual universe but, because of this, the debts I owe to the people who have contributed to my thinking and writing about digital capitalism are especially significant. This book would never have been written had it not been for Ipshita Ghosh, a brilliant young anthropologist whose work on entrepreneurship and digital capitalism in India is already taking the field of economic anthropology by storm. Ipshita played a pivotal role in inspiring me to write about capitalism in the digital age when she suggested I submit a paper for the Society for Economic Anthropology's conference on the convenience economy. Subsequently, Ipshita has offered much constructive feedback on my work, and she has helped me expand my anthropological universe and thinking.

I have also benefited immensely from the camaraderie and intellectual companionship of Zhongjin Li, a brilliant economist at UMKC. Zhongjin was generous and tolerant enough to cross disciplinary lines and form an informal reading group with me. Though I still think and write like an anthropologist (or maybe even sociologist), her analytical rigor and insights into the dynamics of digital capitalism have taught me an immense amount. Zhongjin has also been a generous reader of my work.

Kelly McKowen offered very helpful feedback on chapter 3, and the anonymous reviewers who engaged with this manuscript provided feedback that was unusually constructive and thorough. A special thank you goes to Jonathan Skerrett, one of the most thoughtful, intellectually engaged, and supportive editors I have ever worked with, and to the rest of the Polity team who have helped steer this manuscript into the world. Finally, I want to thank my family. Without you, my spirit would not be able to soar. I love you always and forever.

Prologue: An Occupational Hazard

I am a cultural anthropologist by training, and in all the research and writing I have done so far, I have tried my best to avoid what, among anthropologists, is widely considered to be an occupational hazard: passing judgment and critique on the people who we study and wish to understand. In anthropology, the idea of cultural relativism teaches us to approach our research subjects with tolerance and curiosity. Instead of condemning their beliefs and practices as wrong, we aim to show how they make sense within the cultural context of their lives. This is a message I take very seriously, and it is certainly a lesson I routinely impart to my students.

And yet, in this book, I embrace the hazard. This book is critical, it has an argument to make, and it explores the various ideologies that sustain the era of digital capitalism with the hopes of ultimately helping to dismantle them. I wrote this book because I was frustrated and pissed off. Admittedly, this may have had something to do with being forced into social exile for a year by a global pandemic that still won't go away. However, the real source of my ire stems from coming to recognize, yet again, that our world and society could be so much better. As many of the techno-enthusiasts in this book proclaim, we have the science and technology at hand to solve some of our most pressing problems. We have enough wealth on the planet that, were it distributed differently, we could all live secure and dignified lives. We have the potential for so many things, and yet this potential is continually co-opted and undermined by the imperatives of an economic system that puts the production of profit above the wellness of human beings.

Thus, if I appear a bit cranky in the pages that follow, I hope you will forgive me, and I hope you will remember that it is for good reason. In some small way, not only do I want this book to help us see through the beliefs that keep us wed to a system that does so many people harm, but I also hope it might inspire more creative thinking about what kind of "human economy" (Hart, Laville, and Cattani 2010) can be developed to put people, instead of profits, first.

Introduction: The Digital Age and the Spirits of Capitalism

> If, contrary to prognoses regularly heralding its collapse, capitalism has not only survived, but ceaselessly extended its empire, it is because it could rely on a number of shared representations – capable of guiding action – and justifications, which present it as an acceptable and even desirable order of things: the only possible order, or the best of all possible orders.
>
> Luc Boltanski and Eve Chiapello, *The New Spirit of Capitalism* (2007: 10)

One of the things I love most about being a social scientist is that in the course of pursuing one research project it is almost inevitable that the idea for another one will arise. Such is the case with this book. The idea for this book emerged as I was conducting research on the transhumanist movement in the United States. Transhumanists are committed to using science and technology to overcome the biological limitations of human beings and usher in an enhanced posthuman species and society. As futurists and techno-utopians, transhumanists share a firm belief that science and technology can be used to solve our most intractable problems. But when it comes to other ideological commitments, they are divided. Some transhumanists, for instance, believe democratic socialism provides the best way to ensure that the benefits of science and technology will be shared by all. By contrast, the most influential and outspoken members of the movement, and those who have emerged as some of Silicon Valley's most powerful techno-elites, proclaim free-market capitalism is the only economic system that can efficiently and effectively realize the promise of a radically enhanced future.

In the spirit of "laying my cards on the table," I will confess that my sympathies lie more with the first group, that is, to the extent that I am interested in exploring the possibilities of democratic socialism rather than ushering in a new and enhanced posthuman species. But it was this latter group of transhumanists, those devoted to the promise of capitalism, which led me towards the questions I examine in this book. As I traced the ways transhumanists defend and promote their faith in the free-market system, despite mounting evidence that inequality and economic suffering are rapidly on the rise, I began to ask myself what are the dominant justifications that are used to support and sustain capital accumulation in the current techno-logical age?[1] For those who have made their fortunes by investing in new technologies, and for those who deploy new technologies with the hopes of enhancing corporate profits, what ideas and representa-tions do they use to portray capitalism as the "only possible" or even "best of all possible" economic orders?

Taking these questions as a departure point, in this book I synthesize two approaches to the study of contemporary capitalism with the aim of ultimately demonstrating how social life in the digital age is permeated by a novel set of cultural contradictions. On the one hand, I explore how digital technologies are making possible new forms of capital accumulation, extraction, and domination. On the other hand, I examine the ideological formations that are used to justify the machinations of digital capitalism. As anthropologists and sociologists have long observed, the reproduction of capitalism is never just an economic or technological affair: the reproduction of capitalism requires and gives rise to sets of beliefs that enable its participants to justify and legitimate their participation in "the system." And yet the meanings and ideas that sustain the accumu-lation of capital, that provide justification for the ongoing circulation of M–C–M' as the organizing logic of the capitalist economy, can vary quite considerably across different times and places.[2] As the social and technological composition of capital changes, so too does its "spirit."

This book seeks to explore the spirit of digital capitalism as it is being developed and deployed by business gurus, entrepreneurs, venture capitalists and philanthropists in the contemporary United States.[3] In the pages that follow, I demonstrate how the spirit of digital capitalism justifies and legitimates new forms of capital accumulation, extraction, and domination. I argue that it does this not just by valorizing the spirit of competition, as has long been the case in the capitalist past, or by extolling the role that capitalism plays in the protection of freedom and democracy, another old "trick" from the capitalist "playbook." In addition to drawing upon both of these long-standing and well-examined ideological "moves," the spirit of digital capitalism makes new claims about the way digital technologies contribute to the common good, foster collaboration and connectivity, and render life more convenient, even if this convenience comes at the expense of once cherished values such as privacy and liberty. Thus the central argument of this book is that the spirit of digital capitalism is indeed Janus-faced, and it reveals a new set of cultural contradictions at the heart of contemporary American society.

The idea that American capitalism is beset by cultural contradictions is hardly a novel one. In his seminal work, *The Cultural Contradictions of Capitalism*, sociologist Daniel Bell argued that "the elective affinity" between capitalism and Protestantism, which Max Weber had famously described, no longer held. He proposed that by the latter half of the twentieth century, with the transition from Fordism to the regime of flexible accumulation, a key contradiction had emerged between the imperatives of the capitalist economic order and the values promoted in the cultural "realm." While post-Fordist capitalism still required "ascetic," disciplined subjects who were driven by rational calculation, a dogged devotion to one's work, and acquisitiveness, Bell observed that the cultural sphere was promoting hedonism, consumption, and an "unrestrained self" (Bell 1996 [1976]). By contrast, subsequent scholars have proposed that Bell's analysis no longer rings true and the cultural contradictions he identified over forty years ago have "now been resolved." "The new capitalism," as Eran Fisher has proposed, "does not reject, but quite the contrary – it harnesses self-realization, personal expression, and hedonistic impulses into its mode of operation" (Fisher 2010: 218).

Fisher is not wrong in suggesting that contemporary capitalism "harnesses" the pursuit of self-realization, personal expression, and even hedonistic enjoyment "into its mode of operation." As will be seen in the ensuing chapters, the captains of the digital age promote the idea that digital technologies can unleash the heroes within us all, that work can be a labor of love and means of self and social fulfillment, and that with the aid of new technologies, consumer desires and appetites can be conveniently satisfied without any interfering "friction." However, this book argues that, instead of resolving the cultural contradictions of capitalism, the spirit of digital capitalism reveals a new and deeper set of contradictions at the heart of contemporary American society.

By focusing closely on the pronouncements of its promoters, the chapters in this book will demonstrate that the spirit of digital capitalism utilizes a language that can only be described as double-speak. The spirit of digital capitalism tells us to value our freedom but then demands we sacrifice our privacy. It speaks liberation in the name of "convenience" at the same time as it subjects us to constant digital surveillance. It promises to democratize opportunity but then celebrates situations where the "winners take all" and a new cadre of global elite walk the earth like omnipotent giants. In one moment, it tells us that new forms of technology can unleash the innate human spirit of competition in ever more effective ways. In the next breath, it explains how these very same technologies can harness "our better angels" and engender unprecedented forms of social cooperation. The spirit of digital capitalism celebrates the way new technologies enable corporations to hire "flexible" labor on the cheap, and then it congratulates the techno-elite for their generosity and efforts to achieve social uplift and global "salvation" through philanthropy and "impact investing." Indeed, one of the goals of this book is to consider what the consequences of living with these contradictions might be. However, before moving on to such considerations, I need to first discuss the concepts and questions that frame this analysis, and I want to explain how I have attempted to unearth this rather elusive object of inquiry.

Digital capitalism

Capitalism is an economic system oriented towards the perpetual production of profit. As Robert Heilbroner writes, "the use of wealth in various concrete forms, not as an end in itself, but as a means for gathering more wealth" is what renders capitalism distinct from other social formations premised upon the extraction of a surplus (Heilbroner 1985: 34–5). In the digital age, this remains just as true. The term "digital capitalism" does not refer to a fundamental shift in the logic of our economic system but rather is meant to illuminate the ways digital technologies have become increasingly central to processes of capital accumulation and new forms of ideological justification.[4] The scholarly literature on digital capitalism asks how digital technologies are giving rise to new forms of capital accumulation, extraction, and domination. In turn, how are these technologies "being colonized by the familiar workings of the market system" and therefore being used to enhance elite power (Schiller 1999)?

In his groundbreaking book *Digital Capitalism: Networking the Global Market System*, media theorist Dan Schiller argues that digital technologies and information networks such as the internet "are generalizing the social and cultural range of the capitalist economy as never before" and have given rise to a "new epoch."[5] According to Schiller this is not something to celebrate. He warns:

> As it comes under the sway of an expansionary market logic, the Internet is catalyzing an epochal political-economic transition towards what I call digital capitalism – and towards changes that, for much of the population, are unpropitious . . . The architects of digital capitalism have pursued one major objective: to develop an economy-wide network that can support an ever-growing range of intracorporate and intercorporate business processes. (Schiller 1999: xvii–1)

More recently, Jathan Sadowski has explored "how digital capitalism is extracting data, controlling our lives, and taking over the world." He too argues that the problem is not so much the technologies themselves but the ends towards which they are being put, namely to enhance "corporate technocratic power" (Sadowski 2020: 5). In Sadowski's estimation, digital capitalism doesn't represent an epochal shift in the development of capitalism. "The operations of capital," he writes, "are adapting to the digital age, while also still maintaining the same essential features of exclusion, extraction and exploitation" (ibid.: 50). And yet, while Sadowski argues that digital capitalism still hinges upon the essential features of exclusion, extraction, and exploitation, he also shows how the deployment of "smart technologies" has turned new materials – such as data – into highly sought-after resources that are now central to processes of capital accumulation and extraction.

Shoshana Zuboff echoes this finding. She proposes that if the secret of profit hinged upon the expropriation of surplus labor during the period of industrial capitalism, as Marx famously argued, today the secret of profit hinges upon the extraction of "behavioral surplus." Companies like Google and Amazon reap unprecedented profits by collecting and selling our behavior/data to advertisers. Moreover, Zuboff proposes that these data are always collected with an eye towards enhancing profits in the future. "Surveillance capitalism," as she coins it, is animated by the "prediction imperative." "Its aim is to produce behavior that reliably, definitively, and certainly leads to desired commercial results" (Zuboff 2019: 201) and it relies upon a host of digital "herding" and "nudging" practices to do so.

A number of other scholars have also demonstrated how data collection can be used by corporations and governing bodies alike to establish greater power and control over citizens, particularly the poor (Taylor and Broeders 2015; O'Neil 2016; Cheney-Lippold 2017; Eubanks 2017; Fourcade and Healy 2017).[6] Their work shows how big data is being used to generate "classification situations" that come to intimately, and often detrimentally, shape people's life chances in product and service markets. Fourcade and Healy, for instance, argue that this has led to a "new economy of moral judgment, where outcomes are experienced as morally deserved positions based on prior good actions and good tastes, as measured and classified by this new infrastructure of data collection and analysis" (Fourcade and Healy 2017: 9). Other scholars go even further in their critiques by proposing that data collection and surveillance technologies are generating new forms of "techno" or "digital colonialism," particularly in the Global South where "US multinationals exercise imperial control over the digital ecosystem" and are able to use this control to extract resources and rents while simultaneously "undermining local development" (Couldry and Mejias 2019; Kwet 2019: 3, 7; Madianou 2019; Birch 2020).

While numerous scholars agree that data has become central to processes of capital accumulation, even likening it to the "new oil" (Srnicek 2017), and while they have done much to enhance our understanding of the manifold ways "data is used to create value" (Sadowski 2019: 5), many others point out that in the era of digital capitalism, the exploitation of labor power, or what Nick Dyer-Witheford refers to as the "cyber-proletariat," still plays a pivotal role (Dyer-Witheford 2015). As Mary L. Gray and Siddharth Suri chronicle in their timely study *Ghost Work: How to Stop Silicon Valley from Building a Global Underclass*, the very algorithms used to keep the wheels of digital capitalism spinning rely upon a hidden population of ghost workers who are paid through crowdsourcing labor platforms like MTurk to perform piecemeal tasks such as captioning photos or flagging and removing inappropriate internet content (Gray and Suri 2019). Indeed, the rise of "platform capitalism" has not only fueled the greed and enthusiasm for on-demand labor that is flexible and cheap (Srnicek 2017). It has also enabled companies like Uber and Lyft to further control and regulate labor markets while simultaneously evading the more costly contractual obligations of being a formal employer (Calo and Rosenblat 2017; Rosenblat 2018; Palmer 2020). Although online labor platforms perpetuate the idea that workers are "'independent contractors' or 'digital nomads' who epitomize the neoliberal ideal of flexibility, freedom and autonomy," in reality such platforms often perpetuate a form of labor bondage by "locking their workers in through the provision of immovable assets such as reputation scores, client contacts, and intermediary payment structures" (McKenzie 2020: 6). Moreover, a growing number of scholars propose that in the era of digital capitalism, profits are accrued not only through the exploitation of wage laborers who are bound to digital platforms, but also through the expropriation of "free" or "unpaid labor." As Andreas Wittel contends, "one of the key challenges of digital capitalism" is to consider how "activities that blossom outside of wage-based relations and other forms of commodified labor" contribute to processes of capital accumulation and extraction (Wittel 2017: 68).[7]

Much of the scholarship on digital capitalism thus suggests that despite the enthusiasm of its proponents, the digital infrastructures that mediate contemporary forms of capital accumulation are not in fact leading to a world of greater opportunity where people are free to be "the captains of their own industry" and where information, innovation, and opportunity is happily "democratized," leading to a rich, intellectual commons for all (Benkler 2006; Von Hippel 2006; Sundararajan 2016). Instead, digital capitalism is leading to a world of greater precarity and inequality where everyday people are treated as means rather than ends by a small, yet increasingly powerful, group of techno-elites.[8] In these assessments, domination, rather than liberation, is the true mark of this capitalist order, and digital and "smart" technologies are but the latest weapons capitalists wield to ensure and augment their influence in society.

The spirits of capitalism

The research on digital capitalism has done much to advance our understanding of the way new technologies are being deployed to transform and enhance processes of capital accumulation, extraction, and domination. But this research has paid less attention to an equally important question: how do changes in forms of capital accumulation require and give rise to new forms of ideological justi-fication?[9] This is the central question that sociologist Luc Boltanski and professor of management Eve Chiapello take on in their monumental and now classic study, *The New Spirit of Capitalism*, which was first published in France in 1999 and is currently in its third translated edition.[10]

Boltanski and Chiapello explore the "ideological transformations that have accompanied transformations in capitalism" throughout the twentieth century. Although they base their analysis on French society, they maintain that there is "good reason to believe that rather similar processes have marked the evolution of ideologies accompanying the redeployment of capitalism in the other developed countries," the United States included (Boltanski and Chiapello 2007: 4). Boltanski and Chiapello argue that "the persistence of capitalism, as a mode of co-ordinating action and a lived world, cannot be understood without considering the ideologies which, in justifying and conferring a meaning on it, help to elicit the good will of those on whom it is based, and ensure their engagement" (Boltanski and Chiapello 2007: 3). Invoking Max Weber's famous phrase, they describe this set of ideologies as "the spirit of capitalism."[11] They further propose that "in terms that vary greatly historically, the spirit of capitalism peculiar to each age" must "supply resources to assuage the anxiety provoked by the following three questions":

- How is committed engagement in the processes of accumulation a source of enthusiasm, even for those who will not necessarily be the main beneficiaries of the profits that are made?
- To what extent can those involved in the capitalist universe be assured of minimum security for themselves and their children?
- How can participation in a capitalist firm be justified in terms of the common good, and how, confronted with accusations of injustice, can the way that it is conducted and managed be defended? (Boltanski and Chiapello 2007: 16).

Taking this as a departure point and treating the spirit of capitalism as an "ideal type," Boltanski and Chiapello trace how the spirit of capitalism has transformed over three main historical periods. Surveying these periods will provide us with a comparative perspective from which to assess throughout this book what is distinctive about the spirit of digital capitalism today.

The spirit of capitalism at the end of the nineteenth century

The first period they examine is the end of the nineteenth century. They propose that during this time, the spirit of capitalism was "focused on the person of the bourgeois entrepreneur and a description of bourgeois values. The image of the entrepreneur, the captain of industry, the conquistador, encapsulates the heroic elements of the portrait, stressing gambling, speculation, risk, innovation" (Boltanski and Chiapello 2007: 17). Enthusiasm and commitment to capitalist enterprise were fueled by promises of an opening world of opportunity made possible by new forms of communication and a new pool of wage laborers who had been "liberated" from the servitude of feudal relations in the countryside and who could now be deployed for capitalist projects. While new opportunities for enterprise were highly valued, a sense of security was still linked to the fundamental tenets of "bourgeois morality" and, more specifically, it was anchored in a strong commitment to the family and a sense of obligation to help the poor through acts of charity.[12]

During this period, a number of different ideas and beliefs helped portray capitalist enterprise as being committed to the common good. For instance, they argue that economic science played a key role in contributing to the idea that the pursuit of personal interest would lead to the collective good, thereby revalorizing Mandeville's famous eighteenth-century proclamation that "private vice" spawns "public virtue," an idea also echoed in the works of Adam Smith. Economic science also cast capitalism as inherently more efficient than other systems of production. It framed capitalism as the mode of production that would most readily lead to "progress" and deliver a technologically enhanced future made better by "the benefits of industry." Lastly, free-market capitalism was further justified by the idea that it would serve as a guarantor of political freedom.[13]

Ultimately, Boltanski and Chiapello argue that the spirit of capitalism ascendant at the end of the nineteenth century was indeed a conflicted one, as it brought together an "amalgam of very different, even incompatible propensities and values" (Boltanski and Chiapello 2007: 17). They thus conclude that the "thirst for profit and moralism, avarice and charity, scientism and familial traditionalism . . . underlay what was to be most unanimously and enduringly denounced in the bourgeois spirit: its hypocrisy" (ibid.).

The spirit of capitalism at the height of Fordist production

The second spirit of capitalism they analyze "was most fully developed between the 1930s and 1960s," correlating with the period of Fordist production. Instead of the entrepreneur being the "heroic" figure, it is the manager who oversees the large, centralized, and bureaucratized industrial firm, a figure whom William Whyte depicted in his 1956 classic, *The Organization Man* (Whyte 2002 [1956]). Unlike the entrepreneur seeking to constantly enhance his personal wealth, the manager's enthusiasm and commitment to capitalist enterprise stem from a zeal to "endlessly expand the size of the firm" he is responsible for. Mass production for mass consumption, it was claimed, would pave the way to an improved life for all, liberating consumers from need and fulfilling their desires for the new accoutrements of progress.

According to Boltanski and Chiapello, in this spirit of capitalism a sense of security was provided by "a faith in rationality and long-term planning." They observe "the very giantism of the organizations, which constituted protective environments not only offering career prospects, but also taking care of everyday life (subsidized accommodations, holiday camps, training bodies) modeled on the army (a type of organization of which IBM represented the paradigm in the 1950s and 1960s)" (Boltanski and Chiapello 2007: 18).

They propose that the belief in progress associated with the promise of science and technology, and enhanced productivity and efficiency, became even more pronounced than it was at the end of the nineteenth century. However, Boltanski and Chiapello also argue that these themes were accompanied by a new commitment to the notion of "civic" responsibility. They write, "the stress fell on institutional solidarity, the socialization of production, distribution and consumption, and collaboration between big firms and the state in pursuit of social justice" (ibid.). One of the ways this pursuit of social justice manifested itself was through a growing commitment to protect workers' rights, thereby "attenuating" class antagonisms and struggle.

The spirit of capitalism in the age of flexible accumulation

Though they do not state their findings in these terms, the "new spirit of capitalism" that Boltanski and Chiapello claim emerged during the latter part of the twentieth century was in large part a by-product of what David Harvey refers to as the transition from Fordism to the regime of flexible accumulation (Harvey 1990). The outsourcing of labor, the reliance on leaner and more flexible production models, the dismantling of corporate hierarchy, the loss of secure and stable career tracks, the heightened competition brought forth by the globalization of capital, all of this, Boltanski and Chiapello argue, required a new set of beliefs to help accommodate people to this changed economic order and enable them to "find their everyday universe" inhabitable (Boltanski and Chiapello 2007: 10).

According to Boltanski and Chiapello, under the "the new spirit of capitalism," committed engagement in the process of accumulation is fostered through the idea that one's work is an opportunity to exercise creativity, ingenuity, and vision, rather than subordinate one's self to the hierarchy and domination of the firm manager in the classic scenario of the "organization man" (Whyte 2002 [1956]). Stability and the desire for a lifelong career are rejected in favor of participating in projects and "networks" that enable one to continually develop one's knowledge and skills and enhance one's "employability," rather than move up a preordained corporate ladder. While capitalist firms still justify their existence through "classical arguments" predicated upon the idea of helping to secure freedom and liberty, they also increasingly present themselves as serving the ever-shifting desires and demands of consumers. This, in turn, becomes viewed as key to maintaining profitability and "surviving in a situation of increased competition," which is exacerbated in the context of globalization. Thus, if hypocrisy was the most denounced feature of the nineteenth-century spirit of capitalism, and conformism, alienation, and subordination were critiqued in the mid-twentieth, the new spirit of capitalism evokes concerns over perpetual instability and precarity.

Silicon Valley and the spirit of digital capitalism

As will be seen, the spirit of digital capitalism I explore in this book borrows elements from all three of the ideal types elaborated by Boltanski and Chiapello. For as was the case in the late nineteenth century, the techno-elite who have made their fortunes in the age of digital capitalism very much understand themselves as "heroic" entrepreneurs whose ingenuity and innovation are fueling economic growth and transforming and improving society at lightning speed. Though technological science more than economic science provides the dominant justification for their enterprises, they too, like the robber barons of the late nineteenth and early twentieth centuries, place an emphasis on fulfilling their obligations to help the poor through various philanthropic initiatives. In other words, charity is back (as well as avarice), but as will be seen in chapter 5, this time it too is being approached as a capitalist endeavor. "Impact investing," which encourages donors to approach their philanthropic endeavors with the same kinds of market sensibilities and economic strategies that they approach their businesses pursuits with, is becoming increasingly popular among techno-philanthropists.

Moreover, if the belief in science, technology, efficiency, and progress animated the spirit of capitalism during the early twentieth century, this rings even more true today. The information and technology sector has emerged as one of the most powerful and fastest-growing sectors of the US economy as mega-corporations, such as Google, Amazon, Facebook, and Apple, have achieved unprecedented profits by promising consumers that their technologies and services will make the world a better, more connected, and even more democratic place.[14] Thus, as was the case in the early twentieth century, the spirit of digital capitalism also preserves and perpetuates, albeit in mutated forms, the idea that capitalism can be a guarantor of personal and political freedom.

Finally, many of the features and beliefs Boltanski and Chiapello associate with the "new spirit of capitalism" at the turn of the twentieth century continue to animate processes of capital accumulation in the present day. In many cases, they have become even more intensified. Production models have become even leaner, the demand for flexible labor has become even greater, the imperative of re-skilling to maintain one's employability appears to be at an all-time high, the globalized nature of capitalist competition continues to fuel a race to create and capture new consumer markets, and the predominance of the network as the main organizational figure of contemporary capitalism has become literalized through new communication technologies that enable corporations to appropriate the creative activities of digitally connected enthusiasts and outsource projects across the globe.

However, as alluded to above, over the last two decades the increasing reliance upon digital technologies has also transformed the nature of capital accumulation, extraction, and domination.[15] As such, this book asks: is the digital age giving rise to a new spirit of capitalism? What are "the set of beliefs" that serve to justify, legitimate, and perpetuate this economic order? What are the new sources of enthusiasm as well as insecurity that these ideologies must contend with? Can digital capitalism reproduce itself with the beliefs and ideologies of yesteryear or are we witnessing a new spirit in the making? As stated at the outset, this book argues, yes, we are witnessing a new spirit in the making. While the spirit of digital capitalism certainly borrows liberally from the old capitalist playbook, it also recruits new means of justifying, legitimating, and ultimately celebrating an economic order that increasingly relies upon digital technologies to engage in the continual pursuit of profit.

I also want to emphasize that, in this book, I do limit my discussion of the spirit of digital capitalism to the United States. This is because while the spirit I describe may indeed radiate beyond US borders and find resonance elsewhere, much more research needs to be done to understand how digital capitalism has evolved in conjunction with different ethics and cultural sensibilities. For instance, anthropologist Ipshita Ghosh has begun to explore the way digital capitalism manifests itself in "diverse imaginaries of entrepreneurship and future-making" that may actually work to revive "native cultural practices" (Ghosh 2020, 2021). She shows how the development of digital capitalism in India has been significantly shaped by broader commitments to producing "humanitarian" outcomes and collective progress, often in close collaboration with the state. Similarly, anthropologists working in other parts of the world might ask: what does digital capitalism look, sound, and feel like in places such as China, where both profit making and the use of data-gathering and surveillance technologies are openly touted as means of achieving collective ends like national prosperity and enhanced social control (Zhao and Schiller 2001)? Are the cultural contradictions of digital capitalism as pronounced, or even existent, in places where individual autonomy and freedom have not been historically championed as the ultimate signpost of secular salvation?

In other words, if Weber sought to explore the elective affinity between the Protestant ethic and the spirit of industrial capitalism, I want to ask exactly what kind of ethic has fueled the rise of digital capitalism, and why has Silicon Valley emerged at the epicenter of its development? Is it a matter of mere coincidence that digital capitalism was birthed from the techno-utopian, libertarian worldview of Silicon Valley, or might it be the case that these "extra-economic" influences have played a significant role in shaping the motivations and machinations of digital capitalists and digital capitalism? As Arjun Appadurai points out, "Since the founding of the social sciences, it has been understood that economic activity has a special ethos and that its institutional transformation usually comes from forces that cannot be explained by economic factors or interests alone" (Appadurai 2012: 4).

Indeed, Appadurai takes up a very similar line of inquiry in his research on financial capitalism. He writes:

> We cannot afford to see capitalism as a machine that continues to perpetuate itself after an initial ethical moment. Modern capitalism

keeps transforming its ethics and the question we need to ask ourselves today is whether we can identify the key elements of the capitalist spirit in today's capitalist environment, almost three centuries after the period in which Weber identified its founding ethical moment . . . We need to look again at the nature of capitalist action, especially in the financial sphere, and then ask again what the link between "spirit" and "ethic" might be today. (Appadurai 2016: 22)

Appadurai proposes that, whereas industrial capitalism was driven by "the ideas of vocation, asceticism, methodicality and sobriety" (Appadurai 2012: 7), finance capitalism has "given way to an entirely different spirit." It has emerged as a "magical" realm in which "profits without known causes" have become more celebrated and expected than those accrued through "the methodological rationality of calculation" (ibid.: 6). The finance capitalists Appadurai describes are "heroic," risk-taking, "charismatic players," who use a "series of magical practices" to "divine," manage, and ultimately profit from the uncertainty that lies at the very heart of the global economic order (ibid.: 14).

Appadurai's work provides an important attempt to understand how the spirit of capitalism has changed with the rise of the financial sector, and it represents a highly instructive effort to "'channel' Weber heuristically" (ibid.: 7). It also offers a new theory of profit that places the derivative, instead of labor power, at its center. However, while Appadurai's insights may indeed capture what is going on in the realm of finance capitalism, they do not adequately capture the spirit of digital capitalism analyzed in this book. While there is clearly a long history of crossover between innovations in information technology and innovations in finance (MacKenzie 2018), and while it is also true that "Wall Street and Silicon Valley are converging around data capital as the new frontier of accumulation and circulation" (Sadowski 2019: 5), the fact remains that Wall Street and Silicon Valley are also very different places.

I argue that in the United States, the spirit of digital capitalism is animated by a distinct set of sensibilities that in large part derive from the techno-solutionist and techno-utopian, libertarian ethos of Silicon Valley (Kaplan 1999; Turner 2006, 2013; Fisher 2018; Farman 2020; Chafkin 2021). As will be seen in the ensuing chapters, the realm of digital capitalism has also given rise to its share of "heroic," "charismatic players." However, they do not resort to "magical practices" to combat a fundamental sense of uncertainty, as finance capitalists purportedly do. The heroes of digital capitalism remain strident in their belief in measurable progress and the idea that technology can save the day. Digital capitalists understand themselves as engineers, pioneers, and builders, not as magicians. Instead of staring anxiously at the heavens above, wondering if they will be "saved," as Weber's industrial capitalists did, and instead of trying to read financial tea leaves in their attempts to turn derivatives into profits, the titans of tech cast their gaze across the globe and operate with a supreme confidence that they are the ones doing the saving, or rather doing the solving, of the world's biggest problems. In other words, in the digital age, the "curious transformation of salvational uncertainty into capitalist methodicality – the core of Weber's insight" (Appadurai 2016: 6) – has been replaced by a techno-solutionist certainty that fuels "bold" and aggressive capitalist expansion. If we now live in a world that is disproportionately controlled by a small but extremely powerful group of tech-savvy elites, this is not because of their divinatory prowess, nor even because of their technological prowess. Rather, it is because of their power and determination to remake the world in their techno-solutionist image. Indeed, this, it might be argued, is their true "calling."

Unearthing the spirit of digital capitalism

Yet how does one study something as ethereal as a spirit of capitalism? Here again, I take methodological cues from Boltanski and Chiapello. Boltanski and Chiapello conducted their study of the changing spirit of capitalism, in part, by analyzing changes in the "non-technical" management literature from the 1950s to the present day. As they observe, "this literature . . . emerges as one of main sites in which the spirit of capitalism is inscribed" (Boltanski and Chiapello 2007: 57), as it provides prescriptive and normative claims as to how capitalist firms should be run.[16] In the chapters that follow, I too rely on non-technical management literature as an important source of data. However, in tracking the development of the spirit of digital capitalism, I also use the writings, talks, and lectures of an array of business professionals, entrepreneurs, and philanthropists in the United States who have emerged as "leaders" and influential figures in the business world. As Fred Turner has observed in chronicling the transformation from the counterculture to the cyberculture, these actors have "enabled a multitude of technologies to become widely used and thoroughly integrated into . . . society by establishing not only their material utility but also their semiotic fit with existing systems of discourse" (Turner 2006: 251). What this book provides, therefore, is a qualitative analysis of the discursive landscape in which the spirit of digital capitalism is being produced and promoted in the United States.

Admittedly, this is a research method that comes with limitations and, perhaps even worse, haunting fears that I may be changing my disciplinary stripes! For although I have spent the last fifteen years teaching in a sociology department, I am a cultural anthropologist by training, and most of the time anthropologists gather their data by immersing themselves in their research subjects' lives and getting to know them intimately over prolonged periods of time. This, however, is not the methodological route I have followed. I am skeptical that the questions I pursue in this book could have been adequately addressed by planting myself in one business community and getting to know members of this community intimately over a prolonged period of time. Certainly, this would have yielded insights that my approach cannot, but as my goal is to generate an ideal type of the spirit of digital capitalism in the contemporary United States, a broader sampling of voices and perspectives is indeed warranted. This book, therefore, uses multiple entry points and locations to explore the values and meanings that animate this new era of capital accumulation. I ultimately aim to show how the spirit of digital capitalism brings together its own "amalgam of very different, even incompatible propensities and values" that reveal deeper cultural contradictions in contemporary American society (Boltanski and Chiapello 2007: 17). My hope, moreover, is that my fellow anthropologists will read this book as an invitation for conducting further ethnographic research in the future, and that their work will be able to speak more fully to the ways digital capitalism is being lived, experienced, and even resisted by those who are differentially positioned in its ambit.

Overview of the chapters

The first two chapters explore how and why crowdsourcing has become a highly touted economic strategy among business gurus and entrepreneurs. Chapter 1 focuses on forms of crowdsourcing facilitated through incentive competitions, whereas chapter 2 explores models of "collaborative crowdsourcing." Throughout the book I argue that these two opposing models, based on competition and collaboration, point to more profound tensions animating the spirit of digital capitalism. Moreover, I argue that, although crowdsourcing uses digital technologies to facilitate new forms of capital accumulation, it nonetheless preserves the essential features of exclusion, exploitation, and extraction.

Chapter 3 examines the way smartphone gaming apps are being used to facilitate the digital extraction of surplus value. I argue that it is precisely by blurring the boundaries between work and leisure, and in many cases, "gamifying" tasks, that the app economy is able to perpetuate a classic form of capitalist expropriation. Thus, even though much has changed in the era of digital capitalism, "moments," as Marx noted long ago, are still "the elements of profit" (Marx 1978 [1867]: 366).

Chapter 4 considers how convenience has emerged as an ideology that is integral to new forms of capital accumulation, domination, and extraction. Taking Shoshana Zuboff's work on surveillance capitalism as a departure point, in this chapter I explore this development by focusing on one of Amazon's newest business initiatives, Amazon Go. Drawing upon a range of data, including promotional videos, marketing reports, interviews with the designers of the initiative, and customer comments, I demonstrate how convenience operates not just as a coveted consumer product but also as an ideology that is central to Amazon's abilities to exploit the behavioral surplus of its customers and legitimate new forms of capital accumulation and extraction.

Chapter 5 explores how techno-philanthropists, many of whom have made their fortunes through new forms of digital capitalism, justify and legitimate processes of capital accumulation through philanthropic donations that are themselves guided by the new turn towards "impact investing." Impact investing is premised upon the idea that philanthropy and capital accumulation can go hand in hand; that if one strategically utilizes the logics of market investment, one can "generate a measurable, beneficial social or environmental impact alongside a financial return."[17] Capitalists can thus have their charitable "cake" and profit, too. This chapter asks, what exactly is the spirit of such gifts? How is philanthropy providing a means by which the techno-elite augment and legitimate their power and influence in society? Drawing upon the discussions in chapters 1 through 5, the concluding chapter explores how the spirit of digital capitalism brings together its own "amalgam of very different, even incompatible propensities and values" (Boltanski and Chiapello 2007: 17) that reveal deeper cultural contradictions in contemporary American society.

A note on ideology

Although my analysis of the spirit of digital capitalism is significantly informed by Boltanski and Chiapello's work, and although
I use much of the same conceptual language in describing the
"ideological" changes that have accompanied the rise of digital
capitalism, there is one difference in my usage of this term that I want
to highlight. Boltanski and Chiapello invoke the term "ideology" in
the "Dumontian" sense. They write:

> We stipulate that the term "ideology" is to be construed here not in the
> reductionist sense to which it has often been reduced in the Marxist
> vulgate – that is to say, a moralizing discourse, intended to conceal
> material interests, which is constantly contradicted by practice – but as
> developed, for example, in the work of Louis Dumont: a set of shared
> beliefs, inscribed in institutions, bound up with actions, and hence
> anchored in reality. (Boltanski and Chiapello 2007: 3)

Throughout this book, I also speak of the "beliefs" and "ideologies" that have accompanied the rise of digital capitalism, and I
agree that these beliefs and ideologies are often compelling because
they are experienced as being anchored in reality. This is a point
Terry Eagleton makes when he observes that dominant ideologies
are often dominant precisely because they "engage significantly
with [the] genuine wants, needs, and desires" of those who are
subjected to them (Eagleton 2007: 45). People do not have to be
considered mystified "dupes" because they find a dominant ideology
compelling. However, in this analysis I also want to deploy the term
"ideology" in a more critical spirit. I want to remain focused on how
the ideologies of digital capitalism are used to "conceal material"
interests and thereby help perpetuate relations of domination and
inequality. In this regard, I follow John Thompson who argues that
"to study ideology is to study the ways in which meaning serves to
establish and sustain relations of domination" (Thompson 1990:
56). As the subsequent chapters demonstrate, in the age of digital
capitalism there is no shortage of attempts to make meanings serve
the interests of the powerful.

Indeed, one of the goals of this book is to demonstrate how
the emancipatory potential of digital technologies, or what Yochai
Benkler refers to as "the wealth of networks," is continually co-opted
to foster processes of capital accumulation and enhance elite

power.[18] Benkler proposes that in contrast to the twentieth-century industrial model of information production, the twenty-first-century "networked information economy" represents a "new mode of production" that thrives off of new ways of organizing people in peer-to-peer production. He argues that it has the potential to enhance the autonomy of individuals, further cooperation outside of the market frame, dramatically redistribute power and money from twentieth-century industrial producers, and help create a more robust and democratic public sphere. However, Benkler also warns that the emancipatory promise of the networked information economy is far from inevitable and will only emerge as "as a result of political action aimed at protecting new social patterns from the incumbents' assaults." "None of the industrial giants of yore," he cautions, "are taking this reallocation lying down." "The battle over the relative salience of proprietary, industrial models of information production and exchange and the emerging networked information economy is being carried out in the domain of the institutional ecology of the digital environment" (Benkler 2006: 23).

This book will show that "the battle" is not just being waged on the institutional "front" through corporate attempts to secure policies and practices that favor the interests of capital. It is also being waged on the ideological front. Thus, by closely interrogating the spirit of digital capitalism, and by tracing the ways new forms of accumulation, extraction, and domination are being justified and valorized by business leaders in the contemporary United States, I hope this book will make some contribution to the fight for a more just and equitable future in which "the wealth of networks" can truly be shared by all.

1

The Spirit of Competition: Crowdsourcing through Incentive Competitions

At the turn of the twentieth century, as a significant portion of the rural population began to migrate to industrial cities, social theorists became increasingly concerned with how the crowd was emerging as an agent of social change and unrest in European society. As Gustave Le Bon famously argued in his seminal work, *The Crowd: A Study of the Popular Mind*, "among the special characteristics of crowds there are several – such as impulsiveness, irritability, incapacity to reason, the absence of judgment and of the critical spirit, the exaggeration of sentiments, and others besides – which are almost always observed in beings belonging to inferior forms of evolution – in women, savages, and children, for instance" (Le Bon 2002 [1895]: 11). Le Bon further proposed that the aims and ambitions of the crowd or "masses" were directly opposed to the interests of capitalism. He warned that the crowd seeks to "destroy society as it currently exists" and replace it with a "primitive communism which was the normal condition of all human groups before the dawn of civilization" (ibid.: xi). Le Bon also cautioned that crowds were detrimental to technological progress. "Crowds," he wrote:

> possess conservative instincts as indestructible as those of all primitive beings. Their fetish-like respect for traditions is absolute; their unconscious horror of all novelty capable of changing the essential conditions of their existence is very deeply rooted. Had democracies possessed the power they wield today at the time of the invention of mechanical looms or of the introduction of steam power and of railways, the realization of these inventions would have been impossible, or would have been achieved at the cost of revolutions and repeated massacres. It is fortunate for the progress of civilization that

the power of crowds only began to exist when the great discoveries of science and industry had already been effected. (Le Bon 2002 [1895]: 26)

Whereas Le Bon depicted the crowd as an irrational, "primitive" force that sought to derail capitalism and technological innovation at the dawn of the twentieth century, twenty-first-century business gurus envision the crowd as a very different kind of force, or rather "source," in contemporary capitalist society. For instance, in his 2005 *New York Times* bestseller, *The Wisdom of Crowds,* business columnist James Surowiecki writes, "Gustave Le Bon had things exactly backward. If you put together a big enough group of people and ask them to 'make decisions affecting matters of general interest,' that group's decision will, over time, be 'intellectually [superior] to the isolated individual', no matter how smart or well informed he is" (Surowiecki 2005: xvii).

"The wisdom of crowds" has also been extolled by tech writer Jeff Howe, who first coined the term "crowdsourcing" in a 2006 article published in *Wired* magazine. In this article, Howe discussed how the internet has enabled companies to tap into the "productive potential of millions of plugged-in enthusiasts," rather than relying solely on their contracted employees to get tasks done. Crowdsourcing, he wrote, "is the act of taking a job traditionally performed by a designated agent (usually an employee) and outsourcing it to an undefined, generally large group of people in the form of an open call" (Howe 2006). In his 2008 book, *Crowdsourcing: Why the Power of the Crowd is Driving the Future of Business,* Howe continued to argue that the crowd "is more than wise – it's talented, creative, and stunningly productive" (Howe 2008). Business professor Mark Wexler also casts the crowd as inherently productive. "Crowdsourcing," he writes, "can be understood as a focal entity's use of an enthusiastic crowd or loosely bound public to provide solutions to problems" (Wexler 2011: 11).

One of the leading experts and proponents of crowdsourcing in the United States is Karim Lakhani. Lakhani is a professor at Harvard Business School, the co-director of the Harvard Business School Digital Initiative, and a consultant for the NASA Tournament Lab as well as the Mozilla Corporation. Much of his work involves advising corporations on how to incorporate crowdsourcing into their business models to enhance innovation. Lakhani notes that there are two dominant models of crowdsourcing. The first relies upon the use of incentive competitions where the "winner takes all." In a 2014 talk entitled, "The Crowd as Innovation Partner," given at the NYU Stern School of Business, Lakhani noted that the use of competitions is the preferred model of crowdsourcing when businesses are unsure of who possesses the right knowledge to solve their problems. As he explained, "you have a problem, you set a prize, and you let anyone in the world participate. And you hopefully get a great solution out of it . . . contests are very effective when the problem sponsor does not know who the right person might be to solve the problem, or what the right approach might be, or both."[1]

The second is what he describes as "community" or "collaborative crowdsourcing," which enables businesses to tap into open source communities that can work collaboratively to solve problems and challenges.[2] Lakhani advises that this model works best when innovation problems require "cumulative knowledge building and an aggregation of diverse inputs."[3]

In this chapter and the next, I explore how contemporary business gurus are reimagining and recruiting the crowd as a source of economic utility and innovation. While this chapter focuses on crowdsourcing through incentive competitions, chapter 2 explores the collaborative model of crowdsourcing. The questions that concern me are as follows: By casting crowdsourcing as a solution to the financial and operational challenges that businesses face, what kind of assumptions, values, and interests do contemporary business experts promote? How do these business experts arouse enthusiasm for participation in crowdsourcing initiatives and thereby secure committed engagement in processes of capital accumulation? How do they justify crowdsourcing as contributing to the common good while at the same time assuaging anxieties that crowdsourcing has engendered? What might crowdsourcing reveal more generally about the constant as well as changing nature of capital accumulation, extraction, and domination in the digital age?

Unleashing the spirit of competition, saving the world, and celebrating smartness

Whether wittingly or not, when contemporary business experts extol the use of incentive competitions to organize and motivate the crowd, they frequently reproduce a long history of economic thought and theory that is premised upon the ideas: (a) that competitiveness is an innate propensity among human beings; (b) that capitalism is the economic system that most effectively unleashes and institutionalizes this proclivity, rather than creates it; and (c) that once unleashed and institutionalized, this spirit of competition will pave the way to innovation and progress. Participation in the capitalist enterprise is thus in part justified because it is portrayed as providing a vehicle through which people can pursue and realize an essential aspect of their human nature while at the same time contributing to the betterment of society.[4]

While this idea has long animated justifications of capitalism, indeed Marx himself railed against this idea in his nineteenth-century critique of political economy, it has also taken on some new elaborations and valences in the hands of Silicon Valley's most powerful techno-elites.[5] We can begin to glean how this idea animates the spirit of digital capitalism by examining the works and writings of one of America's most celebrated entrepreneurs, venture capitalists, and self-professed futurists, Peter Diamandis.

Diamandis was born to Greek immigrant parents and grew up in the Bronx. His father, as he likes to recount, represented the epitome of the American Dream. Born into a poor family on the island of Lesbos, he grew up "picking olives and tending goats," but eventually he went to university, emigrated, and became a very successful physician in New York. As an undergraduate, Peter pursued a degree in molecular genetics from MIT and then went on to complete a graduate degree in aerospace engineering. He also holds an MD from Harvard Medical School and is currently known as one of the country's most successful entrepreneurs and venture capitalists, having founded more than 15 high-tech companies and having achieved an estimated net worth of US$200 million. Diamandis is a highly sought-after consultant and public speaker; he has been an invited guest on *The Genius Network Show*, and he is also a *New York Times* bestselling author.[6] In 2008, he joined forces with technology guru and fellow futurist Ray Kurzweil to co-found Singularity University in Silicon Valley, an institution that is explicitly designed to translate technological research and advances into commercial success and vice versa. In 2014, *Fortune* magazine named him one of the "World's 50 Greatest Leaders."[7]

More pertinent to this discussion, Diamandis has also achieved fame by founding the XPrize Foundation, and subsequently co-founding the crowdsourcing platform HeroX. Through his involvement in these initiatives, Diamandis, like Lakhani, has also played a pivotal role in popularizing the use of incentive competitions as a business strategy and practice. His work thus provides a valuable entry point for exploring how incentive competitions are being discursively constructed as a way to not only increase corporate efficiency, innovation, and profitability but also arouse enthusiasm for participation in processes of capital accumulation during the digital age.

Diamandis's interest in incentive competitions was born out of frustration. Having earned a graduate degree in aerospace engineering from MIT, in 1987 Diamandis began a career in space exploration by co-founding the International Space University. He has since emerged as one of the most prominent New Space entrepreneurs and has been integral to the development of space tourism. He serves as the managing director and co-founder of the company Space Adventures, which provides private citizens with opportunities to travel to the International Space Station. As he recounts, his accomplishments in the field of space tourism were in large part facilitated by the use of incentive competitions:

> In 1994, I desperately wanted to get to space. The problem was, NASA was the only name in town and my chances of riding with them were one in a thousand (at 5′5″ in height, I have a better chance of joining the NBA than I do being accepted as an astronaut).
>
> After reading that Charles Lindbergh crossed the Atlantic Ocean in 1927 to win a $25,000 purse (the Orteig prize), I became enamored with the power of incentive prizes. These competitions were the perfect way to excite and leverage the world's most talented, creative people to solve YOUR challenge. That insight led me to the creation of the $10M Ansari XPrize for spaceflight, which was offered for the first commercial, reusable 3-person spaceship.[8]

As Diamandis himself points out, the use of incentive competitions to promote innovation is a phenomenon that far predates the digital age. Some trace it back to the 1714 Longitude Prize which was sponsored by the British government in order to entice mariners to discover a practical way to determine the position of ships at sea (Wexler 2011). Others note that in 1795 Napoleon sponsored a 12,000-franc incentive prize for anyone who could come up with a viable means of preserving food to help feed his army on its march to Russia (Diamandis and Kotler 2015: 245). However, although there are numerous examples of early precursors, the development of digital technologies that enable competition sponsors to widely broadcast their calls and reach an ever more diversified pool of applicants has made the use of incentive competitions far more ubiquitous today. And yet, while acknowledging that digital technologies have given incentive competitions a big push, Diamandis maintains that the popularity and efficacy of incentive competitions also stem from the fact that they tap into one of the most enduring and essential parts of human nature. He explains:

> If you need to accelerate change in specific areas, especially when the goals are clear and measurable, incentive competitions have a *biological advantage*. Humans are wired to compete. We're wired to hit hard targets. Incentive prizes are a proven way to entice the smartest people in the world, no matter where they live or where they're employed, to work on your particular problem . . . such competitions can change the world. (Diamandis and Kotler 2014: 218; my emphasis)

In these remarks, Diamandis doesn't only justify the use of incentive competitions through recourse to human biology, he also suggests that the use of incentive competitions can facilitate moral missions to "change" the world.[9] If late twentieth-century American capitalism was depicted and embodied by cut-throat characters like Gordon Gekko who ruthlessly pursued their own financial gain at others' expense, today's venture capitalists, as will be discussed further in chapter 5, propose that the accumulation of profit can be part and parcel of a much larger mission of worldly, if not galactic, salvation.

For instance, as Christian Cotichini, the co-founder and CEO of the crowdsourcing platform HeroX, noted when commenting on the "Space Poop" incentive competition they helped NASA organize: "NASA's previous challenge, Space Poop, went viral, demonstrating how effective the power of the crowd is to solve galactic problems . . . It's always an honor helping solve 'number two challenges.'"[10] Indeed, as David Valentine has argued in his fascinating research on New Space entrepreneurs, the New Space industry, in which Diamandis is a key figure, is animated by a powerful commitment to securing the survival of our species into "the deep future" by establishing "human settlements in the solar system and beyond" (Valentine 2012: 1047). Valentine proposes that their "cosmological commitments" and desires to ward off species annihilation should be taken as seriously as their desires to turn a profit. Thus, when elaborated by techno-enthusiasts like Diamandis and Cotichini, the spirit of digital capitalism doesn't just "legitimate a new trade-off between social emancipation and personal emancipation" (Fisher 2010: 11). It also recasts emancipation as an urgent matter of species salvation, and it promises collective survival by using digital technologies to harness the wisdom of the crowd.

Moreover, as is generally the case among the Silicon Valley techno-elite, Diamandis arouses enthusiasm for participation in incentive competitions by pitching them as a way to recruit "the smartest people in the world." Jathan Sadowski argues that in the era of digital capitalism smartness itself has emerged as key ideology through which the techno-elite advance their corporate interests and increase their technocratic power. He demonstrates how the development of smartphones, smart houses, and smart cities provides the technological means through which the pioneers of digital capitalism extend their influence in society (Sadowski 2020). Sadowski's observations are indeed apt, but what is equally important to recognize is that for the entrepreneurial "heroes" of digital capitalism, or what Eran Fisher refers to as "the digerati" (Fisher 2010), smartness is not just a technological project. It is also a symbolic badge of honor that they claim and bestow upon each other as a way to mark their "visionary" status and distinguish themselves from the "business as usual" approach to innovation and capital accumulation.[11] Thus, by describing the incentive competition as a means to "entice the smartest people in the world, no matter where they live or where they're employed," Diamandis effectively holds out the promise that by participating in such competitions applicants themselves will be able to join the ranks of the Silicon Valley "genius" elite and play a pivotal role in shaping the future. In this articulation of the spirit of digital capitalism, therefore, democratization of opportunity sits side by side with celebrations of new forms of intellectual distinction.

For instance, in 2018, Diamandis posted the following "call" on his "XPRIZE Visioneering Tech Blog." The message is worth quoting at length:

CALLING ALL INNOVATORS

I often speak about the power of the crowd to drive impact. Whether it's creating Wikipedia, predicting protein folding, or solving XPRIZE Competitions. There is a massive "cognitive surplus" available to do good in the world. So, it's with great pleasure that I call on the smartest and most passionate innovators out there to join me in an experiment . . . Normally, we ask the crowd to SOLVE our XPRIZEs . . . this time, we're asking you to design them as well. Can you write the rules for our next XPRIZE competitions better than our internal team? Or external experts? Here's an open call to innovators around the world to design XPRIZES in five key areas:

• Off-Grid Energy for the Developing World
• Saving Coral Reefs
• Disaster Prediction (Earthquakes & Hurricanes)

- Lifting Farmers Out of Poverty
- Feeding the Next Billion

Why do this? Well, there's up to $100,000 in prizes and awards, but more importantly you get to help shape the future. PLUS, you'll be invited to join alongside our Innovation Board and Vision Circle members (aka our largest benefactors) and participate in our 2018 VISIONEERING Summit this October. I hope you're up to it. And if you're not, would you mind doing me a favor and POST this on your social media, or forward this to a friend who you think might have interest?

Let's dive in . . . [12]

In "calling on" the smartest people in the world and offering them the opportunity to prove their technological and entrepreneurial prowess by joining the circle of elite visionaries, Diamandis uses the XPRIZE as an opportunity to promote the "the California Ideology." As Barbrook and Cameron describe it, the California Ideology "offers a way of understanding" the "so-called virtual class" or "the techno-intelligentsia" emerging from the West Coast. Their techno-optimism and overriding faith in their own intelligence and free-market enterprise lead them to argue that "big government should stay off the backs of resourceful entrepreneurs who are the only people cool and courageous enough to take risks" and effectively solve problems (Barbrook and Cameron 1996: 49). Diamandis, however, doesn't just use the incentive competition as a way to invite the "cool and courageous" into "the club." He also uses the incentive competition to capture and corral them, creating an ever-enriched "circle" of intellectual and economic capital that will purportedly be redeployed to save the species and planet in the future, while at the same time lining the pockets of his visionary investor friends.

Leveling the playing field and accelerating progress

While Diamandis proposes that incentive competitions leverage the most essential parts of human nature, can be used to change the world, and offer a way to recruit a global cadre of intellectual giants, he also argues that incentive competitions level the playing field and actually work to dismantle hierarchies based on accumulated economic and cultural capital. Incentive competitions recruit and reward raw talent based on "objective" results. As he explains:

An incentive competition is straightforward. Set a clear, measurable, and objective goal and offer a large prize to the first person to achieve it . . . Moreover, incentive competitions are brutally objective. They don't care where you went to school, how old you are, or what you've ever done before. Billion-dollar corporations compete as equals against two-person start-ups. They measure only one thing: Did you demonstrate the target goal of the competition? (Diamandis and Kotler 2015: 243–4)

Given the fact that Silicon Valley startup culture is littered with entrepreneurs who possess elite academic degrees or affiliations, Diamandis's celebration of the incentive competition as a meritocratic leveler of symbolic and economic hierarchies calls for greater scrutiny. For although it may be the case that incentive competitions do turn a blind eye to formal credentials, we should also ask how framing the incentive competition in this way further enables the techno-elite to project their own accomplishments as the sole product of their innate "genius" rather than accrued privilege. When we consider the fact that Bill Gates and Mark Zuckerberg both attended Harvard, Steve Jobs graduated from Reed, Peter Thiel and Jeffrey Skoll both hold degrees from Stanford, and Ray Kurzweil (and Peter Diamandis himself) graduated from MIT, it becomes more difficult to sustain the narrative that machinations of digital capitalism have somehow completely transcended the world of Bourdieuan distinctions.

Moreover, despite the suggestion that incentive competitions help ensure meritocracy and equal opportunity for all, upon closer inspection we again find that they function as a means to capture and concentrate intellectual and economic capital in the hands of a powerful few.[13] For instance, former PayPal executive, billionaire futurist, and Stanford law graduate, Peter Thiel is also a proponent of incentive competitions. In 2011, he established the Thiel Fellowship program which offers young entrepreneurs and inventors under the age of 22 US$100,000 if they "skip" or drop out of college to pursue their innovations. Promoted under the slogan that "some ideas can't wait," the Thiel Fellowship program arouses enthusiasm by promising its applicants an opportunity to chart a unique and adventurous path. Quoting an article from the *Wall Street Journal*, the website states, "Not long ago, dropping out of school to start a company was considered risky. For this generation, it is a badge of honor, evidence of ambition and focus."[14]

But it is not just a badge of honor that is used to arouse enthusiasm and secure commitment to "the capitalist cause." The Thiel

Foundation also promises applicants access to the coveted network of the Silicon Valley elite. As stated on the Fellowship webpage, "Our network is yours . . . The hardest thing about being a young entrepreneur is that you haven't met everyone you'll need to know to make your venture succeed. We can help connect you – to investors, partners, prospective customers – in Silicon Valley and beyond."[15] By connecting young entrepreneurs in this manner, the Thiel Fellowship provides participants with opportunities to make their ventures succeed but, equally important, it also provides a select group of venture capitalists with a direct channel to "invest," or rather appropriate, million-dollar ideas and ensure that they are developed through the private sector, thereby giving them a chance to line their pockets as well. Although the Fellowship maintains that they "do not take equity" in any company that applicants develop, they do play a pivotal role in channeling the flow of capital. Under the guise of accelerating innovation, therefore, the Thiel Fellowship also accelerates the accumulation of capital into the hands of a "networked" few.

You pay only the winner!

Diamandis and Thiel present the incentive competition as a key means of ensuring meritocracy, that is, a system where people are justly rewarded and compensated based on the merits of their work and contributions to society rather than on inherited privileges. Yet a closer look at the proliferation of this crowdsourcing strategy suggests that incentive competitions have become such a prominent feature of contemporary business practice precisely because they are able to take advantage of entrenched structural inequalities.[16] As both Juliet Schor and Jeff Howe argue, the corporate deployment of crowdsourcing initiatives must also be understood as part of a larger set of socioeconomic transformations that have thrust Americans and citizens across the globe into situations of increasing economic precarity (Howe 2008; Schor 2020). They note that in the wake of the 2008 global recession, a growing population of un- or under-employed people with college degrees turned to crowdsourcing initiatives as a way to earn or supplement an income. While crowd-sourcing enthusiasts typically celebrate the way digital technologies emancipate the contemporary workforce from "the shackles" of traditional employment arrangements and "soul-crushing" nine-to-five office jobs, others propose that we need to interrogate how crowdsourcing initiatives not only seize upon the economic precarity of others, but actually enhance and exacerbate forms of inequality and exploitation. For instance, how exactly are contestants of incentive competitions compensated for their labor? Here again, Diamandis's remarks are instructive:

> *You pay only the winner.* Prizes are efficient. They generate an enormous amount of innovation – often enough to create an entire industry – but you have to pay only the winner, none of the teams who attempt and fail. (Diamandis and Kotler 2015: 259; italics and bold in original)

Or, as Diamandis explained in a more recent article when listing the five merits of using incentive competitions:

1. Rather than hiring one person or team, imagine having tens or hundreds of teams working tirelessly on your problem.
2. My data shows that teams spend 5×–10× the prize purse amount to develop the solution.
3. You only pay for the solution to your problems, not failures.
4. You set the deadlines. This means that you can incentivize rapid breakthroughs much more quickly than traditional mechanisms might; and
5. You engage communities, organizations, and people by raising awareness and by mobilizing and inspiring.[17]

Thus, in the digital age, incentive prizes retain and perpetuate the fundamentally exploitative nature of capital accumulation. However, instead of expropriating the surplus value created by wage laborers, they replace the dispensation of wages with the dispensation of a singular prize. Whereas more traditional business models would involve having workers bid for a project in advance, in this arrangement the prize sponsor does not have to commit to any contractual agreement beforehand, thereby enabling them to maintain the much-cherished virtue of "flexibility." Instead, the sponsor of the competition retroactively rewards only those who meet the goal first. Emily Fowler, one of the key architects of the HeroX crowdsourcing incentive competition platform, explains:

> HeroX flips that model around and says that the money will be given when the innovation is created, but not before. HeroX inverts the model and offers the funding in a way that motivates the solution.

People put up money and a problem and then they let the various solutions show up. We see an opportunity to use incentive competitions to minimize risk within problem solving and innovation because it allows for safe funding of innovation where the location of the solution is unknown. This is where the power of incentive competitions really comes in – sponsors/funders don't know where the solution is, but . . . as Peter has said before, "Instead of looking for a needle in a haystack, the needle comes to you."[18]

Because the participants are cast as "solvers" or "competitors" rather than workers, or even independent contractors, as is the case with people who earn money on platforms like Uber, Fowler and Diamandis are able to bypass discussions of the way incentive competitions perpetuate "precarious work" or, that is, work that is "uncertain, unpredictable, and risky from the point of view of the worker" (Kalleberg 2009: 2). Instead, Fowler proposes that one of the great selling points of incentive competitions is that they "minimize risk" for sponsors, while offloading it onto the many contestants who, as Diamandis points out, often spend five or ten times the amount of the prize money to come up with a viable solution to the challenge. While sponsors are able to invest their capital with the confidence of having seen proven results, competition participants lay all their resources and energy on the line without any assurances that they will ever be financially compensated for their efforts. In this regard, incentive competitions establish an even more damning form of hierarchy, where "progress" is understood as a race and, at the end of the day or competition, people are divided into two camps: a few winners, who "take everything," and a majority of losers who get nothing, even though their hard work and efforts "generate enough to create an entire industry."[19] In the name of competition, therefore, the incentive prize legitimizes and naturalizes "negative reciprocity" (Sahlins 1972). While most societies have regarded negative reciprocity, or the attempt to get something for nothing, as a threat to the social and moral order, here it is celebrated as a means of enhancing "efficiency" and increasing profit margins by cutting labor costs.

For instance, in discussing the merits of using incentive competitions, Karim Lakhani and his colleague Kevin Boudreau, who is a professor of entrepreneurship and innovation at Northeastern University, also celebrate the way incentive competitions motivate the crowd and enable corporate sponsors to reap the benefits of unremunerated labor.[20] They write:

The most straightforward way to engage a crowd is to create a contest. The sponsor (the company) identifies a specific problem, offers a cash prize, and broadcasts an invitation to submit solutions. Contests have cracked some of the toughest scientific and technological challenges in history . . . Today online platforms such as TopCoder, Kaggle, and InnoCentive provide crowd-contest services. They source and retain members, enable payment, and protect, clear, and transfer intellectual property worldwide. Although a company might in the end use only one of the solutions it receives, the assessment of many submissions can provide insight into where the "technical frontier" lies, especially if the solutions cluster at some extreme. (Boudreau and Lakhani 2013)

Indeed, in his numerous talks and writings, Lakhani repeatedly emphasizes how incentive competitions enable sponsors to reach the "technological frontier" for a fraction of the cost it would require had they followed more traditional employment arrangements. For instance, in a 2014 talk entitled "Collective Intelligence," he discussed his consulting work with NASA and the role he played in helping to organize the NASA International Space Station Longeron Challenge. The goal of the challenge was to "develop a complex algorithm that would allow NASA to position the solar collectors on the ISS to generate as much power as possible during the most difficult orbital positions."[21] Explaining his role in the challenge, Lakhani states:

So what we do with NASA is we take their computational problems, and a range of problems from a range of disciplines and then we use a platform called TopCoder, to get them solved online, and then what we try to do is that once in a while we will run a field experiment on top of it to see what we can learn about social science, but let me show you an example here, and again, the results are very interesting . . . Look at the prize amount 30,000 bucks, like in World Bank parlance that's like decimal dust and same also in terms of what NASA typically spends on a toilet, right?[22]

Lakhani then went on to note that, had NASA relied on an "internal solution" to solve this challenge, they would have likely paid "upwards of US$20 million a year" to develop the answer.

NASA, of course, is not a private sector corporation but rather a government-funded research institution. Indeed, according to Peter Diamandis, this is precisely what makes it so inefficient in promoting space exploration. However, the point I want to emphasize here is that as a highly sought-after business consultant and scholar, Karim

Lakhani pitches the perks of incentive competitions to corporate entities all the time and actively advises them on how to integrate competitive crowdsourcing initiatives into their business arsenal. What his message basically amounts to is that by using incentive competitions, and paying "only the winners," corporations too can save millions of dollars and thereby enhance their profit margins and power. While this clearly contributes to a gross inequity between corporate wealth and labor, Lakhani, like Diamandis and Fowler, celebrates it as a piece of good fortune for the companies he advises. Indeed, he even goes one step further to assuage any anxieties companies might have about using incentive competitions. For instance, in an article entitled "The Crowd as Innovation Partner," published in the *Harvard Business Review*, Lakhani and Boudreau explicitly acknowledge the anxieties that crowdsourcing initiatives engender for corporations. They write:

> Managers remain understandably cautious. Pushing problems out to a vast group of strangers seems risky and even unnatural, particularly to organizations built on internal innovation. How, for example, can a company protect its intellectual property? Isn't integrating crowdsourced solutions into corporate operations an administrative nightmare? What about costs? And how can you be sure you'll get an appropriate solution? These concerns are all reasonable, but excluding crowdsourcing from the corporate innovation tool kit means losing opportunity.[23]

Lakhani thus reassures his corporate clients that incentive competition platforms such as Topcoder, Kaggle, and InnoCentive will lay their fears to rest and "source and retain members, enable payment, and protect, clear, and transfer intellectual property worldwide." What the platforms protect, however, is not just the intellectual property of the contestants (whose potential anxieties are notably not addressed or assuaged by Lakhani and Boudreau) but rather the power and privilege of the corporate sponsor who offers a "decimal dust" prize, or the amount one might spend on a "toilet" for access to a potentially multimillion- or billion-dollar idea.[24]

How are we to understand this bald-faced celebration of negative reciprocity? Are we to assume that business experts and entrepreneurs like Lakhani, Boudreau, Diamandis, Fowler, and Thiel are so steeped in the icy calculative logics of capitalism that the only thing that matters for them is to increase profit margins, and therefore they feel no shame in championing the way profits are accrued through the exploitation of unremunerated labor? This is certainly a possibility worth considering. However, as Thomas Piketty reminds us, "Every human society must justify inequalities: unless reasons for them are found, the whole political and social edifice stands in danger of collapse" (Piketty 2020: 1). As we began to see above, and as I will discuss further, one of the ways contemporary business experts and entrepreneurs justify these extractive and exploitative practices is again by casting their work as part of a larger mission of global salvation.

In the era of digital capitalism, incentive competitions are promoted as one means of unleashing the innovative "hero" within us all, and, as Lakhani himself notes, increasingly incentive competitions are being organized and brokered through the use of third-party digital platforms.

HeroX and platform capitalism

Indeed, the fact that there are now multiple platforms devoted to brokering incentive competitions for corporate clients attests to just how pervasive the incentive competition has become as a business practice.[25] It also illustrates how the platform itself has emerged as a key interface and technology of extraction in the era of digital capitalism. In his book *Platform Capitalism*, Nick Srnicek explains that "at the most general level platforms are digital infrastructures that enable two or more groups to interact. They therefore position themselves as intermediaries that bring together different users: customers, advertisers, service providers, producers, suppliers, and even physical objects" (Srnicek 2017: 43). Moreover, according to Srnicek, the platform is not just a digital infrastructure that facilitates the exchange of services, as its owners typically claim, it also "has emerged as a new business model, capable of extracting and controlling immense amounts of data" that can be sold to generate profits or used in other ways to secure business advantages (Srnicek 2017: 6).[26] He proposes that the rise of platform capitalism must be understood as a response to "a long decline in manufacturing profitability." "Capitalism," he contends, "has turned to data as one way to maintain economic growth and vitality in the face of a sluggish production sector" (ibid.). Given all of this, it is perhaps not surprising that in 2013 Peter Diamandis himself joined forces with "veteran entrepreneur" Christian Cotichini, challenge designer Emily Fowler, and venture capital firm City Light Capital to create

HeroX, a crowdsourcing platform specifically designed to facilitate incentive competitions. As the official origin "story" posted on the website explains:

> On October 21, 2004, Scaled Composites' SpaceShipOne reached the edge of space, an altitude of 100km, becoming the first privately built spacecraft to perform this feat, twice within two weeks. In so doing, they won the $10 million Ansari XPRIZE, ushering in a new era of commercial space exploration and applications.
>
> It was the inaugural incentive prize competition of the XPRIZE Foundation, which has gone on to create an incredible array of incentive prizes to solve the world's Grand Challenges – ocean health, literacy, space exploration, among many others.
>
> In 2011, City Light Capital partnered with XPRIZE to envision a platform that would make the power of incentive challenges available to anyone. The result was the spin-off of HeroX in 2013. HeroX was co-founded in 2013 by XPRIZE founder Peter Diamandis, challenge designer Emily Fowler and entrepreneur Christian Cotichini as a means to democratize the innovation model of XPRIZE.
>
> HeroX exists to enable anyone, anywhere in the world, to create a challenge that addresses any problem or opportunity, build a community around that challenge and activate the circumstances that can lead to a breakthrough innovation . . . HeroX incentive prize challenges are designed to harness the collective mind power of a community to innovate upon any problem or opportunity. Anyone can change the world. HeroX can help. The only question is, "What do *you* want to solve?"[27]

In its very name and narrative, the crowdsourcing platform reinstates the nineteenth-century ideal of the entrepreneur as an innovative "hero" who stands to conquer new frontiers through his or her vision and ingenuity. Indeed, the website itself reads, "HeroX: A Platform for Emergent Heroes,"[28] and CEO Christian Cotichini remarks, "The aspiration of the platform is solvers as heroes. HeroX lets them follow a 'hero's journey' through a career path, expanding from similar knowledge work through smaller prizes."[29] However, we also find some interesting differences between the twenty-first-century entrepreneur/hero innovator depicted here and the nineteenth-century version that Boltanski and Chiapello described.

First, the entrepreneurial hero in the digital age is not just in the business of expanding investment opportunities by laying down railroad lines or creating and catering to consumers' desires for creature comforts. The twenty-first-century entrepreneur is a "social entrepreneur" who keeps the wheels of capital spinning through various forms of "impact investing" (Chiapello and Knoll 2020).[30] By taking on the "world's Grand Challenges – ocean health, literacy, space exploration" – these heroes aim to produce social good *and* inordinate profits. As Peter Diamandis is fond of saying: "I think of problems as gold mines. The world's biggest problems are the world's biggest market opportunities. Solve a big one, you can help a billion people and become a billionaire in the process."[31] Indeed, in the age of digital capitalism, it seems that being a multi-millionaire is no longer enough; in order to legitimate your status among the techno-elite, billions are required.

Second, in seamlessly reconciling the pursuit of profit with progress, Diamandis replays a long-standing justification for capitalist enterprise. However, as the HeroX origin story makes clear, unlike the nineteenth-century entrepreneur, the twenty-first-century entrepreneur is not a towering individual who stands alone. Rather, this is a figure who realizes their heroic potential and fortune by being able to access technologies and institutions that are "designed to harness the collective mind power of a community," technologies and infrastructures which are provided by the platform HeroX. Indeed, given the discussion above, "harness" is an interesting word choice, or rather euphemism, as it presents forms of extraction and expropriation in more palatable terms and produces the illusion that a "community" of innovators really are "in it together," even though incentive competition rules stipulate that at the end of the day only the winners get paid.

Third, if the nineteenth-century entrepreneurial hero was cast as a "conquistador," the twenty-first-century entrepreneur is depicted more as a sleuth or sportsman. Discursive sleights of hand are continually invoked to represent the incentive competition as a game or "challenge" that "solvers" "accept," rather than a task or job that is accomplished through a stealthy expropriation of human labor. Indeed, many of the challenges HeroX facilitates for NASA are conducted as part of their "Tournament Lab."[32] Emily Fowler proposes that pitching the incentive competition as a "game" is precisely what will make them more popular and accessible. In a 2014 interview she noted, "Our business will work only if we get to scale and that requires simplicity and consistency. We need to effectively gamify incentive competitions to make it accessible broadly. Competitions are, essentially, games. So we need to strip it down to the core and go from there."[33]

On a few occasions, Christian Cotichini has conceded that HeroX is ultimately not a game but rather "a new labor model."[34] However, in many of his public pronouncements he too deploys language which downplays or masks this reality. For instance, in a 2020 article chronicling how HeroX was helping NASA advance moon exploration, Cotichini remarked, "Solvers around the world are understandably enthusiastic at the opportunity to contribute to a NASA mission. The ability of our community to solve such incredibly complex problems is a powerful case study for the capacity of crowdsourcing."[35]

Finally, the twenty-first-century entrepreneur, like their nineteenth-century counterpart, is also a person of "vision." However, it is not necessarily their inner fortitude and character, or their commitment to "bourgeois values" that imbues them with the gift which secures their ascent into the future. In the digital age, "one crazy idea" shared and disseminated through the proper technological and social channels can turn "a zero" into "a hero" overnight. Thus, in addition to suggesting that HeroX incentive competitions are a communal affair, here again they are portrayed as a means of "democratizing innovation" and extending creative opportunities to "anyone, anywhere in the world." As Cotichini remarks:

> The beauty of an incentive competition, if it's designed correctly, is that you are allowing anybody, even those who have no credentials, that could never bid on a proposal or win an RFP, to work on your problem and submit their solutions . . . Sometimes it's the crazy idea from the amateur or somebody that doesn't have a lot of experience in the industry that comes up with a breakthrough idea that ends up being the best idea.[36]

Protecting competition and nurturing networks

While incentive competitions are often cast as tapping into the innate human propensity for competition, they are also presented as a vehicle that safeguards competition, thereby ensuring the smooth functioning of "the free-market system."[37] For instance, in a 2019 article, business and tech writer Clive Reffell described the "Mozilla Voice Technology Challenge" that HeroX helped facilitate. This challenge, he wrote, "relates to the voice product market which is heavily dominated by a few giant tech companies. This is unhealthy as it stifles competition and prevents the entry of smaller companies with new and innovative products. The 'Mozilla Voice Technology Challenge!' aims to open up the voice product development process, to make it transparent and accessible to everyone."[38]

HeroX's customer service representative, Kyla Jeffrey, echoes this idea and takes it one step further. She proposes that in addition to hindering the development of corporate monopolies, incentive competitions also shift the balance of power between employers and employees. As she explained in a 2019 interview:

> Crowdsourcing gives the opportunity to prove your talent and genius. We're birthing new careers from these projects that people can put on their resumes – "I was a finalist in the Lockheed Martin AlphaPilot challenge." Millennials get that they're in charge of their own education, learning on demand. We can never stop learning, especially in technical professions. Part of our mission at HeroX is creating job liquidity, moving to an optimum we've already created with the Internet and the knowledge economy.
>
> We want to help make that global market. Once employers have to compete for talent rather than talent competing for jobs, we'll start to see balance in the income disparity, which is a current existential threat to economies and politics. Like social marketing, crowd enablement will eventually be a standard tool because of competitive forces – that's the beauty of the free market. We're also adding to academia and corporate labs what's possible for innovation.[39]

And yet, despite pronouncements that incentive competitions democratize innovation, level the playing field, and maintain the essential element of competition crucial for the flourishing of a free-market system, when we look more closely at how the platform actually works and operates, a slightly different picture begins to emerge.

First, despite its enthusiastic and welcoming language, HeroX does not extend an equally helping hand to "anyone, anywhere" who wants to unleash their innovative potential. HeroX operates as a "two-sided platform" that serves to connect competition sponsors with a varied pool of competition "solvers." According to HeroX, it makes its money from facilitating these exchanges rather than from the products or innovations that incentive competitions yield. The company charges clients for assisting with the contest design, and it charges a commission fee for each competition it brokers. Although HeroX does not stipulate a minimum prize amount in order to use the platform's services, the commission percentage it receives varies with the amount of the prize offered. For prizes between US$10,000 and US$250,000 dollars, the company charges an 18% commission fee, for prizes between US$250,000 and US$1,000,000, it charges 14%, and for prize amounts over one million dollars, the commission fee drops to 10%. Thus, despite its democratic and meritocratic pronouncements, the platform clearly rewards, or rather accommodates, those sponsors with the greatest amount of capital. Just as people with poor credit scores often end up paying the highest interest fees on credit cards, in the world of HeroX, sponsors with more limited means or seemingly less profitable initiatives are subjected to more intense forms of extraction.

Second, HeroX maintains that, unlike other platforms that have achieved staggering profits by selling users' data to advertisers (such as Google, Facebook, and Amazon), they do not regularly sell or "share personal information with companies, organizations and individuals outside of HeroX."[40] However, as it turns out, the various constituencies and corporations that fall within the ambit of HeroX are considerable, as the company routinely "partners" with other crowdsourcing platforms and businesses to expand its network and reach. As they explain:

> HeroX is a turnkey open innovation platform that offers organizations the know-how, the tools and the support to build, develop and manage their own crowd of problem-solvers for any challenges they are facing, internally and externally, bringing fresh innovating minds each time.
>
> We act as the "everything store" for crowdsourcing projects in any field, enabling any organization to solve any challenge, using the power of the crowd.
>
> On our platform, the organization posts the work they seek as an open call, adding guidelines and incentives. Innovators self-select their participation and become your crowd.[41]

Thus, as was the case with the Thiel Foundation, HeroX also arouses enthusiasm to participate in incentive competitions by promising its clients access to a powerful network of "business partners" and "thought-leaders." They maintain that entry into this "globally connected partner ecosystem" will ensure success. However, as Srnicek reminds us in his study of "platform capitalism," platform "network effects" do not just enhance the value of a product or service for users or consumers, as is often explained in the business literature and as is suggested here.[42] They are also central to the way platforms enhance their *own* power and profitability. Srnicek observes:

> With network effects, a tendency towards monopolization is built into the DNA of platforms: the more numerous the users who interact on a platform, the more valuable the entire platform becomes for each of them. Network effects, moreover, tend to mean that early advantages

become solidified as permanent positions of industry leadership. Platforms also have a unique ability to link together and consolidate multiple network effects . . . Platforms also seek to build up ecosystems of goods and services that close off competitors . . . All these dynamics turn platforms into monopolies with centralized control over increasingly vast numbers of users and the data they generate. (Srnicek 2017: 95–6)

This brings me to my final point. In developing the HeroX platform, Diamandis and his co-founders have discovered a way to effectively make incentive competitions available to sponsors who do not have millions to spend. Moreover, their intentions to use this platform to help make the world a better place may indeed be genuine. I am certainly not questioning the authenticity of their enthusiasm for or dedication to improving life on the planet. It is also clear that the thousands of "solvers" who participate in incentive competitions in large part do so because they do derive genuine "rewards" and feelings of satisfaction from working on a challenge, regardless of whether or not they win and get paid. However, in an era where data has become "the new oil" (Srnicek 2017), and where monopolistic tendencies threaten to reduce the platform economy to a few main players who assume an increasingly large role in brokering interactions and transactions between human beings, we must also consider how the platform provides a way to enhance forms of extraction, exploitation, and domination. Christian Cotichini, for example, openly states that achieving such dominance is an explicit business goal for HeroX. As he explained in a 2020 interview:

What I realized was that nobody has figured out how to scale crowdsourcing. Most of these crowdsourcing companies, the ones that were successful, were niche players. What was really needed was a horizontal platform that was going to do what Amazon has done for ecommerce, what Airbnb has done for shared accommodations, etc. "Google it" or "Amazon it" will soon be akin to "HeroX it", in other words our aim is for HeroX to be to crowdsourcing as Amazon is to ecommerce.[43] (my emphasis)

Thus, here again, we find that, even though digital technologies and platform infrastructures are making new forms of extraction possible, in the digital age capital accumulation continues to be animated by the long-standing imperative of continual expansion. Marx's insight that "the necessary result of competition is the accumulation of capital in a few hands, and thus the restoration of monopoly in a more terrible form" is as applicable to today's "platform capitalism" as it was to industrial capitalism during the mid-nineteenth century (Marx 1978 [1844]): 70).[44]

Conclusion: democratizing innovation or exacerbating inequality?

For Gustave Le Bon, the crowd was first and foremost a political problem. His study on the psychology of the crowd was intended as a "resource for statesmen" hoping to govern more effectively during the reign of the unruly masses. By contrast, for today's business leaders, the crowd is first and foremost an economic "opportunity": a solution for enhancing productivity, efficiency, innovation, and profit. As we have seen throughout this chapter, Silicon Valley's entrepreneurial elites and pedigree professors such as Karim Lakhani, also cast the crowd, or rather crowdsourcing, as a means of "democratizing innovation" – a practice that enables heroes of all stripes and backgrounds to use their "cognitive surplus" to crack some of the world's grandest problems. They arouse enthusiasm for participation in processes of capital accumulation by casting the incentive competition as an exciting challenge or game and holding out the promise that, by winning, "the everyman" can also gain entry into a world of genius elites and a circle of prospering investors.[45] They propose that incentive competitions appeal to the most essential parts of our competitive human nature, while at the same time channeling this potentially anti-social impulse into a means of making the world a better place for *all*.[46] Thus a mutation that seventeenth-century philosophers thought only possible through the instantiation of the social contract or the power of an authoritative state is for today's entrepreneurs achieved through a new economic strategy called the incentive competition.[47]

Yet despite business leaders' enthusiastic pronouncements, we must also consider how these ideologies "serve to establish and sustain relations of domination" (Thompson 1990: 56). How do incentive competitions reinstate, if not exacerbate, forms of exploitation, extraction, and domination in the age of digital capitalism? How might they play a role in not just democratizing innovation but also exacerbating inequality?

As we have seen, incentive competitions replace the exploitation of wage laborers with the exploitation made possible by the dispensation of a singular "prize." Competition sponsors benefit from

the "industry-changing" value generated by thousands of unremunerated "solvers" who labor for love and personal enrichment rather
than financial reward. Competition sponsors bear no obligations as
formal employers to the people who work to solve their challenges.
Moreover, by offering a "decimal dust" prize, a tiny fraction of what
they would otherwise spend on hiring formal workers to arrive at a
greater understanding of the "technological frontier," they often save
millions, thereby enhancing their corporate profits and power.

Indeed, although entrepreneurs like Diamandis and Cotichini
argue that incentive competitions are being democratized by
platforms like HeroX, thus enabling innovators with limited means
to reap their benefits, it is also crucial to remember that the use
of incentive competitions is becoming, as Lakhani points out, a
mainstream corporate practice. "Excluding crowdsourcing from the
corporate innovation tool kit" he reminds us, "means losing opportunity." In fact, playing up the democratizing potential of incentive
competitions helps mask the reality that incentive competitions have
become an exploitative staple of the corporate business arsenal.
When corporations such as General Electric, Siemens, L'Oréal,
Colgate-Palmolive, Harley-Davidson (to name but a few) are able
to potentially save millions of dollars a year by crowdsourcing their
business challenges and profiting off the unremunerated labor of
thousands of "digital enthusiasts," we must conclude that incentive
competitions are contributing to the exacerbation, if not production,
of structural inequalities that favor corporate interests.[48]

This is also to say that, although incentive competitions replace
wage labor with prizewinners and although they utilize new forms
of digital technology and platforms like HeroX to facilitate the
process of capital accumulation, "the operations of capital," as Jathan
Sadowski observes, still maintain "the same essential features of
exclusion, extraction and exploitation" (Sadowski 2020: 50). In the
age of digital capitalism, therefore, the secret of profit still hinges
upon negative reciprocity, and the drive for accumulation still leads,
as Marx put it, to "the restoration of monopoly in a more terrible
form."[49] Given this, it seems wise not merely to celebrate incentive
competitions as the new solution to innovation and shared prosperity
but to critically interrogate the role they play in generating a more
stratified and inequitable society. How this is done in the name of
fostering "community" and "collaboration" is the issue that the next
chapter will explore.

2

The Spirit of Collaboration: Crowdsourcing through Communities

While incentive competitions provide business leaders and entrepreneurs with one way to organize, motivate, and ultimately benefit from "the wisdom of the crowd," another is provided by tapping into or creating a community of digitally connected enthusiasts who share a common interest and work together to address a common cause or solve a problem. Indeed, "community," "collaborative," or "open source" crowdsourcing initiatives, as Karim Lakhani variously refers to them, are quickly becoming central to corporate and entrepreneurial business practices. Like incentive competitions, community crowdsourcing initiatives are enthusiastically touted as a means to enhance efficiency, improve and democratize innovation, and increase profit margins by reducing labor costs. However, there are also some interesting differences in the way collaborative crowdsourcing initiatives are ideologically elaborated and justified. Although scholars like Lakhani present "communities and contests . . . as *complementary* approaches to manage innovation," and although they can be, and often are, used together, I contend that these two forms of crowdsourcing are worth interrogating precisely because they point to some of the larger *cultural contradictions* that animate the spirit of capitalism in the digital age.

Thus, with the goal of ultimately illuminating these contradictions, in this chapter I explore how community-based crowdsourcing initiatives are being deployed and promoted by business leaders and entrepreneurs. As was the case in chapter 1, here again I ask: what kinds of assumptions, values, and interests do business experts advance when they promote and utilize community crowdsourcing initiatives? How do they arouse enthusiasm for participation in these initiatives and thereby secure committed engagement in processes of capital accumulation? How do they justify community crowdsourcing as contributing to the common good while at the same time assuaging the anxieties this form of crowdsourcing has engendered? Lastly, what does collaborative crowdsourcing reveal about the constant as well as the changing nature of capital accumulation, extraction, and domination in the digital age?[1]

The community in society

Business gurus will often tip their hats to Gustave Le Bon in their discussions of crowdsourcing, even if it is only to refute him. However, they are far less likely to pay homage to the man who, also writing in the late nineteenth century, foregrounded the concept of "community" as a paramount intellectual concern. In his 1887 publication *Gemeinschaft und Geselleschaft* (*Community and Society*), the German sociologist Ferdinand Tönnies deployed the terms "community" and "society" to reference and describe two very different forms of sociality.[2] Communities, he proposed, reference a world of highly personal relationships where people are bound together by kinship, shared sentiments and beliefs, and the intimacies of daily living. As he wrote, "The real foundation of unity, and consequently the possibility of *Gemeinschaft*, in the first place is closeness of blood relationship and mixture of blood; secondly, physical proximity; and finally, for human beings, intellectual proximity (Tönnies 2017 [1887]: 48). This "intellectual proximity," or as Tönnies also phrased it, "*Gemeinschaft* of the mind," expresses "the community of mental life" forged through shared devotion to "sacred places and worshipped deities," and through participation in "cooperation and coordinated action for a common goal." Indeed, Tönnies proposed that in many cases the most powerful bonds that develop in communities result not from kinship or neighborhood but, rather, "from similarity of work and intellectual attitude." "Friendship," he wrote, "comes most easily into existence when craft or callings are the same or of similar nature" (ibid.: 43). Tönnies further pointed out that in communities, loyalty and fulfilling one's obligations to others, rather than pursuing individual interests, is paramount.

Societies, by contrast, reference a very different world of sociality where people are bound to each other by impersonal and instrumental relations. Dis-embedded from the organic ties and obligations of kinship and close living, in societies, Tönnies wrote:

> everybody is by himself and isolated, and there exists a condition of tension against all others . . . nobody wants to grant and produce anything for another individual, nor will he be inclined to give ungrudgingly to another individual, if it be not in exchange for a gift or labor equivalent that he considers at least equal to what he has given . . . In *Gesellschaft* every person strives for that which is to his own advantage and he affirms the actions of others only in so far as they can further his interest. (Tönnies 2017 [1887]: 65, 77)

In societies, as Tönnies observed, self-interest is pursued through recourse to rationality rather than sentiment, and social relationships are increasingly mediated by money, markets, and contracts.[3]

While Tönnies viewed community and society as antithetical to each other, and indicative of two very different periods in human history, contemporary proponents of crowdsourcing suggest that in the digital age community and society coexist in very fruitful ways. Indeed, they propose that digital technologies have made possible new kinds of "communities." Instead of being produced through the intimacies of daily life, kinship bonds, and shared locales, digital technologies such as the internet enable groups of people who share a passion for a common interest or cause to come together, cooperate, and form, in Tönnies's words, "relationships of mutual affirmation" (Tönnies 2017 [1887]: 33). Business experts argue that these communities, in turn, can be used in manifold ways to enhance market enterprise and drive innovation, thereby furthering the instrumental needs and interests of society.

For instance, in discussing the role communities can play in fostering innovation, Karim Lakhani notes that "like contests, collaborative communities have a long and rich history. They were critical to the development of Bessemer steel, blast furnaces, Cornish pumping engines, and large-scale silk production." He further proposes that far from representing the antithesis of instrumental ends, communities, like "companies," can and do work together to achieve instrumental outcomes. As he explains, "communities are organized to marshal the outputs of multiple contributors and aggregate them into a coherent value-creating whole – much as traditional companies do. And like companies, communities must first assess what should be included in the final aggregation and then accomplish that through a combination of technology and process."[4]

And yet, as Lakhani observes, the key difference between communities and companies is that for communities the instrumental outcome, or the market value created by their efforts, is not the *ultimate* end. Instead of pursuing economic gain, he proposes that communities are motivated primarily by "intrinsic" rewards, such as "enjoyment, the stimulation associated with intellectual challenge, the satisfaction from completing a task at hand" (Lakhani 2016: 121) and "the desire to burnish one's reputation in a community of peers." Lakhani proposes that this, in turn, helps explain the puzzle of why "actors would make private investments and then willingly give away and share the results of their efforts" (ibid.: 113). If corporations have long run on the model that private vice spawns public virtue, among communities, Lakhani suggests, the formula is flipped; public virtue, as demonstrated through acts of sharing and cooperation, can lead to private gains, like an enhanced reputation, recognition from one's peers, or just the sheer joy of participating in the creative process. For instance, in contrasting the success of open source communities with the Apple company, Lakhani writes:

> Now Linux, Apache and the open-source movement have the same kind of rabid fans, people who really love it – it's a religious conviction for them – and they can contribute to it, can contribute source code, can contribute patches, can help each other out. And it is amazing to think that people can have this strong affection for open source and actually help it evolve. That's why Linux and Apache have taken off, and Apple reached a plateau and then dropped off the radar.[5]

Indeed, Lakhani notes that, increasingly, companies are looking for ways to harness the advantages of open source communities and integrate them into their business models. As he points out:

> In June of 1998 IBM shocked the global software industry by announcing that it intended to abandon its internal development efforts on web server infrastructure and instead join forces with Apache, a nascent online community of webmasters and technologists . . . IBM reasoned that the crowd was beating it at the software game, so it would do better to join forces and reap profits through complementary assets such as hardware and services.[6]

Lakhani thus arouses enthusiasm for community crowdsourcing initiatives by proposing that they enable companies to recruit the best, most enthused, and most efficient talent. If the incentive competition provides winners with a financial reward and a way to be a hero to humanity, Lakhani proposes that community crowdsourcing initiatives promise their participants the opportunity to engage in their craft alongside a group of like-minded peers. Unalienated labor is the ultimate prize that community crowdsourcing initiatives confer on their members.

Indeed, Jeff Howe suggests that we should view the emergence of community crowdsourcing initiatives in part as a response to the rise of amateurism and the increasingly alienated nature of wage labor, or what anthropologist David Graeber refers to as the massive proliferation of "bullshit jobs" (Graeber 2018).[7] As Howe observes, participants in such communities, are "not primarily motivated by money . . . they're donating their leisure hours to the cause. That is, they're contributing their excess capacity, or 'spare cycles,' to indulge in something they love to do." He proposes that as people have become more educated and yet are expected to compete in a labor market that "requires ever greater degrees of specialization," it has ultimately left them feeling "overeducated and underfulfilled." He thus asks, "with job satisfaction rates reaching all-time lows, is it any wonder they're seeking more meaningful work outside the confines of the workplace?" (Howe 2008: 29).

Wired to collaborate

As we have seen, economic and societal factors are frequently presented as one reason for the flourishing of community crowdsourcing initiatives but, as was the case with incentive competitions, they are also justified through recourse to claims about human nature. If incentive competitions promote the idea that human beings are "hardwired" to compete, community crowdsourcing initiatives propose that human beings are "wired" to collaborate. As Jeff Howe notes, "crowdsourcing capitalizes on the deeply social nature of the human species . . . people derive enormous pleasure from cultivating their talents and from passing on what they've learned to others. Collaboration, in the context of crowdsourcing, is its own reward" (Howe 2008: 1–15). Or as Christian Cotichini, the co-founder of HeroX, remarked when reflecting upon his involvement with crowdsourcing:

I had a background in B2B start-ups, and when I first started with crowdsourcing, I had anxiety at first. I've learned a lot in the past five years. When you give people a chance to participate, don't micromanage it – there's a fundamental human desire to compete. It's not about winning; it's about inclusion, which is powerful. *I'm also amazed to learn that we're wired to collaborate;* we're social animals. We see that desire a lot in these crowdsourcing projects, bringing talent to our customers. That's the egalitarian nature of HeroX.[8] (my emphasis)

As was the case with Lakhani, who expressed "amazement" at the fact that people might donate their labor and time to help develop open source code, Cotichini also suggests that discovering this natural propensity to collaborate was an "amazing" revelation. However, as he confesses, the revelation itself was not enough to ward off the "anxiety" he experienced when he first began experimenting with crowdsourcing. Moreover, such anxiety is hardly exceptional. As Lakhani and co-authors note in an article entitled "Overcoming Cultural Resistance to Open Source Innovation" (Winsor, Paik, Tushman, and Lakhani 2019), the turn to community crowdsourcing initiatives is often experienced as "a threat." It challenges the "prestige and creative talent" of firm members. It is often regarded as something that will "upend" a company's "old ways of doing things." Open source innovation, it is feared, might "lessen the value" of company employees' expertise and experience. Despite these "very real concerns," Lakhani and his co-authors maintain that if companies want to stay competitive, this resistance must be overcome. They explain:

Companies that let their old culture reject the new risk becoming obsolete if doing so inhibits their rethinking of their future using powerful tools like crowdsourcing, blockchain, customer experience-based connections, integrating workflows with artificial intelligence (AI), automated technologies and digital business platforms. These new ways of working affect how and where work is done, access to information, an organization's capacity for work and its efficiency. *As important as technological proficiency is, managing the cultural shift required to embrace transformative industry architecture* – the key to innovating new business models – may be the bigger challenge. (Winsor, Paik, Tushman, and Lakhani 2019: 1; my emphasis)

There are two points worth emphasizing here. First, Lakhani and his co-authors clearly demonstrate that digital capitalism is not just a technological or economic project; it is also, as Eran Fisher reminds us, an *ideological* one (Fisher 2010). In addition to integrating new technologies to facilitate the accumulation of capital, it requires participants to accept beliefs and commitments to news kinds of social arrangements. As people who are actively involved in the business *and* consulting world, Lakhani and his colleagues play an influential role in facilitating such ideological transformations. Second, while the incentive competition mobilizes the language of "the game" or "contest" and refers to participants as "solvers" here, we get an explicit acknowledgment that what crowdsourcing initiatives introduce is not so much a new game as a new business model, which in turn is predicated upon new kinds of labor relations. Indeed, Lakhani and his co-authors go as far as to provide explicit advice on how to introduce this new model to nervous employees and thereby "assuage" their anxieties and secure their commitment to participating in a form of capital accumulation that deploys open source initiatives as part of its business strategy. They write:

> Begin by clearly communicating how adopting open systems will affect the larger ecosystem of the organization. Share that the traditional way of doing business will not change and is in fact core and essential to the overall strategy, which ensures traditional employees that their professional identities will not be threatened. Addressing unspoken fears in this way increases the likelihood that employees will emotionally engage and be more open to the overall vision adopting open systems and tools. (Winsor, Paik, Tushman, and Lakhani 2019: 3)

As was the case with incentive competitions, here again we find that Lakhani and his co-authors work to assuage the anxieties of company employees who fear that their traditional power and privilege will be diminished by the adoption of crowdsourcing initiatives. The potential concerns of the community members, whose "free labor" is integral to the company's success, are notably *not* addressed. This omission may be accidental, or it may reflect an awareness of the fact that the audience for this article is by and large comprised of business owners and managers, so it is their concerns that need to be spoken to. However, the ideological effects of such an erasure are potentially powerful. They not only *naturalize* the idea that one need not concern oneself with the potentially exploitative dynamics of open source labor arrangements, especially when they are consistently appropriated as part of the corporate business arsenal to increase profits. They also reinstate the idea that in this new "sharing economy," which itself often operates as "a floating signifier for a diverse range of activities" (Nadeem 2015) and as a euphemism for various forms of capitalist extraction, the powerful will benefit from the free labor and "gifts" of others but not be expected to share their "traditional" wealth and privileges in return.[9] Once again, therefore, it appears that negative reciprocity emerges as an enduring logic of capital accumulation.

Putting community crowdsourcing to work

As academics and consultants, management professors such as Karim Lakhani and others associated with the Harvard and MIT Innovation Labs or the Harvard Business School Digital Initiative do play an influential role in producing and disseminating the ideologies associated with the spirit of digital capitalism. But their ideas are also inspired by empirical examples and by observing how forms of community crowdsourcing are being deployed by actual businesses and investors. As such, in the remainder of this chapter I want to focus on two companies that have embraced community or open source crowdsourcing models as a central component of their business practice. How do they justify and legitimate such initiatives? How do they arouse enthusiasm for participation in them? And what can their deployment of community or open source crowdsourcing initiatives teach us about the nature of capital accumulation, extraction, and domination in the digital age?

"The accidental business"

Though it has lost some of its former glory among its community members, one of the most widely acclaimed pioneers of crowd-sourcing, and the "textbook case" that Lakhani and colleagues themselves use when teaching in the Harvard Business School, comes from the Threadless T-shirt company.[10] As company founders Jake Nickell and Jacob DeHart tell the story, the Threadless T-shirt company was very much an "accidental business." "Threadless," Nickell writes, "was never intended to be a business. When Jacob DeHart and I started out it was all just a hobby – a fun thing to do for the other designers we were friends with" (Nickell 2010: 12). The idea for Threadless developed in 2000, after Nickell, who was an art school student and web designer, had won an online T-shirt design competition hosted by the New Media Underground Festival in London. After participating in the competition, Nickell contacted Jacob DeHart and proposed that they sponsor an ongoing online competition where fellow artists and designers could submit T-shirt designs. They posted their first call for entries as a thread on the dreamless.org forum but, as the competition and number of entries began to grow, they built their own website.

The website not only enabled users to submit their T-shirt designs, it also introduced a voting system so that people visiting the site could score the different entries. The shirts that received the highest scores, or that were deemed most interesting and/or controversial by Nickell and DeHart, would then be printed and sold online. The copyright to the design and the profits accruing from the sales of the T-shirts went to the company and, in exchange, the designer would receive "prize money" and usually a store credit towards T-shirts.[11] In addition to the voting system, the website included forums and blogs where designers could comment on each other's works, read interviews, and browse photo galleries.

At the outset, new T-shirts were being issued "every couple of months" (Nickell 2010: 14); however, by 2004, "the Jakes" had moved their operation into a larger warehouse and were printing six new design T-shirts every week. "Everything we made sold," Nickell recounts. "It makes sense. It's simple. If we only make the stuff people tell us they'd like to buy before we even make it, then we should be able to sell it once we do make it" (ibid.: 50). They began earning enough money to quit their day jobs, with a total annual revenue of "around $1.5 million." As Nickell recounts, "By the end of 2004, we fully realized that Threadless had huge potential to become a significant business. We started to focus more on it. We took a step back, and looked at what we were doing right, and how we were able to build such an incredible business almost accidentally" (ibid.: 15).

Indeed, in 2005 the success of the operation garnered the attention of business experts like Lakhani. "The Jakes" were invited to speak at a user innovation conference at MIT. As Nickell recalls:

> We really didn't know what we were getting ourselves into. Apparently, some people at the school had been researching this new idea of "user innovation," and "crowdsourcing," and came across us: the first business they'd really seen implement it in the real world. Huge businesses such as General Mills and Pitney Bowes were represented at the conference, discussing this new business model.
> We were the only ones who actually ran our business that way. (Nickell 2010: 48)

While onlookers identified a promising new business model in Threadless, the Jakes themselves continued to emphasize that "Threadless is a community of people first, a T-shirt store second." Nickell explains:

> Most day-to-day visitors on Threadless are not there to shop. They are there to submit designs, score designs, talk in the forums, read interviews, browse the photo galleries, and just generally be inspired by other members in the community. There may be these new, fancy words and ideas to describe what we're doing in an academic way, but we try not to let it change us. Threadless really is just a giant group of friends making cool designs; not an "innovative crowdsourcing platform." (Nickell 2010: 51)

Considering the fact that revenues jumped to US$6.5 million by 2005, Nickell's depiction of Threadless as a "community" first and a business second may rightfully invite some skepticism. However, this way of depicting Threadless is frequently echoed by the artists who design T-shirts for the company. For instance, an artist named Sonmi explained, "When I found Threadless it became like an addiction. It's a rare community, in that its members are super-friendly, passionate about art, and just really cool and diverse" (Nickell 2020: 183). Nor are the Threadless community members confined to interacting online. As part of their attempt to further a feeling of community among their "members," in 2007 the Jakes began sponsoring annual in-person meetups. The first gathering, which was held at their warehouse, was called the "the Family Reunion" and was attended by members from around the world. They also opened a "bricks-and-mortar" store in Chicago "that only carries the newest two weeks' worth of designs, and an LCD monitor displays information about each tee that is sold"(ibid.: 104).

While the Threadless community is bound together by a passion for art, and as evidenced from the T-shirt designs, a playfully ironic hipster sense of humor, they are also motivated by a spirit of competition. Indeed, at the very heart of the Threadless business model is the incentive prize, and it does provide an apt example of Lakhani's point that "contests and communities" can be used in complementary ways to organize the crowd. However, whereas Diamandis and even Lakhani frequently praise the incentive competition as a means to discover the technological frontier on the cheap by paying only the winner, the Jakes deploy the incentive prize as a means to strengthen the bonds of the Threadless community by tapping into artists' desires for recognition from their peers. Indeed, as one designer fondly recalls, "I remember trying for months to get my first print, it was a badge of honor and every print after it was as amazing a feeling as the first time." Or as another explains, "I used to be really proud of getting printed here, of being part of the Threadless family. I remember that when I went to Chicago to hang out with everyone and also win the Bestee award was, with no doubt, one of the best fucking days of my life, it was magical!"[12]

In the hands of the Jakes, the incentive prize not only plays a pivotal role in conferring prestige upon community members, it also enables them to eliminate the need for advertising their products. Indeed, the incentive prize is touted as the ideal way to achieve the elusive economic goal of the perfect match between supply and demand. As Nickell points out, by only producing shirts that received high votes, they were more or less guaranteed sales. The Jakes's secret to arousing committed engagement in this process of capital accumulation thus hinges upon their abilities to transform T-shirt *customers* into *community members* who feel committed to a common goal, and who use their votes and design contributions to actively shape the products that are produced. The Jakes's business mantra boils down to the idea that if you can use technology to harness people's passions, profits will follow.

Blake Mycoskie, the founder and CEO of Toms Shoes, describes the Threadless business model as "simple, yet revolutionary." He writes:

> Artists submit designs that, by the nature of the selection process, must be clever/different/innovative to stand out from the pack; the community sparks the conversations about the ideas that they like best; and to complete the cycle, Threadless listens to these conversations, and prints the shirts with the most fanfare and buzz. Wash, rinse, and repeat. Because of this unique model, Threadless transforms its customers into both fans and evangelists. (Nickell 2010: 211)

The Threadless case study provides an apt example of the need to consider how "activities that blossom outside of wage-based relations and other forms of commodified labor" contribute to processes of capital accumulation and extraction in the digital age (Wittel 2017: 68). Digital technologies may not have created the ability to appropriate such activities. For instance, as the anthropologist Robert Foster points out, the process of creating valued brands or "love marks" has long relied upon appropriating sentiments and feelings that are produced by consumers in their daily lives and homes (Foster 2007). However, digital technologies have certainly enhanced abilities to capture non-commodified value-generating activities for the purposes of capital accumulation.[13] By providing tools to build online communities and forums where company owners can "listen in" and appropriate the ideas, information, and products created by community members, entrepreneurs like the Jakes can more readily ensure that the wheels of profit will continue to spin and everyone will walk away feeling that they have got exactly what they desired. Indeed, a look at the blog forum over the past few years reveals that one of the biggest perceived threats to the company's continued success and sustained profits has been a loss of feeling of community among many of its members. In a 2017 post entitled, "What is Happening?," which elicited over 200 comments from Threadless community members, one blogger laments:

> Back in the days that I remember, Threadless was a company with a model to be followed by others. It was friendly, the staff and the community were so close that it felt more like a bunch of friends, and everyone worked together to suggest new improvements that were both good for the designer and the company. Threadless would do every-thing in their range to compensate the designer as fair as possible. And because of that, everyone worked as hard as possible to come out with both great ideas and a great product. There was passion on both sides. I just don't see this anymore here, and I don't see Threadless standing out from other t-shirt sites as they once did.[14]

This blogger's lament, and the many others like it, can be read as a symptom of Threadless's fall from "grace." However, it is more interesting to consider what these remarks reveal more generally about the dynamics of capital accumulation in the digital age. If capital accumulation increasingly comes to depend upon the ability to extract value from a community of digitally connected enthu-siasts, then the real crisis this form of accumulation must contend with is not just one of overaccumulation, as Marx proposed, but it is also the diminution of affect. When passion fades, profits fall.[15] When the affective bonds of community begin to feel like the instrumental relationships of society, businesses like Threadless face declining fiscal returns. In contrast to incentive competitions, therefore, community-based crowdsourcing initiatives must not only harness the "the cognitive surplus of the crowd," as Peter Diamandis proposed, they must also harness the *emotional surplus* to ensure committed engagement in processes of capital accumulation.[16] In the era of digital capitalism, therefore, information and affect both emerge as central to processes of value creation. Eran Fisher, for instance, astutely observes that collaborative crowdsourcing initiatives enable participants "to bring their personal, lifeworld qualities of creativity, intimate relationships, and deep personal engagement to bear on their work activities and reeroticize the disenchanted world of (industrial) work" (Fisher 2010: 6).

Community crowdsourcing goes corporate

As the Jakes tell the story, Threadless was an "accidental business" that emerged from a group of digitally connected enthusiastic designers who were all pursuing the same passion in life. However, in the time since their business emerged, community crowdsourcing has become a mainstream corporate practice. One of the best-known examples, and again one that has become a classic "case study" for Karim Lakhani and his colleagues, comes from General Electric (GE). As one of the longest-standing companies in America, and as the founder of one of the oldest corporate universities, GE offers a valuable entry point through which to explore how community-based crowdsourcing initiatives are being appropriated and ideologically justified at the corporate level.[17]

GE's forays into community crowdsourcing began in the second decade of the twenty-first century. As was the case with so many companies that experienced declining profits in the wake of the 2008 global economic recession, GE was eager to find new ways to boost its business, and in 2012, under the new management of CEO Jeffrey Immelt, it hired entrepreneur, consultant, and author of *The Lean Startup*, Eric Ries, to help reformulate its business model. The premise of the movement and the book boils down to the idea that by taking a more "entrepreneurial" approach to business management, and by becoming more "capital efficient" and leveraging "human creativity more effectively," corporations can better adapt to the uncertainties and disruptions that drive the contemporary business world, and thereby become more innovative and profitable (Ries 2014).[18] Ries recommends that instead of investing heavily in fixed capital and deciding beforehand what products should be produced and brought to market, companies can gain a competitive edge by deploying processes of "co-creation" and soliciting and utilizing consumer input much earlier in the production process. As one journalist describes it, Ries essentially proposes that companies should "act like a startup," but "make money like a Fortune 500."[19] Indeed, Jeff Immelt was so impressed by Ries's approach to management and innovation that he not only hired him as a consultant, he also wrote the foreword to the 2014 edition of his book and provided an endorsement on the jacket cover that states, "I make all of our managers read *The Lean Startup*."

One of the first changes GE made in their attempt to become a "leaner" company was to begin crowdsourcing some of their innovation challenges. For example, in 2013 GE aviation engineers wanted to create a lighter jet engine bracket, but they lacked the knowledge and resources to do so.[20] Instead of spending millions of dollars from their research and development budget to recruit the right specialists and acquire the necessary technology, GE turned to GrabCAD, an "online community of more than a million engineers and designers" and sponsored an incentive competition. As Liz Stinson reported, "Whoever could redesign a bracket that reduced the most weight while still supporting the engine would win $7,000." More than a thousand entries came in, and a 21-year-old PhD student from Indonesia won the prize. The competition was heralded as a "triumph of crowdsourcing." As Stinson wrote:

> For a nominal price, GE used the knowledge of someone they would have never otherwise met to innovate its way out of a design problem . . . Under Immelt, GE has invested a sizable chunk of its annual $6 billion R&D funds into taking advantage of a simple, internet-enabled truth: Now, more than ever, it's possible to connect with people around the world, so why not take advantage of that to solve some engineering problems?[21]

Or, as Alex Tepper, who then served as the global director of innovation for GE, commented when reflecting on the contest, "What we learned was not only that open innovation can work, but part of the reason why it works is that you're tapping into a very different group of people."[22]

Indeed, subsequently, GE has not only deployed incentive competitions to organize and motivate the crowd to solve its problems, in 2014 they partnered with Local Motors and also developed their own community-based online crowdsourcing platform called FirstBuild. As the website announces, FirstBuild is "changing the way products come to market by letting a community influence the product from the very beginning." Their stated purpose is to "invent a new world of home appliances by creating a socially engaged community focused on the next great idea."[23] The platform provides a space for engineers and designers to submit ideas for new products, browse and comment upon ideas that others have submitted, and compete in innovation contests. It arouses enthusiasm for these activities by promising participants a trifecta of rewards: a vibrant sense of community, recognition for one's talents, and protection of intellectual property under the Creative Commons License. Describing the communal nature of FirstBuild, the website states:

> The community is the heart of FirstBuild. It is what drives creativity and inspires innovation. FirstBuild is an online community of like-minded individuals as well as a physical location where community members can work on projects. It is a place to bounce your ideas off one another or just take a break and hang out with other creative minds.[24]

Here again, we find that in the era of digital capitalism, community is not construed as antithetical to market rationality, but rather it is portrayed as the means of furthering the interests of the corporation by inspiring creativity and enhancing innovation. Moreover, as was the case with Threadless, FirstBuild also offers its online community members opportunities to socialize and collaborate in person. The physical location "where community members can work on projects" is called "the microfactory" and is located at the University of Louisville Kentucky.[25] It is described as an open-sourced "maker space" where designers and engineers are given access to materials and tools to rapidly develop their prototypes into products.[26] As the website states, "Think of it as a playground for adults. A collaborative maker space where ideas come to life. Open to the imaginations of all students, engineers, artists, developers, entrepreneurs."[27] Indeed, the GE "microfactory," or rather "playground for adults," provides a paradigmatic example of the "rebranding of work as play that underwrites the labor control mechanisms of the dot-com and startup industries of the late twentieth and early twenty-first centuries" (Benzon 2020: 98).

In addition to arousing enthusiasm by promising participants an opportunity to be a part of a vibrant maker community, GE's FirstBuild initiative also secures committed engagement in processes of capital accumulation by tapping into members' desires for recognition and rewards. While the workers, or rather "makers," in the microfactory do not receive any wages or salaries for the products they create, and while their ideas can be freely used by others, they are guaranteed that the innovations they develop will be credited to them under the creative license agreement.[28]

Furthermore, although makers do not receive wages, they can earn money by becoming a "concept leader" or "key contributor" in the production process. Upon the first sale of the product, the "concept leader," or person who played the main role in developing the idea for the product, receives a US$1,000 award and a 0.5% royalty commission "for a period of not more than three years beyond the date of sale of the first product." "Key contributors," or those who have played a significant role in helping to refine or develop the product, receive a US$500 award and 0.25% royalties for the same time period.[29]

Through awards, recognitions, and even royalty agreements, there is some attempt, albeit often small, on the part of GE to compensate community members for the creative energies and the labor they expend to "bring new ideas to life." Provided, that is, that their innovations end up selling. Moreover, as members of the FirstBuild community themselves frequently emphasize, they derive multiple benefits (psychological, social, and economic) from participating in this community and having the opportunity to develop their product in a setting where they are given the opportunity to network with peers and are granted free access to the means of production. Thus it seems like a win–win situation for both the corporation and the community, and I am sure there are many GE executives as well as FirstBuild community members who actually experience it this way.

However, the job of the social scientist is not just to elicit the emic or insider's point of view. It is also to highlight relations and dynamics which the "natives" themselves may not be fully aware of and consider current socioeconomic developments within their appropriate structural context. In this spirit, therefore, we must also ask what kind of ideological work is done to present this community crowdsourcing initiative as a win–win situation. In justifying and valorizing community-based crowdsourcing as a new mode of capital accumulation, what other realities or inequalities are downplayed or ignored? When community-based crowdsourced initiatives are scaled to corporate size, and indeed become an industry-wide practice, what effect does this have on the millions of workers (not digitally connected, enthusiastic makers) who now find themselves without a job?

I argue that in the era of digital capitalism, it is precisely through such semantic sleights of hand that corporations like GE are able to mask practices of extraction and exploitation and re-present them as benevolent forms of "investment" in an innovation community. These ideological formations work to "justify and normalize flexible and precarious work through an ambiguous association between capitalist exchange and altruistic social values" (Cockayne 2016: 73).[30] For instance, by referring to their "members" as "makers" and not workers, GE is able to defend deploying (again *not employing*) hundreds of designers and engineers to labor in their "microfactory" for *free*. GE's monopoly over the means of production is presented as a "gift" to curious enthusiasts who are bound together by a passion to innovate and would like nothing more than to spend their "spare" time or "cycles" testing prototypes in a "playground for adults." Factory production, once the paradigm of alienation, is now recast as an opportunity for deepening the ties of community and enhancing one's personal growth and development, all the while having fun in the process.

Again, such depictions may indeed resonate with the experiences of FirstBuild community members. I am not suggesting that "the makers" get *nothing* out of the deal. However, these framings also work to serve the interests of the powerful. For despite the celebration of communal energy and passion, at the end of the day makers enter these microfactories, just as they did during the period of industrial capitalism, because they do not have access to the means of production. They comprise a surplus army of sorts, but instead of competing for wages, they compete for often paltry prizes and limited royalties. While their labor may be experienced as enriching and self-affirming, the value they collectively produce and the cognitive and emotional surplus they generate is nonetheless being expropriated to augment GE's profit margins. The microfactory, therefore, as well as the online FirstBuild platform which has numerous built-in features to collect innovation ideas from community members, is not just a community maker space "that helps people collaborate economically at scale," as "the sharing economy narrative" so frequently proposes (Cole and Rosenblat 2017: 1635). It is also a corral in which various forms of social, intellectual, and emotional capital are captured for minimal sums and then redeployed in the name of profit seeking and commercial expansion.

Conclusion: the wealth of networks or corporations?

Ferdinand Tönnies deployed the terms "community" and "society" to reference and describe two very different forms of sociality.

Writing amidst the emergence of industrial capitalism, he worried that the bonds of community – based on shared sentiments, mutual interests, and relations of reciprocity – were being rapidly displaced by the instrumental and impersonal relations of market society. However, as we have seen in this chapter, contemporary business leaders propose that in the era of digital capitalism, these two ways of relating to human beings are not antithetical but, rather, complementary. Digital technologies have made possible new forms of community that can be harnessed by corporations to pursue instrumental ends. In return, participants in community crowdsourcing initiatives are promised opportunities to realize an essential part of their cooperative human nature while finding meaning, purpose, and passion amidst a community of like-minded peers. In contrast to the incentive competition, where "the winner takes all," in community crowdsourcing initiatives everybody purportedly wins!

However, by framing these crowdsourcing initiatives as win–win situations for businesses and communities alike; by invoking the language of "makers" not workers; and by presenting the microfactory as a communal playground rather than a colonizing space where various forms of value are captured for the purposes of capital accumulation, corporations like GE are ultimately able to re-present extractive relationships as if they were based on real rather than negative reciprocity. Indeed, one wonders what Marcel Mauss might make of all of this. Almost a century ago, the French sociologist admonished, "those who have benefited from" the worker's "services have not discharged their debt to him through the payment of wages." "The worker has given his life and his labor, on the one hand to the collective, and on the other hand, to his employer" (Mauss 1925: 67). If Mauss, like Marx, was able to see through the hypocrisy, or rather inequities, of industrial capitalism, what might he say today, as both workers and wages are increasingly displaced by "digital enthusiasts" who donate their "excess capacities" and "spare cycles" for the opportunity to collaborate with peers or win a "nominal" incentive prize?[31]

Indeed, such language itself warrants scrutiny because it serves to further justify and legitimate the extractive practices of digital capitalism and the so-called "sharing economy." As author and entrepreneur Alex Stephany writes in his book, *The Business of Sharing: Making It in the New Sharing Economy*, "The sharing economy is the value of taking underutilized assets and making them accessible online to a community, leading to a reduced need for ownership of those assets" (Stephany 2015: 9). Yet, while it might make sense to argue that a car sitting idle in a parking lot, or a chainsaw hanging dormant in a garage, could be more productively "utilized" by being lent out or rented to others, what are the consequences of treating human, conscious, creative life activity (that is, all the good unalienated stuff that Marx told us to hold sacred way back in 1848) this way? Isn't it precisely by discursively transmuting our conscious life activity into "unutilized" surplus that proponents of crowdsourcing are able to justify and legitimate the expropriation of human labor for their crowdsourcing initiatives?

It is not particularly surprising to discover such language in the writings of journalists and technology experts like Jeff Howe or Alex Stephany – though to be fair, Howe does discuss some of the ways crowdsourcing initiatives stand to exacerbate inequality. However, it does sound alarm bells when this language comes from a scholar who has devoted his career to considering the ways digital technologies might be used to enhance "peer-to-peer" or "social" production, and thereby emancipate human beings from the exploitation and domination of commercial industries.

In his seminal book, *The Wealth of Networks: How Social Production Transforms Markets and Freedoms*, Yochai Benkler considers how digital technologies and the emergence of the "networked information economy" are potentially giving rise to a more democratic society. He proposes that, as individuals are increasingly able to enter into cooperative relations with each other, and use digital technologies to collectively create our information environment, they are able to challenge the hegemony of the old "industrial information economy" and play a much larger role in shaping the world we dwell, think, and create in. Moreover, like Howe, Benkler also asserts that one of the great perks of living in the networked digital age is that communication technologies make it possible to harness individuals' "excess capacities" or "activities and judgments" that are "unrelated to making a living" and use them to fuel a variety of projects that stand to bolster our "intellectual commons." Benkler proposes that as complicated projects are increasingly broken down into "modular tasks" that take only minutes of deliberation, an ever-expanding portion of the networked community can play its role in contributing to the collective welfare of society. From solving NASA space challenges, to creating the next Wikipedia, to even discovering a cure for cancer, Benkler sees great promise in a future where social production, sustained through the cooperation, sharing, altruism, and the passion of networked individuals, comes to rival the efficacy of the market. His perspective is worth quoting at length:

With the right institutional framework and peer-review or quality-control mechanisms, and with well-modularized organization of work, social sharing is likely to identify the best person available for a job and make it feasible for that person to work on that job using freely available information inputs. Similarly, social transactional frameworks are likely to be substantially less expensive than market transactions for pooling large numbers of discrete, small increments of the excess capacity of the personal computer processors, hard drives, and network connections that make up the physical capital base of the networked information economy. In both cases, given that much of what is shared is *excess capacity from the perspective of contributors, available to them after they have fulfilled some threshold level of their market-based consumption requirements,* social-sharing systems are likely to tap into social psychological motivations that money cannot tap, and indeed, that the presence of money could nullify. Because of these effects, social sharing and collaboration can provide not only a sustainable alternative to market-based and firm-based provisioning information, knowledge, culture, and communications, but also an alternative that more efficiently utilizes the human and physical capital base of the networked information economy. (Benkler 2006: 116; my emphasis)

By way of conclusion, I want to wrap this chapter up with three observations on "the wealth of social networks." First, the problem I have with this depiction is neither its optimism nor its vision. Indeed, I hope the potentialities Benkler describes are actualizable in the future. However, the examples in this chapter suggest the need to temper our enthusiasm. For what they clearly demonstrate is that in an era of digital capitalism we are witnessing *both* the triumph of social networks *and* the steadfast ability of corporate entities to co-opt social production for the purposes of capital accumulation. As business professor Henry Chesbrough put it in the subtitle of his 2006 book, open innovation is the "new imperative for creating and *profiting* from technology" (my italics). In the era of digital capitalism, it is not just sharing and cooperation that are being scaled to corporate proportions, but extraction. This is a point Robert McChesney also makes in his insightful book, *Digital Disconnect: How Capitalism is Turning the Internet Against Democracy.* He concludes, "the democratization of the Internet is integrally related to the democratization of political economy. They rise and fall together" (McChesney 2013: 22).

Second, the more successful corporations become at this, and the more pervasively they embrace using unremunerated labor as a standard business practice, the more precarious the world becomes for all of the people who do *still require* a paycheck to meet "the threshold level of their market-based consumption requirements." If social production and market production are likely to coexist in the future, as Benkler anticipates they will, then we need to consider the larger structural context in which community-based crowd-sourcing initiatives are touted as a means of social and economic "progress." Indeed, as Benkler himself advises, moving forward we will need to "adjust our expectations, assumptions, and ultimately, policy prescriptions to accommodate the emerging importance of social relations in general, and sharing in particular, as a modality of economic production" (Benkler 2004: 358). Will corporations like GE offer their "makers" any assurance of assistance or existence after they gift them their labor?[32] Will "makers'" free labor exacerbate the precarity and poverty that the underemployed and unemployed increasingly face today? If the "rise of crowd-based capitalism" ushers in "the end of employment," as NYU business professor, Arun Sundararajan speculates (Sundararajan 2016), where will people turn to meet their market needs? Without carefully considering these questions, it seems premature to herald social or peer-to-peer production as the remedy to social and economic ills.

Lastly, while Benkler is optimistic about the emancipatory potential of social production and the new networked information economy, he is cautiously so. He argues that progress will only be won "as a result of political action aimed at protecting new social patterns from the incumbents' assaults." "None of the industrial giants of yore," he cautions, "are taking this reallocation" of power and privilege "lying down." "The battle over the relative salience of proprietary, industrial models of information production and exchange and the emerging networked information economy is being carried out in the domain of the institutional ecology of the digital environment" (Benkler 2006: 23).

What I have hoped to demonstrate in this chapter is that the battle is not just being waged on the institutional "front" through corporate attempts to secure policies and practices that favor the interests of capital. It is also being waged on the ideological front, and in this regard Benkler himself is complicit in perpetuating the rhetoric of the "incumbents." For it is precisely through semantic maneuvers that turn workers into "makers," factories into "playgrounds," and creative, human life activity into "excess capacities" and "spare cycles" to be productively recouped (or rather expropriated) by corporate actors that the pioneers of digital capitalism attempt to convince us that our current economic system is not just the "only possible order," but the "best of all possible orders." Thus, if we are going to work towards a more equitable future where the wealth of social networks can truly be shared by all, then the words and language of "the incumbents" deserve the same level of scrutiny as the institutional policies they pursue. With this in mind, the next chapter will explore how the smartphone gaming app industry also attempts to legitimate the expropriation of surplus labor by further blurring the boundaries between work and leisure.

3

The Spirit of the Game: Smartphone Apps and the Digital Extraction of Surplus Value

More than 150 years ago, Karl Marx famously unveiled the secret of profit in the age of industrial capitalism. He argued that the relationship between capital and wage labor was not based on real reciprocity, as many political economists of his time had proposed. Rather, it was rooted in a form of time theft that resulted in the worker laboring for "free" for varying portions of the day and thereby producing surplus value for the capitalist. Indeed, Marx argued that in order to grasp this dynamic, it was necessary to move from "the sphere" of the marketplace, where the buying and selling of labor power is celebrated in the name of "freedom," "equality," and "property," and enter into the "hidden abode" of factory production, where the "greed for surplus labor" and hence surplus value, leads factory owners to "pilfer" and "steal" as many precious moments from their workers as they can (Marx 1978 [1867]: 343). In Volume 1 of *Capital*, Marx used the reports of factory inspectors to illustrate his point. He wrote:

> Let us listen, for a moment, to the Factory Inspectors. "The fraudulent mill-owner begins work a quarter of an hour (sometimes more, sometimes less) before 6 a.m., and leaves off a quarter of an hour (sometimes more, sometimes less) after 6 p.m. He takes 5 minutes from the beginning and from the end of the half hour nominally allowed for breakfast, and 10 minutes at the beginning and the end of the hour nominally allowed for dinner. He works for a quarter of an hour (sometimes more, sometimes less) after 2 p.m. on Saturday. Thus his gain is . . . 5 hours and 40 minutes weekly, which multiplied by 50 working weeks in the year (allowing two for holidays and occasional stoppages) is equal to 27 working days" . . . It is evident that in this atmosphere the formation of surplus-value by surplus-labour, is no

secret. "If you allow me," said a highly respectable master to me, "to work only ten minutes in the day over-time, you put one thousand a year in my *pocket*." "Moments are the elements of profit." (Marx 1978 [1867]: 366)

Do Marx's insights still hold up today? In the era of digital capitalism where must we look, and who must we "listen" to, to uncover the secret of profit? As the platform economy displaces factory production, as wage labor gives way to on-demand piecemeal tasks, and as the precariat class overtakes the proletariat, how do capitalists ensure that "the greed for surplus-labor" and hence surplus value will not be impeded by changes in the social and technological composition of capital?[1]

As we have seen in previous chapters, in the digital age the pursuit of surplus labor and hence surplus value frequently takes place outside of factory walls. Crowdsourcing technologies enable capitalists and corporations to expropriate the labor of digitally connected enthusiasts in exchange for nominal prize money or a range of intangible rewards. They arouse enthusiasm for participation in processes of capital accumulation by discursively transforming workers into "solvers" and "makers" who puzzle and "play" against and amidst a community of like-minded others. And yet, if crowd-sourcing initiatives conjure enthusiasm by promising to make labor more meaningful and fun, digital technologies are also frequently touted by companies as a way to "make downtime more productive." One of the places this is most readily visible is in the proliferation of the smartphone gaming app industry.[2]

Over the last two decades, while the ranks of the under- and unemployed have swelled, and as the commercial demand for more precise data has skyrocketed, the smartphone task and gaming app industry has exploded.[3] Likened to a portable Mechanical Turk, or a veritable "data enrichment" industry, apps such as Spare5, Taps for Money, InboxDollars, Cash Karma, Mistplay, Bingo Box, Solitaire Cube, Swagbucks, Survey Junkie, Lifepoints, PrizeRebel, and TreasureTrooper, to name just a few, are advertised to e-commerce and AI companies as ways to get the most direct access to potential consumers and as ways to gain a "cost-effective" leg up in the "arms race in training data."[4] They are also presented to consumers or users as a means to "win" or "earn some money by performing simple tasks irrespective of the place where you are." Companies propose that by downloading these apps onto smartphones, users can render their "free time" economically productive. In a review article entitled

"25 Apps that Pay You Real Money in 2021," entrepreneur and investor Brian Meiggs echoes this point. He writes: "By spending just 5–10 minutes per day on this (either on your lunch break or during TV commercial breaks) you can earn an extra \$50/month just for playing games. They also offer you the opportunity to earn cash for sharing your opinion and completing surveys. More people should be doing this."[5]

In this chapter, I explore how the smartphone app industry is facilitating the digital extraction of surplus value. I argue that it is precisely by blurring the boundaries between work and leisure, and in many cases, "gamifying" tasks, that the app economy, which is inextricably tied to the platform economy, is able to perpetuate and extend a classic form of capitalist expropriation into the most intimate reaches of daily life. Drawing upon an analysis of some of the most popular smartphone "earning" apps, I will demonstrate that although much has changed in the era of digital capitalism, moments, as Marx recognized long ago, are still the elements of profit. And yet, while moments remain the elements of profit, I also want to use this chapter to consider how digital capitalism is fundamentally reconfiguring our relationship to time. For if alienated industrial workers came to feel alive only in their time outside of work, as Marx suggested, today truly free time is experienced by many as something that generates intolerable anxiety. Thus I want to propose that in the era of digital capitalism, the smartphone app industry's attempt to render "downtime more productive" may not only serve economic interests but psychological ones as well.

Earning with apps

One of the first things to emphasize is that although many of these companies describe themselves as "on-demand work platforms," these apps are not touted as a means to secure a livelihood. They are advertised as "side hustles," "micro-incomes," and ways to make some "extra pocket change" or "spending money." As one of the founders of Spare5 explains:

> Spare5 is not a job, nor does it aspire for it become one . . . How much people make varies widely depending on the complexity of their tasks, quality and productivity. We prefer not to think of it in terms of an hourly wage, but people in the community have made several hundred dollars. It's probably helpful to think of Spare5 as more of

a marketplace and snack-sized task platform, than a job or even job supplement.[6]

Companies like Spare5 thus make no attempt to assure "taskers" or "fives," as they are euphemistically called, that this work will enable them to reproduce that very special commodity that "Mr. Moneybags" so greedily coveted in the era of industrial capitalism.[7] Indeed, as the quote above makes clear, smartphone app companies *proclaim* that what they purchase and pay for is not labor power – or the *capacity* to work for a designated period of time – but rather, the *completion* of a task. This is a claim I will return to later. However, for now, I simply want to point out that by deferring any official responsibility for providing "taskers" with a living wage, and by emphasizing that they are *not* in the business of generating jobs, these companies are better able to justify the minimal amounts that they do pay out.

These tasks, or "micro-tasks" as they are often called, range from tagging photos, taking surveys, playing games, identifying products, watching videos, guessing prices of products, reading emails, and a variety of other activities that typically take anywhere from a couple of seconds to twenty, thirty, or even forty-five minutes to complete. The shorter tasks yield a few cents per task, whereas the longer ones can pay up to a couple of dollars. Taskers can also earn money by recruiting others to sign up for the app. Earnings occur in a piecemeal fashion and to receive a "payout" most of these companies mandate that taskers accumulate a certain amount of income which, in many cases, is deposited in a PayPal account, before being able to collect it. Spare5, for instance, initially set the payout amount at US$5 but then reduced it US$1. Other companies, such as InboxDollars, require a US$30–$40 minimum to receive a payout. If an InboxDollars tasker opts to collect their earnings at US$30 rather than US$40, they are also charged a US$3 processing fee. The payouts, moreover, are slotted for a particular day of the week, thereby creating the sense that even though it is not an official job, taskers can still enjoy the satisfaction of anticipating a "payday," minimal though it might be.[8]

To get started, taskers first need to download the apps onto their smartphones, fill out a questionnaire, and perform a few "unpaid tasks" as part of an informal "training session." As tech writer Taylor Soper observes:

> We spend a lot of time on our mobile devices – almost three hours each day for the average American, in fact. Some of that time is for more important tasks, like accessing email, texts, phone calls, bank accounts,

and more. But many of us spend hours every day playing Candy Crush, scrolling through social media feeds, or surfing the web.

Spare5 wants to help qualified people make money in that "down time" by giving them easy, video game-like projects that can be completed while they sit in line for their latte, or during that 45 minutes on the bus home from work.[9]

The company itself describes its mission in very similar terms. Spare5 states, "A tremendous opportunity exists to better people's lives by making time they spend on mobile devices more valuable. A host of companies can benefit immediately by tapping the nearly unlimited resources of people's time and expertise to improve their data and understanding of their customers."[10]

In the era of digital capitalism, therefore, people's habituation, or rather addiction, to technology is actively harnessed as a way to draw them further into processes of capital accumulation. For instance, InboxDollars transforms the daily routine of checking one's email into an opportunity to extract data and labor from its users. Once a person signs up for the InboxDollars app and establishes an account, they receive a minimum of three "paid emails" per day. These emails variously contain advertisements or offerings from brand-name companies or provide recipients with opportunities to take surveys. By clicking on the emails or "confirming" them, recipients earn a few cents. They also pay users for browsing the web or shopping online. Thus, if Marx proposed that it was necessary to enter into the "hidden abode" of factory production in order to unveil the secret of profit, in the era of digital capitalism, we must also examine how the greed for surplus value leads capitalists to use technologies to extend their tentacles into the most intimate spaces of our daily lives. With a smartphone on hand, waiting in line, riding the bus home from work, sitting through commercial breaks, and even checking one's email all become opportunities to transform "downtime" into time that is marginally productive for taskers but, as will be seen, inordinately productive for capital.

Indeed, by devoting their spare moments to these tasks, taskers play a direct role in producing the very forces that perpetuate their own subjugation. They not only agree to have their labor exploited for a few pennies here and a few pennies there. They also agree to engage in labor that is integral to producing the digital infrastructure that Shoshana Zuboff refers to as "Big Other" (Zuboff 2019). "Big Other," she writes, is the "ubiquitous digital apparatus" through which "surveillance capitalism imposes its will . . . it is the sensate, computational, connected puppet that renders, monitors, computes, and modifies human behavior" (Zuboff 2019: 376). By producing data that can be utilized to enhance the power of corporations and fine-tune the algorithms and AI that increasingly assess, shape, and control human behavior, taskers, as Marx observed of wage labor long ago, produce something that ultimately comes to dominate them.[11]

In fact, in the age of "surveillance" (Zuboff 2019) or "platform capitalism" (Srnicek 2017), as it is variously called, it is not "the slave driver's lash," or the factory overseer's "book of penalties" that are used to discipline and evaluate workers (Marx 1978 [1867]). It is algorithms, which again, taskers play a key role in fine-tuning or "training" with their "human intelligence."[12] Many of these companies use algorithms to assess the taskers' work and determine whether they are suitable for more "complicated" assignments. If the algorithm discerns that the quality of work or a tasker's answers is poor, it can prevent the tasker from gaining access to future tasks. Alternatively, the more tasks they successfully complete and the more "experience points" (XP) they accumulate, the more they are rewarded by being given earlier access to tasks and chances to perform tasks with higher payouts.[13]

Blurring the boundaries and gaming the tasks

Indeed, earning points, and thus granting users an opportunity to progress to higher levels, is but one of the many ways these apps work to gamify tasks and thereby further blur the boundaries between work and leisure. For instance, when asked, "how does Spare5 secure engagement, or commitment" from taskers, Matt Bencke, a founder of the company, explained that one of Spare5's key strategies is to make the work "fun," and this is achieved "through various gaming approaches."[14] InboxDollars deploys a similar strategy. They offer users multiple opportunities to enter "sweepstakes contests" while getting paid a few cents for doing menial tasks such as surfing the internet. They encourage participants to take on "scratch and win" tasks where they have the *potential* to win larger prizes or amounts of cash if they scratch off the correct box.[15] When a tasker is disqualified from taking a particular survey because they have performed poorly or do not meet the desired demographic criteria, InboxDollars gives them an opportunity to spin "Billy's Wheel" "for a chance to win a cash prize."[16] In all of these subtle ways, taskers are encouraged to focus on how many opportunities there are to *win* by doing this work instead of reflecting upon what is being *taken* from them or what they might be losing.

In addition to gamifying tasks to make them more "fun," these companies also offer innumerable opportunities for taskers to get paid or receive "rewards" for playing actual games.[17] InboxDollars, for instance, features its own array of games like Monkey Bubbler Shooter, Mahjong Solitaire, Outspell, and Candy Jam, which they pay users a few cents to play. They also partner with the GSN Casino, which offers access to hundreds of online games. For every dollar a tasker spends on a GSN game, they earn "18% cashback with InboxDollars."[18] By playing these games, taskers not only generate data that will be used to further commercial interests but they also become products themselves who are "sold" to various corporate actors.

In fact, many of the apps that are marketed as games and that enable players to win "real money," such as Solitaire Cube, are in essence mechanisms for exposing players to advertisements. Lured in by the possibility that the game will enable them to win some cash, or even just "kill time" (a promise that has taken on greater appeal during the COVID-19 pandemic), players discover that, once they begin, they are bombarded with advertisements. As one disgruntled player of Solitaire Cube commented, "the ads are total BS and the winning money part is too." Another remarked, "It's stupid how you people scam people just so we watch your ads and enrich yourself . . . Your game is ugly and the ads annoying, so I hope no one downloads it."[19]

The pushback and criticism that players often express also lead gaming app companies to devise ever more skillful ways of ensuring that players will want to return. One way they do this is by rendering the games more social by enabling users to play against each other in real time, or by sponsoring multiplayer tournaments that pay out bigger prizes.[20] Another way they do this is by personalizing games to each player's gaming habits, thereby making them ever more "addictive," a word that continually comes up in players' reviews. Mistplay, "the app that lets you earn gift cards while playing games," draws players in with the promise that they provide "mobile games that are curated just for you!"[21] Players are provided with a "Mixlist" or personalized game library that is curated based on their previous gaming history.[22] For instance, in an article posted on *MoneyTamer*, a blog that aims to help people get out of debt and "take control" of their finances, Steffa Mantilla, a Certified Financial Education Instructor, writes:

How is it possible to get paid to play games? The mobile app industry is extremely oversaturated, and there isn't a lot of space open for new games. Game developers understand this problem and use reward platforms, such as Mistplay, to showcase their game to a broader audience. Mistplay gets paid by the game developers in exchange for these games being featured on the Mistplay platform. As a Mistplay user you're earning part of this money in the form of rewards. Developers also use Mistplay to conduct research and gather feedback from gamers. Using Mistplay allows the game developers to take the information provided by the players and tweak the app and make it better suited for their target audience.[23]

This is also to say that the companies that deploy these apps don't just *harness* the addictive properties of gaming in order to ensure that play and profit will continue undisturbed; they also purposefully try to *produce* these properties. As Trevor Haynes, a researcher for Harvard Medical School, reports in his article "Dopamine, Smartphones & You: A Battle for Your Time": "similar to slot machines, many apps implement a reward pattern optimized to keep you as engaged as much as possible . . . If you pay attention, you might find yourself checking your phone at the slightest feeling of boredom, purely out of habit. Programmers work very hard behind the screens to keep you doing exactly that."[24] Thus, while propaganda has long provided a means for securing committed engagement in processes of capital accumulation, in the digital age this is equally accomplished by technological interventions designed to target and tinker with our brain chemistry. If people like Edward Bernays had their sights set on influencing the unconscious of millions of Americans, people like Chamath Palihapitiya, the former vice president of user growth at Facebook, confesses that his goal has been to create "the short-term, dopamine-driven feedback loops" that keep Facebook users incessantly returning to their digital devices and social media platforms.

Similarly, in her fascinating book, *Addicted By Design: Machine Gambling in Las Vegas*, anthropologist Natasha Dow Schüll explores how the digitization of machine gambling is purposively designed to keep players in a "zone in which time, space, and social identity are suspended in the mechanical rhythm of a repeating process." She argues that while these technological innovations have resulted in dramatic profits for casinos, their appeal to consumers lies not in the potential for a big cash payout or win, but rather in the way they provide a "reliable mechanism for securing a zone of insulation from a 'human world'" that is often experienced as "capricious, discontinuous, and insecure." "The continuity of machine gambling," she writes, "holds worldly contingencies in a kind of abeyance, granting . . . an otherwise elusive zone of certainty." The aim of machine gamblers "is not to *win* but simply to *continue*" (Schüll 2012: 12–13).[25]

Clearly, there are significant differences between playing games on a digitized slot machine in a Las Vegas casino and playing games on one's mobile phone. However, Schüll's research is worth considering because it prompts us to ask how the gaming app industry plays off of desires to not only render downtime economically productive but also to "kill time," as many of the reviews of these apps proclaim.[26] Might it be the case that in the era of digital capitalism, as people have become increasingly habituated to technological devices and constant internet stimulation, truly "free time" is no longer appealing, or is experienced as something that prompts anxiety? Considering the fact that many of these apps are advertised to people in precarious situations who struggle with the threat of constant economic insecurity – single moms, millennials trying to cope with student debt, retirees who are scrounging to make do with their dissipating savings and pensions, it seems worth asking, how is the proliferation of this industry linked to psychological needs, as well as economic ones?

Multiplying moments and multiplying millions

And yet, if the smartphone app industry is in some way addressing the psychological needs of taskers and gamers who increasingly feel overwhelmed by their economically precarious lives, it is also abundantly clear that for the companies themselves the bottom line is profit. According to numerous online reports, Spare5, which now goes under the company name of Mighty AI, reported revenues of over US$5 million in 2017 and InboxDollars' annual revenue is now estimated at over US$20 million dollars.[27] Which returns us to the question: wherein lies the secret of profit in the era of digital capitalism? How exactly do these companies turn moments into millions?[28]

To answer this question, I propose that we must leave the realm of the platform "marketplace" (as Spare5 founder Matt Bencke describes it), where tasking and gaming are presented as a win–win situation for users and companies alike, and listen to the taskers themselves. The fact that tasks, not time, provide the official means of coordinating and compensating labor in the app/platform economy might lead some to conclude that in the app economy moments are no longer the elements of profit. However, when we look and listen to the tens of thousands of reviews posted online by users of such apps, a different picture begins to emerge.

One of the ways app companies augment their profits is through the use of what I call predatory technocracy, a term inspired by Noelle Stout's eye-opening account of the 2008 financial and housing crisis. In *Dispossessed: How Predatory Bureaucracy Foreclosed on the American Middle Class*, Stout chronicles the way middle-class homeowners in California were robbed and cheated out of their homes by corporate scandals and interests. She argues that one of the ways homeowners lost control of their homes was by being continually subjected to predatory bureaucracy that made settling their claims and securing their property near impossible. Describing this process, she writes:

> Corporate lenders were charging the US Treasury and taxpayers, by extension, for bailouts to homeowners who never received relief . . . Individual cases when corporate lenders misplace a homeowner's paperwork or offer misinformation on a claim might seem innocuous annoyances typical of interactions with modern corporations. But when these bureaucratic failures reach epic proportions, in the millions, a pattern emerges: they become forms of *predatory bureaucracy*, a collection of private-sector bureaucratic techniques aimed to extract profits while masking these goals through a rhetoric of assistance. (Stout 2019: 10)

Although there is no "rhetoric of assistance" in the smartphone task and gaming app economy, a similar pattern can be detected. However, instead of being the product of misplaced paperwork and bureaucratic techniques, "the failures" that taskers complain of are often of a technological nature. For instance, consider the following reviews from users of the InboxDollars app:

> Absolute ZERO. My account hasn't worked for many months, so I quit using it. I tried the live chat to figure out what I need to do to reactivate my account so I can start using it again and I didn't receive any response! Tried many times and I can see employees join the chat and leave without saying anything or acknowledging me at all. How do I contact this company? At this point, I'm just going to cancel my account and delete the app. So frustrating!! Surveys are broken half the time. It sends you to sign up for InboxDollars which you already signed up for if you have downloaded it, sometimes you get promised extra money if you continue the survey and you don't get it.

This is a scam app do not install. Your chances of getting money disappear when you type in your validation code. It won't send you a code. It just says you have exceeded your verification attempts after 1 try! That was a week wasted waiting for a nonexistent payment to be available. Do not waste your time!

I would not recommend this app. Finally got enough to cash out. Won't let me verify via my phone and then also saying my email and password combinations not correct when I know it is. This has been a waste of time.

I was supposed to get a $50 PayPal redemption code and never got it after many requests. Every time I make a new request, it brings up a page with my email and a spot for the claim code but it's empty. Can't ever talk to a human, and the bot tells me to talk to PayPal who has no idea what I'm talking about. Time to delete this useless app.

Scam. TIME FOR A CLASS ACTION LAWSUIT. If you have a high payout due they will deactivate your account and not reply to your request to reopen it. The links and instructions in the support section of their website are broken or missing. There is no real way to reactiv[at]e. STAY AWAY! THEY JUST END UP STEALING YOUR EARNINGS FROM YOU.[29]

These technological "glitches," impasses, or even purposeful designs help ensure that companies like InboxDollars are able to profit from the unremunerated labor of taskers. In many cases, they make taskers so frustrated that they give up on any attempt to claim their compensation, which means that at the end of the day, or week, or month, or year, the labor they performed was for free.

While there are certainly taskers who are satisfied with the app, a look at the tens of thousands of user reviews definitely reveals "a pattern . . . aimed to extract profits." It also points to one of the many ways that "the agentless" quality of automation "can induce an emotional state of rage" as the inability to collect payments from digital infrastructures turns the game into a source of aggravation rather than pleasure (Gusterson 2019: 21).

Another way these companies augment their profits is through stealing data. In the digital age, as numerous scholars have proposed, data have become the "new oil," a commodity or resource that is bought and sold to keep the wheels of profit spinning.[30] Companies like Spare5 and InboxDollars make no secret of the fact that the buying and selling of data is the cornerstone of their business model, or rather, "data enrichment" industry. However, even though they are transparent about this, they still find ways to stealthily extract surplus data from their taskers. In addition to utilizing predatory technocracy, they also establish other barriers that prevent taskers from being compensated for the labor and data they provide. For example, one reviewer of InboxDollars reports, "Their game play minutes are legit. The surveys are absolute fraud. You can answer 50+ questions where they collect all your data to later say you're disqualified after product and service questions. Grab this only if you want to make legit nickels playing games." Another reviewer writes, "It makes you answer a ton of questions before telling you 'Sorry, you don't qualify for this survey.' A lot of time answering questions and end up not getting payment. Seems like a scam."[31] Such comments and experiences also suggest that, although these companies *claim* they are paying for the completion of a task, and although they claim that they are not in the business of buying *labor power*, or the *capacity* to work for a certain period of time, in actuality they do end up getting access to this very special commodity. In the examples mentioned above, it is not the completion of a task but rather *the stealing of labor power* that fuels the accumulation of capital.

Moreover, even when companies keep their promise to pay taskers for the work they have done or games they have played, we find that the compensation they receive is abysmal. While Spare5 executives like Matt Bencke celebrate the fact that some "community members have made hundreds of dollars," users of apps like Spare5 and InboxDollars report a very different economic reality. One reviewer reports he received US$0.20 for completing a twenty-minute survey, which works out to being paid 60 cents an hour. Another reviewer reports that even after becoming a "Gold Member" of InboxDollars, he was paid only US$0.25 for completing a nine-minute survey which works out at US$2.50 per hour. Yet another writes:

> The whole process of taking the surveys can be frustrating. InboxDollars serves up surveys for which you aren't qualified. Before I got through a single episode of Fuller House, I was disqualified from four surveys. Survey providers are looking for a specific demographic, you don't meet their qualifications, blah, blah, blah. When I finally found a survey I could take I earned a whopping $0.25. The survey took about 10 minutes. At that rate, I was earning about $1.50 per hour.[32]

Very few Americans would agree to work for such appalling wages and tolerate such an extreme "rate of surplus value," as Marx would put it. But the "trick" here, as Matt Bencke again noted, is that these companies "prefer not to think of it in terms of an hourly wage."

They rely upon others to provide their taskers with a livable wage or salaried employment so that they can pay them pennies for taking surveys, tagging photos, watching videos, reading emails, and playing games that are variously promoted in the name of having fun, killing time, and making "downtime" more productive. As Greg Gottesman, one of the angel investors in Spare5 puts it, "The idea of giving people the freedom to use their spare time to make enough money for that date night or enough money for gas – that's an exciting proposition that has big implications."[33]

Conclusion: free time or free labor?

Greg Gottesman is correct. All of this does have "big implications." In concluding this chapter, I want to discuss what some of these implications are. First, it is clear that if we want to understand the secret of profit in the era of digital capitalism, it is necessary to move from the sphere of the "marketplace" where the buying and selling of *task* labor is celebrated in the name of "freedom," "opportunity," and "reciprocity," and into the intimate spaces of daily life where taskers' smartphones and "free time" are colonized by the digitized tentacles of capitalist expropriation. With the right app on hand, waiting in line, taking a lunch break, checking one's email, riding the bus home from work, and even sitting through a television commercial all become opportunities for companies like Spare5 or InboxDollars to extract data and thereby generate profits from their users.[34]

Second, while it is abundantly clear that data are crucial to the accumulation of capital in the digital age, the examples discussed in this chapter also suggest that we must continue to attend to the role that surplus labor plays in the production of surplus value. Although the app industry promotes itself as a way for taskers to render their free time more productive, what ultimately transpires in the exchange between companies and taskers is an expropriation of surplus labor. Companies like Spare5 and Inbox find numerous ways to engage in forms of "pilfering" and "time theft." From uses of predatory technocracy that makes it impossible for many taskers and gamers to claim their earnings to paying out what would be the equivalent of starvation wages, these companies are able to significantly extend that portion of the day that taskers, as Marx put it, labor "for free." Indeed, one might even argue that it is precisely because they can rely on other employers to provide taskers or gamers with the requisite income and wages to reproduce their existence that *all of the labor* taskers and gamers perform becomes surplus labor to be expropriated by the smartphone app industry. Thus, even though much has changed in the 150 years since Marx took us into "the hidden abode" of factory production, and even though factory production is being significantly displaced by the platform economy, in the era of digital capitalism, moments are *still* the elements of profit. While surplus labor is now extracted through digital means, as others have argued, Marx's basic insights into the nature of capital accumulation remain as germane today as they did over a century and a half ago (Fuchs and Fisher 2015).

Third, the emergence of the smartphone gaming app industry again illuminates just how blurred the boundaries between work and leisure have become in the era of digital capitalism, and it suggests that this blurring is not just incidental but rather central to processes of capital accumulation. As Paul Benzon points out:

> The inseparability of work and play in the global economy is nothing new within the critical study of digital culture. On the one hand, work – particularly the knowledge work that forms a key component of the digital economy – has long been masked and rebranded as play . . . On the other hand, critical approaches rooted in political economy have made clear that the social play that has become increasingly central to digital culture . . . is ultimately a form of work. (Benzon 2020: 97)

Indeed, in a provocative article entitled, 'Games without Play," David Golumbia proposes that many of the digitally generated games people participate in today "do not resemble other ludic or playfully imaginative activities that we have seen before in our culture" but rather "much more nearly resemble something like *work*" (Golumbia 2009: 179). He writes:

> What emerges as a hidden truth of computer gaming – and no less, although it may be even better hidden, of other computer program use – is the human pleasure taken in completing of activities with closure and with hierarchical means of task measurement. Again, this kind of pleasure surely existed before computers, but it has become an overriding emotional experience for many in society only with the widespread use of computers . . . A great deal of the pleasure users get . . . is a digital sense of task completion and measurable accomplishment, even if that accomplishment only roughly translates into what we may otherwise consider intellectual, physical, or social goal-attainment. (Golumbia 2009: 191–2)

Thus, in the era of digital capitalism the spirit of the game is far from playful. Smartphone games have become one more means through which human beings are "trained" to become productive members of the capitalist system and one more means through which they learn to not only position themselves within a hierarchy but also derive pleasure from doing so (ibid.: 194).

And yet what strikes me as most interesting about the emergence of the smartphone gaming app industry is the possibility that it not only serves the economic needs of capital, which it clearly does, but that it might also serve the psychological needs of the subjects that digital capitalism has created. People have become so dependent upon their technological devices that the anxiety they experience when separated from their cell phone is now a diagnosed psychological condition called "nomophobia" (Bhattacharya et al. 2019). The smartphone app industry is very much aware that people have become deeply habituated to constant technological stimulation, and they do everything in their power to engineer and reproduce that dependency by developing games that can more effectively hijack the dopamine system and keep users returning for more. While enthusiasts like Greg Gottesman celebrate "the idea of giving people the freedom to use their spare time to make enough money for that date night or enough money for gas,"[35] in practice, they aggressively use gaming app technologies to ensure that people spend more and more of their time at the behest of capital. It is not freedom they produce with their smartphone gaming apps but, rather, dopamine-induced addiction.

Indeed, the gaming technologies that are now deployed to keep people in a constant state of "productivity" and "play" recall a critique made by Theodor Adorno over 75 years ago. In an essay entitled "Free Time," Adorno lamented:

> The lack of imagination which is cultivated and inculcated by society renders people helpless in their free time . . . The reason why people can actually do so little with their free time is that the truncation of their imagination deprives them of the faculty which made the state of freedom pleasurable in the first place. People have been refused freedom, and its value belittled, for such a long time, that now people no longer like it. They need shallow entertainment . . . . (Adorno 2007 [1977]: 167)

Adorno's critique is unapologetically snobby, but it also strikes me as incredibly timely and perhaps even more relevant today than when he first penned it. In the era of digital capitalism, technologies are increasingly used to discourage people from cultivating their imagination. The smartphone technologies discussed in this chapter provide users with opportunities "to kill time." They provide not just "shallow entertainment" but a comforting cocoon which enables precarious taskers to shelter themselves from the demands and difficulties of everyday living and derive some sense, even if only digital, of accomplishment. Thus, at the risk of making a claim that clearly warrants further research, I propose that for many people working and playing in the era of digital capitalism, free time has become something they "no longer like"; it increasingly provokes anxiety and listlessness. Thus, if Marx argued that one of the tragedies of industrial capitalism was that the worker only came to feel free in his time off, and in pursuing his most basic animal needs (eating, sleeping, fornicating), perhaps the tragedy today is that people no longer even welcome free time. It reminds them of their structurally enforced idleness and their diminishing capacity for imaginative play.[36]

However, while the gaming app industry arouses enthusiasm for participation in processes of capital accumulation by promising users that smartphone apps can help them render their downtime more productive and even stave off the anxiety of daily life, other captains of the digital age suggest smartphone apps and technologies are the key to making our busy and anxious lives more convenient. As will be seen in the following chapter, by integrating smartphone apps and technologies into their "no checkout" shopping experience, Amazon Go seeks to create the ultimate "frictionless" shopping experience by removing human sociality and connection from the equation. In the name of convenience, Amazon Go also justifies using technology to enhance processes of capital accumulation and domination.

4

In the Spirit of Convenience: Amazon Go and Surveillance Capitalism

The spirit of digital capitalism is not only reflected in new means of organizing labor and production. As evidenced by Amazon, it can also be gleaned in new forms of retail and consumption. Since its inception in 1994, Amazon has achieved staggering financial success. As of 2018, it became the second company after Apple to reach a market value of US$1 trillion dollars, making it more valuable than Walmart, Target, Best Buy, JC Penny, and all other publicly traded retailers *combined* (Hyken 2018: 29).[1]

As scholars and journalists alike have noted, the secret of Amazon's success in large part derives from its ability to render the shopping experience more convenient. Indeed, in less than thirty years, Amazon has revolutionized the way Americans shop, it has devastated the competition from brick and mortar stores, and it has given rise to novel distribution systems that promise more efficient and cost-effective delivery. In a world where "convenience is king," Amazon has emerged as the emperor (Hyken 2018).

Yet despite all the attention Amazon has received, *the product* it sells – convenience – warrants further academic scrutiny. While business analysts and marketing gurus attempt to explain *how* Amazon delivers convenience to its customers, they have yet to ask a crucial anthropological question: *what exactly is convenience?* How does convenience operate not just as a highly coveted consumer good that stands to mitigate the demands of life in a fast-paced society, but also as an *ideology* that is integral to attempts to justify new forms of capital accumulation, domination, and extraction?[2]

In this chapter, I explore this question by analyzing one of Amazon's newer business initiatives, Amazon Go. Drawing upon a range of data, including promotional videos, marketing reports, interviews with the designers of the initiative, and customer comments, I show how convenience operates as an ideology that is central to Amazon's abilities to exploit the "behavioral surplus" of its customers (Zuboff 2019). I argue that just as the ideology of freedom supported and perpetuated exploitative relationships between capital and labor during the period of industrial capitalism, as Marx famously argued, in the era of "surveillance capitalism" the ideology of convenience plays a crucial role in supporting, perpetuating, and legitimizing extractive relationships between capitalists and consumers. By interrogating how convenience functions in this capacity, this chapter seeks to further our understanding of "the convenience economy" – which is frequently touted as one of the main perks of capitalism in the digital age – and it returns us to one of the central questions of this book: what role do ideologies play in sustaining and perpetuating exploitative economic systems? "Is it indeed the case," as Terry Eagleton asks, "that advanced capitalism can be said to operate all by itself, without any need to resort to *discursive* justification?" Or, is "the end-of-ideology thesis," as Eagleton contends, "implausible" (Eagleton 2007: 37, 41)?

Amazon Go

Launched in Seattle in 2018, Amazon Go represents the cutting edge of in-house convenience store shopping. Built around "walk-out technology," the stores are intended to enhance customer convenience by weaving "machine learning, computer vision, and AI into the very fabric of the store," so customers "never have to wait in line. No lines, no checkouts, no registers."[3] In order to enter the store, customers must first download an app on their smartphones and then scan their personalized QR code (which verifies the shopper's identity) over an electronic turnstile to gain entry. Once inside, customers can put their phones away and begin shopping. Every item they take off the shelf and put in their bag or walk out with is recorded through the app, and customers can leave with their goods, again exiting through an electronic gate, without having to interact with a cashier or scan items at an automated register. Purchases are billed to customers' Amazon account, and receipts are delivered directly to the app. Receipts also inform customers of the exact amount of time they spent in the store.

The stores range from 1,800 to 2,100 square feet, and all of the stores have high ceilings to accommodate the cameras and sensors that are used to meticulously track the movements of merchandise and shoppers.[4] While the stores offer items that would typically be found in other convenience stores, such as toothpaste or dental floss, they specialize in "ready-to-go" fresh foods and offer a small selection of beer and wine. In contrast to the donuts, hotdogs, and warmed-over frozen pizza slices that one might grab from a convenience store like 7 Eleven, Amazon Go markets itself as a convenience store that simultaneously accommodates hectic lifestyles and consumers' desires for "good taste." As noted on the Amazon Go website:

> We offer delicious ready-to-eat breakfast, lunch, dinner, and snack options made by our chefs and favorite local kitchens and bakeries. Our selection of grocery essentials ranges from staples like bread and milk to artisan cheeses and locally made chocolates. For a quick home-cooked dinner, pick up one of our chef-designed Amazon Meal Kits, with all the ingredients you need to make a meal for two in about 30 minutes.

As of January 2021, Amazon had opened 30 stores across the nation, but numerous reports speculate that in the coming years the company could open thousands more.[5] It is projected that, with more opening, the stores will gross more than US$4.5 billion dollars.[6]

Surveillance capitalism

The Amazon Go initiative provides an apt example of surveillance capitalism, a term which has been deployed several times throughout this book but here warrants further explanation.[7] In *The Age of Surveillance Capitalism: The Fight for a Human Future at the New Frontier of Power*, Shoshana Zuboff argues that digital infrastructures and technologies have made possible a new form of capital accumulation based on the ceaseless pursuit and extraction of digital data and "behavioral surplus." Referring to this infrastructure as "Big Other," Zuboff sets out to identify "the laws of motion" (Zuboff 2019: 66) that animate this new digitally mediated economic order, and also to warn readers of its potentially devastating consequences. Her argument, in a nutshell, is that surveillance capitalism poses an existential threat to democracy and human nature.

Zuboff's book covers a lot of ground, but there are four aspects of her argument that have particular relevance for the ensuing analysis.

First, Zuboff proposes that if, under industrial capitalism, the secret of profit hinged upon the exploitation of surplus labor, today, in the age of surveillance capitalism, the secret of profit increasingly hinges upon the extraction of "behavioral surplus." Zuboff uses the term "behavioral surplus" to refer to the behavioral data that corporations gather and use to augment machine intelligence and create "prediction products that anticipate what you will do now, soon, and later." These prediction products are then "traded in a new kind of marketplace for behavioral predictions" that Zuboff refers to as "behavioral futures markets" (ibid.: 8). Corporations like Google and Facebook, that provide the primary case studies for her analysis of surveillance capitalism, increasingly make record-level profits by engaging such markets and selling users' data/behavior to advertisers. For instance, she notes that "within less than four years," the discovery of behavioral surplus led Google's revenues to skyrocket by over 3,500%, increasing from US$347 million in 2002 to US$3.2 billion in 2004, the year the company went public (2019: 87). This leads Zuboff to conclude: "The discovery of behavioral surplus marks a critical turning point not only in Google's biography but also in the history of capitalism" (ibid.: 91).

Second, Zuboff argues that with the discovery of behavioral surplus, companies like Facebook, Google, and Amazon have become ever more aggressive in pursuing it. Instead of just selling the "digital exhaust" generated from internet browsing, now more and more of users' lives are colonized by surveillance capitalism. For instance, Google and Amazon have developed technologies to put in people's cars, neighborhoods, and even homes in their efforts to extract more data from their users.

Third, Zuboff argues that the goal of surveillance capitalism is not just to track human behavior but to *shape* it. Surveillance capitalism, Zuboff argues, is animated by the "prediction imperative." "Its aim is to produce behavior that reliably, definitively, and certainly leads to desired commercial results" (ibid.: 201). Moreover, it relies upon a host of "herding" and "nudging" practices to do so. For example, a customer may be presented with an advertisement and direct order link for a product they browsed on the internet the night before. Or, as has happened to me, they might receive a message on their iPhone reminding them that one of the items they intended to purchase is still "waiting" in their cart.

Fourth, Zuboff argues that the rise of surveillance capitalism and the digital infrastructure that sustains it have also ushered in a new form of instrumentarian power. She writes: "Big Other combines these functions of knowing and doing to achieve a pervasive and unprecedented *means of behavioral modification*. Surveillance capitalism's economic logic is directed through Big Other's vast capabilities to produce instrumentarian power, *replacing the engineering of souls with the engineering of behavior*" (ibid.: 367; my emphasis).

According to Zuboff, the real tragedy of surveillance capitalism is that by tracking and shaping human behavior in ever more pervasive arenas of life, Big Other ultimately *automates us*. It robs people of the will, volition, awareness, and autonomy to make decisions on their behalf. Human beings become akin to pinballs that are digitally nudged, prodded, and directed into lines of behavior that serve others' commercial interests.[8] Thus, if one of the dominant critiques of industrial capitalism was that it fostered alienation, for Zuboff, the main critique of surveillance capitalism is that it fosters automation.

As will be seen, Zuboff's work on surveillance capitalism provides a useful departure point for analyzing Amazon Go's new fleet of high-tech convenience stores, and her explication of the digital infrastructure that makes this new mode of capital accumulation possible is indeed instructive. However, before proceeding, there are two points of her analysis I want to take issue with. First, although Zuboff is correct in noting that the exploitation of behavioral surplus becomes increasingly central to processes of capital accumulation in the digital age, as the previous chapters have made clear, it is crucial to remember that surveillance capitalism, like industrial capitalism, still feeds off the exploitation of labor power. This is a point that anthropologist Mary Gray and computer scientist Siddharth Suri make in their equally important book, *Ghost Work: How to Stop Silicon Valley from Building a New Global Underclass*. Their ethnography focuses on the global population of platform workers who are paid piecemeal on sites like MTurk to provide the human labor that trains the very algorithms that keep the digital infrastructure of Big Other in operation. As Gray and Suri explain, their labor "can be hard to see – in fact, it's often intentionally hidden" (Gray and Suri 2019: xi). Indeed, as will become evident, one of the biggest obfuscation tactics that Amazon Go deploys is to generate the illusion that there are no workers being exploited at their stores as the technologies they deploy by and large do away with the need for human labor.

Second, and more central to the analysis that follows, Zuboff suggests that surveillance capitalism achieves its hold and power less through ideological means than through technical ones.[9] Indeed, as

Terry Eagleton has pointed out, a number of scholars share this belief. They argue that in the age of advanced capitalism, domination and consent are increasingly achieved through economic and technical means rather than ideological ones and that "discursive justification" is no longer necessary to keep the wheels of profit spinning and the interests of capital protected (Eagleton 2007: 37).[10] If, for instance, Amazon can get people to spend their money with digital nudges and links that take them directly to their checkout carts, then they do not have to exert a lot of energy trying to "engineer" their "souls" or convincing them that they have their best interests in mind. Or, as we saw in the previous chapter, if the gaming industry can figure out how to create "short-term, dopamine-driven feedback loops" to keep users playing, they do not need to work as hard to "sell" them on the idea that their apps will improve their lives.

Zuboff is not wrong in emphasizing how aggressively technologies are being used to shape human behavior, and I agree that this is one of the new and defining features of digital or surveillance capitalism. As will be seen, Amazon has become a master at deploying digital nudges to influence consumers' behaviors. However, Amazon also spends *a lot* of effort trying to win over "the souls" of their customers. Their central message, from Jeff Bezos on down the entire executive chain of command, is that customers come first, and that *accommodating* customer needs and customer desires drives their business model. As their mission statement reads: "Our vision is to be earth's most customer-centric company . . . We strive to offer our customers the lowest possible prices, the best available selection, and the utmost convenience."[11] Given the amount of work Amazon does to promote this message I, like Eagleton, am skeptical of the end-of-ideology thesis.

In the remainder of this chapter, I show how convenience is not just woven into the products and services that Amazon Go provides, I also demonstrate how convenience functions as an ideology that is used "to establish, sustain and legitimate relations of domination" (Thompson 1990: 56). I argue that invoking "convenience" is one of the ways that Amazon Go discursively justifies a new set of extractive technologies and practices that ultimately serve the interests of capital. In the name of convenience, customers surrender their right to privacy, allow their behavior to be rendered and very likely sold, and effectively pay for their own subjugation. The question then becomes: what kind of ideological strategies does Amazon invoke to try and make this reality appear more palatable?[12]

The ideology of convenience

Naturalization

One of the key ideological strategies that Amazon deploys is naturalization. As Eagleton notes, "successful ideologies are often thought to render their beliefs natural and self-evident – to identify them with the 'common sense' of a society" (Eagleton 2007: 58). In the case of Amazon, one of the primary "self-evident" claims it promotes is that Amazon exists to serve and accommodate the needs of its customers. As Jeff Bezos himself declares: "We're not competitor obsessed, we're customer obsessed. We start with what the customer needs and we work backwards."[13] The idea that capitalism exists to *satisfy* consumer needs rather than *create* them has been questioned by a long line of theorists whose names are too numerous to mention here.[14] However, their various attempts to denaturalize this ideology are instructive when considering the development of Amazon Go.

For instance, the first Amazon Go convenience store opened in Seattle on January 22, 2018. However, long before the first store opened, Amazon had already begun advertising the new chain of convenience stores, and in 2016 it released a widely watched promotional video advertising the features of the store. The text of the video reads:

> Four years ago, we started to wonder, what would shopping look like if you could walk into a store, grab what you want and just go? What if we could weave the most advanced machine learning, computer vision and AI, into the very fabric of a store so you never have to wait in line? No lines, no checkouts, no registers. Welcome to Amazon Go. Use the Amazon Go app, to enter, then put away your phone, and start shopping. It's really that simple. Take whatever you like. Anything you pick up is automatically added to your virtual cart. If you change your mind about that cupcake, just put it back. Our technology will update your virtual cart automatically. So, how does it work? We used computer vision, deep learning algorithms and sensor fusion much like you would find in self-driving cars. We call it Just Walk Out Technology. Once you've got everything you want, you can just go. When you leave, our Just Walk Out Technology adds up your virtual cart and charges your Amazon account. Your receipt is sent straight to the app, and you can keep going, Amazon Go. No lines. No checkout. No, seriously.[15]

The fact that Amazon invested so much time and energy preemptively advertising the new store concept suggests that Amazon was not just *responding* to consumer demand but actively *creating* it. Indeed, as Gianna Puerini, one of the chief architects of the Amazon Go initiative, noted in an interview, for many first-time shoppers, the "walk-out" technology used in the store to make the shopping experience more convenient was not something they immediately or intuitively embraced, but rather something they experienced as profoundly *unnatural*, something that butted up against their commonsense notions of how to conduct themselves. As she remarked:

> You know, one of my favorite things is actually, we thought, well, we want to make this shopping experience as natural as possible. We want the customer to have to learn as little as possible, but entering the store is new, so we have a great team of associates, and we have some who are dedicated to that area of the store to help customers. What we didn't necessarily expect was how many people would stop at the end on their first trip or two and ask, "Is it really okay if I just leave?" Or, "Are you sure it's alright?" And our associates would say "sure." We even actually wrote it above the door: "You're good to go. Thanks for shopping." So that's been fun to see. It tends to wear off after the first or second trip. It becomes more natural, but even I – I go to the store every day, once in a while, I tend to stop as I'm putting things in my handbag and look around because that behavior is something we've all done our whole lives. So watching customers pause and ask and then see the excitement when they get to just leave has been really fun.[16]

Puerini's remarks recall a more general point that scholars and critics of capitalism have long appreciated: new forms of capital accumulation require new kinds of subjects. Indeed, Puerini's reflections raise many interesting questions about how "the convenience economy" is actively reshaping the habits and habitus of American consumers. Initiatives like Amazon Go not only involve training consumers to develop new sensibilities when shopping *in* the store, they also habituate customers to a grab-and-go lifestyle that is predicated upon ever more entrenched forms of technological dependence and *privilege*. For, in order to even enter the store, shoppers must have their smartphones with them or be with a friend or family member who can scan them in. Those who find themselves on the less fortunate side of the digital divide, therefore, will not be reaping the benefits of this new convenient lifestyle. Indeed, in February of 2019, Amazon Go threatened to scrap its plan to open a store in the city of Philadelphia after the city council approved legislation that would require all businesses to accept cash. Proponents of the legislation argued that cashless stores discriminate against lower-income shoppers who are less likely to pay for goods with credit or debit cards.[17] While Amazon has subsequently claimed that it intends to concede to this requirement and make "additional payment mechanisms" that include the use of cash available to consumers, a smartphone with the requisite app will still be necessary to gain entrance to the stores, and thus will still exclude those who lack the means to afford such technology.[18]

Moreover, by notifying shoppers afterwards of how much time they spent in the store, Amazon Go encourages shoppers to embrace new forms of time management and discipline. Indeed, if the smartphone gaming app industry promotes itself around the idea of making downtime more "productive," the watchword of the convenience economy is efficiency. Instead of lingering through the aisles, shoppers are implicitly encouraged to treat their shopping experience almost like a race. Can I get in and out of the store more quickly on my next trip? As Chris, a shopper from Seattle, remarked:

> It's confusing at first, but rule of thumb is that if it feels like you're shoplifting, you're doing it right. . . . Scan a QR code, walk in, pick up what you want, and leave. You're being tracked by artificial intelligence fed by weight sensors under the food and more cameras than Caesar's Palace. Bear in mind that products are billed to whoever takes them off the shelf – if you hand something to your friend who buzzed in with their own account, you'll still pay for it. If you put something BACK on the shelf and your friend grabs it, they will pick up the tab. One nifty feature is that your receipt (when it does arrive) actually clocks how long you were in the store. I was able to see that it took me less than 20 seconds to grab and pay for a Red Bull this afternoon. The future is now![19]

What is being fostered and naturalized through Amazon Go is not just a new relationship to time and technology but to people as well. Through its product offerings (many of which are geared towards individual meals and serving sizes) and technological design, Amazon Go renders shopping a profoundly individualizing experience. Whereas previously, shoppers may have been inclined to assist another shopper by handing them an item from the shelf, in Amazon Go stores the technological imperative forecloses such assistance by mandating that whoever removes the item from the shelf foots the bill. And yet many shoppers find the *lack* of "human interaction" to be one of the store's greatest appeals. As Lisa remarked after visiting a store in Florida, "The future is now. Amazon Go is such a neat concept. A convenient store where you can leave your wallet at home while you shop and check out without any human interaction." [20]

Obfuscation

The second ideological strategy that Amazon Go relies upon to discursively justify its use of new extractive technologies that are again offered up in the name of providing convenience for customers is obfuscation. As theorists of ideology have long observed, power asymmetries are often legitimated through strategies of obfuscation or mystification; by masking exploitative social relations or arrangements, or presenting them in a more favorable light, the consent of the dominated can be won. However, with literally thousands of cameras and sensors plugged into the ceiling, walls, and shelves of the Amazon Go stores, it would be difficult, if not impossible, to mask the fact that Amazon Go deploys surveillance technology to constantly monitor shoppers' experiences and take information from them. As Chris remarked above, there are "more cameras than Caesar's Palace!" Or as shopper Monica Chin playfully remarked in a 2019 article, entitled "My Trip to Amazon Go: The Surveillance State is Sure Convenient":

> Imagine a grocery store with no cash registers. No tedious checkout lines, no mixing up your items on the conveyor belt, no fiddling around for your credit card or counting out your change. It sounds almost too good to be true. So I paid a visit to Amazon Go, Amazon's cashier-less convenience store, on its opening day in New York City . . . The only sacrifice you make: near-constant surveillance . . . But if you can get past the surveillance, and you don't mind Amazon gaining even more information about what you buy and eat, Amazon Go is convenient . . . It's creepy and it's awesome. I'm totally going back.[21]

Monica's remarks might lead us to conclude that Amazon Go customers are willing to accept the creep factor and loss of privacy in exchange for greater convenience, and there is, thus, little need for ideological persuasion to keep the company–customer relationship intact. But when we look once again at the way Amazon Go executives discuss the company–customer relationship, we find that efforts at obfuscation and mystification are very much in play; quite a bit of discursive work is done to justify the expropriation of behavioral surplus, and to reframe the company–customer relationship as being based on reciprocity rather than extraction. For instance, as Gianna Puerini further explained in her interview:

> You know we've been delighted with customer response and because it is, the store is, very geared towards people who are hungry and in a rush, you know it's a lot of grab 'n' go food to eat right now. Obviously, the Just Walk Out Technology is a *convenience play for customers*, to *hopefully give them some valuable time back*.[22] (my emphasis)

The idea that the company–customer relationship is based on reciprocity rather than data plundering and expropriation is again reinforced in Puerini's discussion of the "feedback" app that customers are encouraged to use after shopping. The app, which is installed on their phones, enables customers to send in their suggestions and product preferences. For instance, when asked what has changed since the first store opened, Puerini answered:

> The thing that probably has changed most has been learning about what customers like. What are they buying? What are their favorite things? We have this fantastic app on their phone. They can give us feedback directly. So they write in for brands they wished we had or gosh, "We wish you had that same sandwich in a half size," or "Why don't you carry this soda?" And when it makes sense, we listen, and they are very good about giving us a constant stream of feedback.[23]

The feedback app not only keeps the wheels of surveillance capitalism turning by providing a concrete technology for rendering more behavioral surplus, it also enables customers to feel that in "The Surveillance State" of Amazon Go, where their most minute behaviors are tracked and recorded, there is still a space for *choosing* to disclose information about themselves. The genius of the feedback app, therefore, is not just as a data-gathering device but as an *ideological* device that produces the *illusion* of democratic participation. It transmutes the experience of being *listened in on* through invasive surveillance technology into the sense that customers are actively be listened *to*. Indeed, if we substitute the word "convenience" for "comforts" of life, the feedback app provides a perfect illustration of an observation Herbert Marcuse put forth in his seminal work, *One-Dimensional Man*. He wrote, "In this universe, technology also provides the great rationalization of the unfreedom of man and demonstrates the 'technical' impossibility of being autonomous, of determining one's own life. For this unfreedom appears as neither irrational nor as political, but rather as submission to the

technical apparatus which enlarges the comforts [*convenience*] of life"
(Marcuse 1964: 158).

Moreover, while Puerini celebrates the way the feedback app
provides the company with an opportunity to listen to their customers,
she also notes that customers are listened to "when it makes sense,"
that is, when their recommendations translate into the possibility of
greater profits for the company. For instance, when asked, "What are
the metrics for success? How do you know that you have delivered
on your mission for Amazon Go?" Puerini replied:

> You know I think it's like what it is for a lot of people in this room.
> Do customers like what we are offering? Do they like the price we're
> offering it at? And that's just based on what's selling, pretty old school
> kind of stuff. And when we first talked about this, at Amazon we've
> always talked about price, selection, and convenience, and Just Walk
> Out Technology, and being able to walk in and kind of take it as if it
> were my own pantry was definitely a convenience play, but we also
> knew from the get-go that – and Dillip and I talked a lot about this –
> that that would not matter if customers didn't like the food assortment
> and our pricing. So I think that's our primary focus is making sure that
> we're really understanding what do customers like, listening to their
> feedback, and continually iterating and adapting to make sure that it's
> serving their needs and *that they come back often.*[24] (my emphasis)

Thus, by using technologies such as the feedback app to constantly
monitor and ascertain consumers' desires, Amazon Go is able to
stock their shelves with products that customers will be more likely to
buy. That is, Amazon Go uses the app to not only track consumers'
behaviors but, as Zuboff points out, to *shape* them: "to produce
behavior that reliably, definitively, and certainly leads to desired
commercial results" (ibid.: 201).

Moreover, although it is impossible to obscure the ubiquitous
presence of surveillance technologies in the store, Amazon does go
to considerable lengths to obscure what they do with the data they
collect from their customers. While the company claims to use this
data to personalize and enhance customer service and products, it
could easily follow the lead of Google and Facebook and decide
to sell this data to third parties thereby amassing even more astro-
nomical profits in the future. Indeed, Zuboff notes that "evidence
suggests that Amazon has veered in this direction" (ibid.: 9). With the
proliferation of its new behavior tracking technologies, Amazon, she
claims, is establishing itself "not only as an aggressive capitalist but
also a surveillance capitalist" (ibid.: 267).

Promotion

The third ideological strategy that Amazon Go executives deploy in their efforts to discursively justify and legitimate this new form of capital accumulation, domination, and extraction involves promotion. As Eagleton writes, "A dominant power may legitimate itself by *promoting* beliefs and values congenial to it" (Eagleton 2007: 5). In the case at hand, the first idea promoted by Amazon Go executives is that traditional forms of convenience store shopping that involve things like interacting with a human cashier or having to wait in a line are indeed a "problem." Although many consumers derive pleasure from developing relations with a neighborhood cashier, and although anthropologists have documented instances where waiting in line breeds highly valued forms of sociality (Jeffrey 2010; O'Neill 2017), Amazon Go executives assume that both are inherently problematic for customers. As Dillip Kumar, who leads the Amazon Go technology team, remarked when asked whether or not "Walk Out Technology" would become ubiquitous in the future:

> Well, it's hard to have a crystal ball to predict the future, but I think the way, as Gianna said, we . . . its spectacular to be able to invent on behalf of customers, to solve a customer problem, and if you do it often enough and you do it well, that's what we draw our energy from, and how big it gets, or how popular it gets, customers get to decide that. So whether it becomes ubiquitous or not, I mean customers are the ones who are going to eventually decide.[25]

Having defined traditional ways of shopping as problematic, the second idea Amazon Go actively promotes is the belief that the use of surveillance technologies provides the best means of solving this problem. While Zuboff warns us of the existential threat Big Other poses to democracy and human nature, conjuring up images of an Orwellian or Foucauldian nightmare, Dillip Kumar celebrates the way this "state-of-the-art technology" emancipates us from many of the daily grinds of shopping and can be used to create an utterly "effortless" shopping experience. For instance, in commenting upon the challenges the technology team faced in designing the store, Kumar remarked:

> Yeah, so as Gianna said, we had a very simple problem to solve; people come in, take what they want, and just leave. But there were . . . challenges that we had. . . . The first one is how do you do this in a way that makes it effortless? Where the technology just recedes into

the background, where you are not really fighting it, it's not inter-
ruptive, you don't have to scan every item, you don't have to go take it
somewhere else, there's no stopping or waiting in line.[26]

Kumar is not just promoting the belief that surveillance technologies
should be used to make shopping more convenient or "effortless."
What is also being promoted here is a larger ideological vision
in which the ubiquitous use and development of new computing
technologies are again cast as an unquestioned social good. As Eran
Fisher and others reminds us, in such cases, "technology becomes
an unquestionable 'good,' a 'religion' (Noble 1999), and a 'myth'
(Robins and Webster 1999: 151; Mosco 2004), which suggests that
virtually any social problem is subject to a technical or technological
fix (Aronowitz 1994; Segal 1985)" (Fisher 2010: 19). Indeed,
Kumar's remarks raise the question: is the real problem improving
customer convenience, or is the real problem cracking "the holy grail
of computer vision" so that Amazon Go can establish itself as part of
the technological vanguard and extend its surveillance technologies
ever further into nooks and crannies of our social lives? As Kumar
himself suggests, Amazon Go customers provide a valuable training
opportunity for scientists to develop ever more precise algorithms
and thereby "push the boundaries" of computer vision. They are
instrumental not just to the pursuit of profit, but to the advance of a
science that will further serve the interests of a powerful techno-elite.
Whereas entrepreneurs such as Diamandis use the incentive competition to discover the technological frontier on the cheap by paying
only the winner, designers like Kumar use convenience stores like
Amazon Go as a natural laboratory for developing and fine-tuning
their technologies. For instance, when asked to talk about the hardest
technology problem he had to solve, Kumar responded:

Oh, how much time do you have? [Laughing] Well, there were many.
I'll distill it to you, you know the holy grail of computer vision; it's a
tough computer science problem as well, to be able to take an arbitrary
scene and to be able to interpret it. To know what exactly is happening
in a scene. It is not a fully solved problem. In our case the scene is
shoppers shopping around everywhere in the store, and us figuring out
who took what. To do that, you need to be able to understand all of
the activities that are happening, and you need to have a much greater
understanding of what is current state of the art, in understanding
and interpreting video. So understanding a scene, and inventing the
algorithms that go and solve and push the boundaries of computer
vision, is what we had to solve.[27]

Kumar is quite open about his technological ambitions, and he proposes that unlocking "the holy grail of computer vision" is precisely what is necessary to discern "who took what" and thereby make the no-checkout shopping experience possible. However, what Zuboff would again remind us of here is that this computer vision technology is not just being used to catalogue the merchandise customers buy but, ultimately, it is being used to survey and *shape* their behavior so that in the future merchandise will more seamlessly move off the shelf and into their virtual shopping carts.

Indeed, business analyst Shep Hyken refers to this as "reducing friction" and he argues that it is "the first principle" of what he calls "the convenience revolution." He writes that reducing friction means "taking down as many barriers as possible to buying or using a product or service. Reducing friction means anticipating and removing any barriers that stand between the customer and the product or service experience. This principle leads the list because it is the essence of convenience, and serves as the foundation for the five principles that follow" (Hyken 2018: 16).

In this formulation, the essence of convenience also conveniently turns out to be the essence of augmenting sales and profits. Though "friction" is cast as a problem because it stands to hinder consumer satisfaction, it is equally problematic because it stands to hinder desired commercial results. According to Hyken, Amazon's unparalleled ability to reduce friction is precisely what has led to its staggering commercial success, and it is also what has earned Amazon the title of "The Most Convenient Company on Earth."[28]

Conclusion: ideology, extraction, and the convenience economy

What does all of this suggest about the nature of the convenience economy, and what does it reveal about the role ideology plays in the maintenance and reproduction of economies of extraction? I will begin with the first question. First, it is important to recognize that the convenience economy, as Thomas Tierney chronicles, far predates the era of Amazon. Indeed, he proposes that ever since the industrial revolution, convenience has been touted as an ultimate value (Tierney 1993). One need only recall how Betty Crocker cake mixes, or TV dinners, microwaves, dishwashers, washing machines, and an endless array of other consumer products and services were advertised with the promise that they would render life more convenient. Throughout the twentieth century, corporations used the promise of convenience as a way to increase sales and move their products into the homes of millions of Americans. What strikes me as different today is that business ventures like Amazon Go are not just interested in using the promise of convenience to move products (though this undoubtedly remains one of their top priorities). They are also interested in using convenience as a way to develop and expand their technological control over society. Indeed, this is one of the reasons why I have argued that in the era of surveillance capitalism, convenience can be usefully conceptualized as an ideology. As Kumar himself suggests, Amazon Go customers provide a valuable training opportunity for scientists to develop ever more precise algorithms and thereby "push the boundaries" of computer vision. They are instrumental to the advance of a science that will further serve the interests of a powerful techno-elite that is, in turn, becoming ever more implicated in the machinations of surveillance capitalism. What this chapter thus suggests is that, in the era of surveillance capitalism, the alliance between technocrats and capitalists is becoming ever more entrenched, as "cutting-edge" technologies make new forms of capital accumulation possible and as new capital ventures provide valuable training grounds for pushing the frontiers of science and technology.

Second, this chapter indicates that the convenience economy is not just a response to the quickening pace of social life and the consumer demand for more convenient products and services. The convenience economy is also playing an active role in *shaping* the habits and desires of twenty-first-century American consumers. Most significantly, it is habituating us to a way of life where the desire to save time trumps the desire to interact with people. It is habituating us to a way of life where consumer access is not just a question of how many dollars one has in one's bank account, but also whether or not one has the right technological gadgets in hand. Indeed, this analysis suggests that to partake of the fruits of the convenience economy, one must possess both. This instantiation of the convenience economy further normalizes the idea that one's smartphone is one's ticket to freedom, pleasure, and empowerment. With the simple swipe of a smartphone app, the gates of consumption open and a world of quick and tasty treats is there for the taking. What could be more convenient than that?

And yet, while Amazon prides itself on being "the most convenient company on earth," Zuboff's work on surveillance capitalism also suggests the need to interrogate how the *ideology* of convenience has become integral to the workings of new forms of capital accumulation, domination, and extraction. The technology being used in Amazon Go convenience stores does indeed provide an apt example of surveillance capitalism, and it does illustrate Zuboff's point that, in the age of surveillance capitalism, corporations like Amazon are increasingly aggressive about finding new ways to extract behavioral surplus from the people who use their services. (Importantly, Zuboff reminds us that the real customers of surveillance capitalism are not the Amazon users but the advertisers who buy their data.) Cameras in stores, in neighborhoods, and even in our homes provide part of the digital infrastructure through which Big Other gathers, and most likely sells, information about us.

However, even though much of surveillance capitalism hinges on the technological infrastructure of Big Other and the ability to use technologically induced "nudges" to influence consumer behavior, it would be remiss to argue that ideology plays no role in ensuring the interests and operations of surveillance capitalism. I have argued that, in the name of convenience, executives such as Jeff Bezos, Gianna Puerini, and Dillip Kumar go to significant lengths to discursively justify and legitimate these new forms of capital extraction and accumulation. Indeed, by justifying these practices in such terms, Amazon Go designers and executives effectively "recuperate" (Chiapello 2013) Zuboff's critique of surveillance capitalism by recasting the tragedy of automation as the ultimate gift of convenience.[29] Convenience, therefore, is not just a consumer good; it also operates as an ideology that is used to establish, sustain, and legitimate relations of domination. Like Terry Eagleton, therefore, I am also highly skeptical of the claim that the stage of advanced capitalism marks the end of ideology. Indeed, as I have been arguing throughout this book, it seems more likely that digital/surveillance capitalism, just as was the case with industrial capitalism, is developing its own unique set of ideologies to ensure its interests, and that social scientists should be viewing this development with a critical eye. While Marx was able to show how the ideology of freedom masked and perpetuated exploitative relationships between capital and labor during the age of industrial capitalism, social scientists today must ask how the ideology of convenience masks and perpetuates exploitative relations between capitalists and consumers in the age of surveillance capitalism. When technologies are aggressively used to keep the wheels of profit spinning in a "frictionless" manner, whose interests does it serve and what forms of domination does it engender?[30]

And yet to argue that convenience operates as an ideology is not to argue that all the customers shopping at Amazon Go are duped. As Eagleton again reminds us, dominant ideologies are often dominant precisely because they "engage significantly with [the] genuine wants, needs, and desires" of those who are subjected to them (Eagleton 2007: 45). Most people who shop at Amazon Go are fully aware that they are surrendering their privacy and having their behavior plundered in the name of gaining more convenience – the creep factor is not lost on them.

This brings me to the last point I want to make. Over time, as shoppers become habituated to these new technologies and conveniences, it may increasingly become the case that the creep factor fades. The "exchange," if you will, may not be perceived by customers as an exploitative relationship but rather one of mutual interest. One is reminded of James Scott's writings on the moral economy of the peasant and his insightful critique of Marx's concept of exploitation. As Scott observed, for peasants, extraction, in and of itself, wasn't the problem; they were quite okay with the idea that the value they produced was being expropriated by the landed classes. Rather, for peasants, exploitation was experienced as problematic when the landed classes failed to meet their obligations to provide them with the necessary services and means to ensure their existence. Scott thus reminds us:

> If the analytic goal of a theory of exploitation is to reveal something about the perceptions of the exploited – about *their* sense of exploitation, *their* notion of justice, *their* anger – it must begin not with an abstract normative standard but with the values of the real actors. Such an approach must start phenomenologically at the bottom and ask what the peasants' or workers' definition of the situation is. (Scott 1976: 160)

My hope is that this chapter will serve as an invitation for future research which ethnographically attends to the way consumers living in the age of surveillance capitalism define and understand their situation. For "the laws of motion" of surveillance capitalism that Zuboff skillfully lays bare do not necessarily equate with the lived experience of it. Exploitation, as Scott reminds us, is still a category of experience that needs to be ethnographically interrogated. For now, however, I want to examine yet another way capitalism is legitimated in the digital age and presented as "the best possible order" for organizing economic and social life. As will be seen, the stewards of digital capitalism not only purport to use technology to gift us a more convenient lifestyle, increasingly, they also propose to use their technologies and wealth to solve a range of social and environmental problems and thereby make the world a better place. As the next chapter explores, in the digital age, acts of techno-philanthropy increasingly provide a justification for the ceaseless accumulation of capital and the staggering inequality that it generates.

5

The Spirit of the Gift: The Work of Techno-philanthropy

"Philanthropy is a problem posing as a solution."[1]
Comment left by blogger (phosda, 2018) in response to Peter
Diamandis's talk, "The Robber Barons vs the Technophilanthropists"

In the United States, one of the most outspoken champions of modern-day "techno-philanthropy" is entrepreneur and venture capitalist, Peter Diamandis, who we met in chapter 1. In numerous talks and lectures, as well as in his *New York Times* bestselling book *Abundance: The Future is Better Than You Think*, which he co-authored with Steven Kotler, Diamandis argues that today's "new breed" of techno-philanthropist is playing an unparalleled role in making the world a better place. Describing this new breed, Diamandis and Kotler write:

> what seems to unify them [is] . . . a high level of optimism, a magnan-imous sphere of caring, and a hearty appetite for the big and the bold. Perhaps this is to be expected. These are the same captains of the digital age who, with the stroke of HTML code, have reinvented banking with PayPal, advertising with Google, and commerce with eBay. They've seen firsthand how exponential technologies and the tools of cooper-ation can transform industries and better lives. They now believe that the same high-leverage thinking and best business practices that led to their technological success can bring about philanthropic success. Taken together, they constitute a significant force for abundance and a new breed of philanthropist: a technophilanthropist; a young, ideal-istic, iPad jet-setter who cares about the world – the whole world – in a whole new way. (Diamandis and Kotler 2014: 132–3)

While the last chapter explored how the ideology of convenience is used to justify new forms of extraction in the era of digital capitalism, this chapter examines how philanthropy is used to justify and legit-imate unprecedented levels of capital *accumulation*. As Boltanski and Chiapello propose, in any age the spirit of capitalism not only has to arouse enthusiasm to secure "committed engagement in the process of accumulation." It also has to be "justified in terms of the common good" and, when "confronted with accusations of injustice," find ways to "manage and defend" capitalism as "an acceptable and even desirable order of things: the only possible order, or the best of all possible orders" (Boltanski and Chiapello 2007: 16). This chapter thus asks how does philanthropy provide such a justification? In what terms do proponents of techno-philanthropy manage and defend capitalism as contributing to the common good? How do they use philanthropic endeavors to disarm or "recuperate" critiques of capitalism and thereby further legitimate capitalist business ventures and practices (Chiapello 2013)?[2]

Drawing upon an array of philanthropic initiatives and the writings and talks of philanthropy enthusiasts, in what follows I seek to illuminate the various ways techno-philanthropy is promoted as a *solution to*, rather than *symptom of*, pervasive social problems. I contend that in the current era it is not so much the case that the spirit of digital capitalism legitimates "a new trade-off between social emancipation and personal emancipation," as Eran Fisher has argued (Fisher 2010: 11). Rather, in its most recent manifestations, the spirit of digital capitalism achieves its efficacy, in part, by *pledging* a renewed commitment to the social, albeit in transmuted form. By casting their philanthropic efforts as part of a global and even galactic mission of salvation – an attempt to "take on the world's biggest problems" with science and technology at their sides – and by blurring the boundaries between commerce and care, digital capitalists are able to present their philanthropic ventures as acts of social uplift, even while their business practices contribute to ever more entrenched forms of precarity and inequality. Indeed, as will be seen, the "work" of techno-philanthropy not only justifies the accumulation of capital into the hands of a networked few. It also serves as a vehicle through which the titans of tech are able to further disseminate their techno-solutionist approach to the world, while at the same time valorizing capitalism as an economic order. One of the key ideological tricks techno-philanthropy performs is that it turns occasions of giving into opportunities to further cultivate and celebrate an economic system and an economic habitus devoted to ceaseless accumulation. In the era of techno-philanthropy, therefore, the spirit of the gift, far from representing the antithesis of the logic of capitalism, as Marcel Mauss famously proposed, becomes an extension of it (Mauss 1925).

Hyper-agents

As was the case in the early twentieth century when robber barons like Andrew Carnegie and John D. Rockefeller were sowing their philanthropic oats, today's era of techno-philanthropy has also been made possible by savage inequality and the massive accumulation of wealth in the hands of a few. In *The Givers: Wealth, Power, and Philanthropy in a New Gilded Age*, David Callahan examines the context in which this "new wealth" has emerged, arguing that a "confluence of factors – globalization, technological change and public policies favoring capital – have worked together to create this Second Gilded Age" (Callahan 2017: 17). Coupled with the "declining ability," or rather will, "of the government to solve big problems and provide public goods," billionaire philanthropists, "who have amassed such vast fortunes that philanthropy is the only real place the money can go," have stepped in to fuel a "rising tide" of philanthropic "mega-giving" (Callahan 2017: 16). Callahan further notes that "No industry is producing more big donors these days than tech, which has spawned enormous fortunes in an era of rapid digital breakthroughs and expanding global markets" (Callahan 2017: 44). Indeed, the fortunes and, in some cases, "largesse" of techno-philanthropists have accelerated during the coronavirus pandemic. In 2020, while millions of Americans sank further into economic precarity, reports abounded on "the winners of the pandemic economy" and the "tech giants" who were "profiting and getting more powerful," even as the global economy tanked.[3] For instance, in December of 2020, Jeff Bezos's ex-wife, Mackenzie Scott, made international headlines by donating an estimated US$4 billion in just four months as the value of her Amazon stock options skyrocketed.[4]

And yet, while this massive disparity in wealth certainly warrants comparisons with the first Gilded Age, there are some interesting differences, particularly regarding the way philanthropy was, and is, regarded. As numerous scholars have observed, the philanthropic initiatives of business tycoons in the early twentieth century elicited skepticism and concern. For instance, commenting on John D. Rockefeller's attempts to establish his philanthropic foundation, President Theodore Roosevelt quipped, "No amount of charities in spending such fortunes can compensate in any way for the misconduct in acquiring them" (Reich 2018: 4). Nor was it just the case that these philanthropists were criticized because their wealth was viewed as ill-gotten. Philanthropic foundations were regarded by many as a fundamental threat to democracy, a means by which pluto-cratic power could undermine American civic and political life. The idea that philanthropic initiatives should be welcomed as a solution to widespread social problems was further criticized in the aftermath of the Great Depression as New Deal legislators increasingly argued that relief from poverty should be construed as a "right" of citizens and "a duty" of government, "not a gift" from private charities (Zunz 2012: 128).

By contrast, today, in the opening decades of the twenty-first century, a far less critical attitude prevails.[5] As neoliberalism has eroded many of the government-funded safety nets citizens rely upon, techno-philanthropists are being heartily encouraged – through tax incentives as well as enthusiastic praise and peer pressure – to direct their inordinate wealth and influence towards solving societal problems. For instance, shortly after announcing his decision to step down as chief executive of Amazon, an editorial appeared in the *New York Times* encouraging Jeff Bezos to follow in the footsteps of his robber-baron predecessors and embrace large-scale philanthropy as a way to "transform his public image." The author proposed that if Rockefeller's philanthropy could become "a justification for amassing his great fortune in the first place," it could likely do the same for Bezos.[6]

Indeed, the stark inequality that New Deal policies sought to, and in many cases did, successfully eradicate is now offered as a *rationale* for philanthropic interventions in social life.[7] In the academic and popular press, today's philanthropists are being heralded as "hyper-agents" whose unparalleled wealth and influence make them particularly well suited to tackle social problems, "transform the global aid industry," and even "save the world" (Schervish 2003; Bishop and Green 2009; Diamandis and Kotler 2014; Kumar 2019). Matthew Bishop and Michael Green are among the numerous thinkers to champion this idea. In their book *Philanthrocapitalism: How Giving Can Save the World*, they write:

> Philanthrocapitalists are "hyperagents" who have the capacity to do some essential things far better than anyone else. They do not face elections every few years, like politicians, or suffer the tyranny of shareholder demands for ever-increasing quarterly profits, like CEOs of most public companies. Nor do they have to devote vast amounts

of time and resources to raising money, like the heads of NGOs. That frees them to think long term, to go against conventional wisdom, to take up ideas too risky for government, to deploy substantial resources quickly when the situation demands it – above all, to try something new. (Bishop and Green 2009: 12)

Instead of critiquing "the laws of civilization" which have "thrown" wealth "into the hands of a few," as Andrew Carnegie wrote in his 1889 philanthropic treatise, *The Gospel of Wealth*, promoters of techno-philanthropy celebrate techno-philanthropists' status as hyper-agents, and in so doing cast radical inequality as a force for the common good.[8] Better to leave society's challenges in the hands of super-rich elites than trust them to be solved by the nonprofit sector or democratically elected government officials. Moreover, it is not only proposed that these hyper-agents are effective because they command enough financial wealth to shape the future without interference from other actors in society. Techno-philanthropists' ability "to do essential things" "far better than anyone else" is also explained as a by-product of their visionary, daredevil, entrepreneurial spirit. As Diamandis and Kotler explain in the quote that opened this chapter, the experience and confidence that techno-philanthropists have gained from their industry-transforming success in business is frequently accepted as an indicator of their future success in philanthropy. Who better to give money away than those who have learned how to accumulate the most of it?

MarketWorld

Social critic Anand Giridharadas refers to this do-gooder "ascendant power elite," and the accompanying "culture and state of mind" it promotes, as "MarketWorld." He observes:

These elites believe and promote the idea that social change should be pursued principally through the free market and voluntary action, not public life and the law and the reform of the systems that people share in common; that it should be supervised by the winners of capitalism and their allies, and not be antagonistic to their needs; and that the biggest beneficiaries of the status quo should play a leading role in the status quo's reform. (Giridharadas 2019: 30)

Giridharadas's description of the MarketWorld elite and "the culture and state of mind" that animates their philanthropic initiatives does indeed permeate the worldview of techno-philan-thropy. While techno-philanthropists are not totally averse to working with government entities and nonprofit organizations, and while they frequently espouse the idea that philanthropy works best when local people are "empowered" to make decisions for themselves, they also actively promote the message that market mechanisms and solutions can play the most effective role in solving the world's biggest problems. As Peter Diamandis is fond of saying, "the world's biggest problems are the world's biggest market opportunities . . . Solve hunger, solve water, solve energy, solve healthcare, and you get a billion dollars while helping a billion people."[9] Life becomes a win–win situation for the poor and rich alike.

Furthermore, the MarketWorld ideology encourages techno-philanthropists to view the poor not as victims in need of charity, or citizens in need of representation, but rather as consumers or "customers" in need of products. As Raj Kumar writes in his book, *The Business of Changing the World: How Billionaires, Tech Disrupters, and Social Entrepreneurs are Transforming the Global Aid Industry*, "The aid industry today is increasingly targeting funds and tailoring programs to specific individuals and communities. These programs are set up like a retail business would be. They're designed to react and iterate based on customer feedback. This is part of a major shift towards seeing aid recipients as 'customers' of aid instead of nameless, voiceless 'beneficiaries'" (Kumar 2019: 3).

One of the most outspoken proponents of this idea, and someone whose writings have had a profound influence on Peter Diamandis, Bill Gates, and other techno-philanthropists, was Coimbatore Krishnarao Prahalad, a highly regarded professor of corporate strategy at the University of Michigan. In his award-winning book, *The Fortune at the Bottom of the Pyramid: Eradicating Poverty through Profits*, Prahalad set out to "build a framework for poverty allevi-ation" that starts with a "simple proposition":

> If we stop thinking of the poor as victims or as a burden and start recognizing them as resilient and creative entrepreneurs and value-conscious consumers, a whole new world of opportunity will open up. Four billion poor can be the engine of the next round of global trade and prosperity. It can be a source of innovations. Serving the BOP consumers will demand innovations in technology, products and services, and business models. (Prahalad 2004: 1)

As I will discuss below, Prahalad's MarketWorld message is changing the way many techno-philanthropists think about and practice philanthropy. However, Prahalad himself proposed that philanthropy is *not* the solution to solving global poverty. "Poverty reduction," he writes, can result "from co-creating a market around the needs of the poor," and from incorporating "these underserved consumers" into a "system of inclusive capitalism" (ibid.: xiv–xv). Indeed, if enthusiasts like Green and Bishop cast radical inequality as a force for the common good by arguing that it leads to the development of billionaire "hyper-agents" who can do things far more effectively than others, Prahalad makes the inverse argument. He proposes that it is the power of the "rising billions," the mass population of destitute people who live on less than US$2 a day, who will spur innovation and growth in the future. In Prahalad's MarketWorld, therefore, the goal of "inclusive capitalism" is not to restructure "the pyramid" but rather to recuperate "the bottom" as a viable market that can fuel ongoing capital accumulation for those at the top.

Techno-solutionism can save the world

In the discursive universe of techno-philanthropy, it is not just MarketWorld ideology that rules the roost, it is also what a number of scholars have referred to as "solutionism" or "techno-solutionism" (Morozov 2014; Appadurai and Alexander 2020; Haven and boyd 2020; Sadowski 2020).[10] As Janet Haven and danah boyd observe:

> The tech sector's runaway financial success – enabled by a deafening regulatory silence – has propped up the economy, and philanthropy's endowments, for the last two decades. This has birthed a new class of philanthropists informed directly by the tech-solutionist logic of the tech industry. During this time, philanthropy has spent uncounted millions advancing and funding a narrative that posits new technologies as the solution to our most pressing problems. (Haven and boyd 2020: 68)

In addition to placing a premium on the ability of technology to solve the world's biggest problems, thereby downplaying the need for social or political reforms, techno-solutionism also promotes a vision of the world as a constellation of "concrete problems to be solved" (Žižek 2006). Taking on the problems of water, energy, healthcare, hunger, pollution, climate change, disease, and education, to name but a few of the issues that typically populate the agendas of techno-philanthropists, will pave the path to progress. Collective salvation is presented not as a matter of consensus building among differently vested social groups (though, in the world of techno-philanthropy, technological "collaboration" is highly valued), or as an attempt to radically reform existing social structures and systems. It is presented as a checklist of technical projects that can be successfully solved or engineered by the world's smartest people. If the Gates Foundation can just get enough toilets and malaria nets to the Third World, or Google.org (the philanthropic arm of Google) can provide internet technologies to be disseminated amongst the world's poor, the world will become a better place.

For instance, in a video produced for the Gates Foundation, advertising their "World's Grand Challenges" incentive competition, both the MarketWorld ideology and techno-solutionism come to the fore. A male voice with a British accent narrates an animated video that breaks down the world's grandest challenges into more digestible or solvable steps, a method that, as Ethan Rasiel documents in his book *The McKinsey Way*, has also been widely adopted in the business world (Rasiel 1999). The narrator proclaims:

> The future is in close research; we might even go to Mars within the next century, but before we step onto the red planet there are a myriad of small steps we need to take to make that dream come true. That also applies to scientific breakthroughs that affect our daily lives. Take healthcare: we tend to forget what it takes to turn a eureka moment into an actual prescription. It starts with the process of discovery, often by a researcher with government funding of research and development. Then there is a long development process, including lots of lab tests, small and big test trials, lengthy regulatory approval and marketing before there is finally a finished product. This journey can take years and sometimes the idea gets stuck along the way, or loses funding and sometimes never sees the light of day. *What if we could help turn those ideas into reality by bringing together people with great ideas and experts who know how to make them happen? That's the mission of the Grand Challenges program, an open call for innovative ideas to solve some of the world's biggest problems.*[11] (my emphasis)

The narrator then goes on to provide an example of this, discussing how the Gates Foundation sponsored an initiative by the organization Zana Africa, to develop cheaper sanitary napkins for girls in developing countries. By making sanitary napkins more accessible, they reasoned, girls would be more inclined to stay in school after reaching puberty and thereby have an opportunity to "reach their full potential" in the future. The narrator explains that when the Gates Foundation Grand Challenges program started supporting the initiative, "experts from across the entire development process worked together to create several potential solutions," and the new product was brought to market far more quickly, and at a significantly lower cost, than had it been developed through traditional channels. The video ends by proclaiming, "Only with teamwork and investment can we quickly take it from an idea to impact. Innovation done well can help solve the world's biggest challenges."[12]

This video is but one of countless examples of the way in which techno-philanthropists frame their mission as "taking on the world's biggest challenges." In fact, given how frequently "the world" and "taking on the world's biggest challenges" is invoked in techno-philanthropic discourse, it is worth pausing to ask what exactly does this "world" reference and signify. What and who falls in and out of the frame, when "the world," rather than say "society" or "the oppressed and exploited" – two terms that are typically absent in techno-philanthropic discourse – becomes the object of philanthropic intervention?

In part, these recurring allusions to "the world's biggest challenges" may just be an example of hyperbole. Or, as Diamandis suggests, a reflection of the "bold" ambition, vision, and "magnanimous sphere of caring" that motivates techno-philanthropists today. Perhaps we shouldn't be surprised that the same people who "reinvented banking . . . with the stroke of HTML code" are used to thinking at scale and swinging for the fences. Perhaps the mission to combat the "world's biggest challenges" is a means by which techno-philanthropists seek to re-enchant the world with meaning and compassion after their entrepreneurial commitments to rational calculation, technical mastery, and inordinate capital accumulation have jeopardized these very things.

My concern, however, is that by continually invoking "the world's biggest challenges," the discourse of techno-philanthropy also, in a curious way, de-socializes the very world it purportedly aims to save. If the poor in the Third World can be saved with toilets, mosquito nets, antiviral drugs, sanitary pads, and cell phones, as is often proposed, then there is little need to consider how the machinations of digital capitalism might contribute to their poverty and suffering. Moreover, when the world is mapped as a constellation "of concrete problems," as Slavoj Žižek observes, it becomes increasingly difficult to see or understand the systemic relations between these problems. In an opinion piece entitled "Nobody Has to be Vile," Žižek refers to this do-gooder "power elite," of which he cites Bill Gates as a prime example, as the new breed of "liberal communists." "Liberal communists," he writes, are "pragmatic; they hate a doctrinaire approach. There is no exploited working class today, only concrete problems to be solved: starvation in Africa, the plight of Muslim women, religious fundamentalist violence" (Žižek 2006: 2).

To be clear, I am not suggesting that the global problems techno-philanthropists identify are not real or pressing. Nor am I suggesting that they shouldn't be addressed, or that techno-philanthropists haven't made some valuable contributions in trying to solve them. Rather, I am proposing that we must also consider how this way of framing and "solving" problems enables techno-philanthropy to "maintain the status quo," while deflecting or recuperating more damning critiques of capitalism that would ultimately call for changing the system itself.[13] If the very business practices techno-philanthropists engage in are in part responsible for creating conditions of global poverty, inequality, and ecocide, as Žižek and many others point out, then perhaps the solution to these problems is not to try and solve them through philanthropy, but rather to change the practices that contribute to them in the first place.[14]

And yet, instead of critiquing or questioning the capitalist system, I contend that techno-philanthropy has emerged as one of the central vehicles through which the logics of capitalism are valorized and reinscribed. This can be discerned through celebrations of techno-philanthropists as "hyper-agents," as discussed above, but it can also be gleaned in their recent embrace of "venture philanthropy," "impact investing," and "social entrepreneurship." Increasingly, these are the terms through which today's techno-philanthropists articulate their work and their approach to philanthropic "giving." As such, I want to explore how these concepts have come to permeate the thinking and initiatives of techno-philanthropists. I contend that by integrating these market principles into their philanthropic practice and discourse, techno-philanthropists blur the boundaries between commerce and care, and cast their philanthropic "gifts" not as the antithesis to the logic of capital accumulation but as an extension of it. By transmuting giving into a form of investing, techno-philanthropists are able to maintain and spread an essential element of the spirit of capitalism, even as some of the initiatives they promote defy the economic imperative of M–C–M′ or the continual pursuit of profit.

The business of giving

The idea of applying insights from business in order to yield more effective philanthropic results is certainly not new. Sociologist Linsey McGoey, for instance, argues that "a businesslike approach to charity has been dominant within large-scale organized philanthropy for at least 120 years" (McGoey 2016: 15). She reminds us that Frederick T. Gates, who served as the philanthropic advisor to John D. Rockefeller was a "major adherent of the Efficiency Movement, a school of thought that sought to apply Taylorist principles of management to all spheres of social business and life" (ibid.). Similarly, sociologist Nicolas Guilhot notes that Rockefeller and Carnegie both claimed "to apply the rational methods of business to the administration of charitable deeds, which they considered to be outdated" (Guilhot 2007: 451). And yet, while scholars have noted that there is a precedent for running philanthropies like businesses, it is also clear that during the late twentieth century and certainly within the first two decades of the twenty-first century the business influence has become far more pronounced. McGoey attributes this development, in part, to the intervention of management scholars who in the 1980s began to shift their attention to the nonprofit sector. She writes:

> From the 1980s onwards, a new generation of management scholars, accustomed to scrutinizing the bottom line turned their gaze to the non-profit sector, and they found the field wanting. The problem with traditional foundations, they proclaimed, was their failure to meet or even clearly state objectives, to adopt clear performance measures, or to reduce operating overheads.
>   The ideas of these management scholars have been instrumental in the rise of trends such as social innovation and social entrepreneurship, as well as a bewildering array of new terms for describing the 'business' of giving: venture philanthropy, catalytic philanthropy, strategic philanthropy, philanthrocapitalism, philanthroentrepreneurism. (McGoey 2016: 62)

Others propose that the most significant impetus came from Silicon Valley startup culture which took the US economy by storm in the late 1990s. The explosion of venture capitalism in the tech industry not only produced a generation of super-wealthy elites with newfound millions to spend. It also provided a model of how to get the greatest returns on an investment. For instance, in 1997,

Christine Letts, William Ryan, and Allen Grossman published a landmark essay in the *Harvard Business Review* entitled, "Virtuous Capital: What Foundations Can Learn from Venture Capitalists." The article began by observing that venture capitalists and philanthropic foundations share similar challenges. They are both charged with "selecting the most worthy recipients for funding, relying on young organizations to implement ideas, and being accountable to the third party whose funds they are investing" (Letts, Ryan, and Grossman 1997). The authors then went on to suggest some ways foundations could incorporate practices from venture capitalism to improve their philanthropic impact. These included providing longer funding periods for the organizations they support; developing a more involved working relationship with the nonprofits they fund; developing more rigorous "performance measures" to assess impact and accountability, and coming up with a viable "exit strategy" after which foundation involvement would be terminated.

Peter Frumkin, who is a professor of public policy at Harvard, proposes that it wasn't just Silicon Valley startup culture that rendered "the investment metaphor" so popular among philanthropists. He also attributes its allure to the rise of the "New Democrats" who in the 1990s wanted to "veer away from images of wasteful government spending" and sought to exchange the language of "higher taxation and spending" to one of making "contributions" and "social investments" (Frumkin 2003). In a widely cited essay entitled "Inside Venture Philanthropy," Frumkin wrote:

> The rhetoric of the New Democrats and the practices of Silicon Valley were ultimately wed together in the field of philanthropy and the result is what is now generally termed venture philanthropy. It was a marriage made in heaven, in that sophisticated donors have long sought to turn their gifts and grants into something more concrete and scientific. Rather than simply being a purveyor of charitable funds for deserving organizations of all sorts, venture philanthropy promised to turn donors into hard-nosed social investors by bringing the discipline of the investment world to a field that for over a century relied on good faith and trust. (Frumkin 2003: 8)

According to Frumkin, by the dawn of the twenty-first century a whole "new language" had emerged that reflected the "deep seated desires of these new donors to have an impact and measure the effects of their philanthropy." In the language of venture philanthropy, donors were "reinvented as social investors," grants became "investments," impact was recast as "social return," grant lists were referred to as "investment portfolios," evaluation was replaced by "performance measurement" and grant review process became "due diligence' (ibid.: 15). And yet Frumkin also proposed that the "frenzy of verbiage that has accompanied" the turn to venture philanthropy did not necessarily bespeak a real or significant change in philanthropic practice. In 2003, he lamented, "For now it is very difficult to find authentic innovations that justify the new terms that have been introduced." He concluded his essay by writing:

> Although only a few critics have to date pointed to the holes in the venture philanthropy industry, time will tell how durable the business metaphor ultimately will prove to be. For now, one thing is impossible to deny: By seeking to move concepts and language from the world of business to the world of nonprofit organizations, venture philanthropy must be viewed as a marketing triumph. (Frumkin 2003: 15)

In the two decades since Frumkin's essay was published, the business metaphor has proved to be incredibly durable, and a growing number of critics have emerged to question the way techno/venture philanthropy enables mega-donors to undermine civil society, to compromise democratic forms of social governance, and to use philanthropy as a tool for penetrating new consumer markets, thereby increasing their profit margins (Eikenberry and Drapal Kluver 2004; McGoey 2016; Birn and Richter 2018; Reich 2018). While these issues are certainly relevant to any critique of techno-philanthropy, what concerns me here is of a slightly different nature. As stated at the outset, I am mainly interested in the ideological work techno-philanthropy performs. I argue that by moving "concepts and language from the world of business to the world of nonprofit organizations," techno/venture philanthropy doesn't just achieve a "marketing triumph." It also achieves an ideological coup – which admittedly, for some people, might be one and the same thing. Techno-philanthropy becomes the means by which capitalism is once again presented and promoted as the "best of all" economic systems, and techno-philanthropy is portrayed as a solution to, rather than symptom of, pervasive social problems. To illustrate this point, I now want to focus on one prominent example where the ideological work of techno-philanthropy can be gleaned: the Silicon Valley Social Venture Fund.

Teaching the techno-elite how to give:
the Silicon Valley Social Venture Fund

The fortunes made in the tech industry have not only led to a new era of mega foundations and billionaire donors. They have also given rise to a new wave of community foundations and venture philanthropy organizations that basically understand their work as teaching the techno-elite how to give and making it easier for them to do so by providing a ready-made infrastructure to pursue philanthropic endeavors. As Jeff Skoll put it, these organizations provide "training wheels for young philanthropists." Indeed, by the dawn of the twenty-first century, journalists were observing that philanthropy had become "another Silicon Valley growth industry" (quoted in Elkind 2000).

Two of the most influential champions of this cause were Peter Hero, who has been heralded as "the man who sold Silicon Valley on giving" and served as the president of the Silicon Valley Community Foundation from 1988 to 2006, and Laura Arrillaga-Andreessen who, in the late 1990s as a business student at Stanford, became interested in why young tech leaders "were amassing great fortunes but giving comparatively little back."[15] Concluding that there was "simply no model of giving that addressed their unprecedented circumstances," Arrillaga-Andreessen approached Peter Hero with the idea of starting the Silicon Valley Social Venture Fund (SV2).[16] With the support of Hero and some of Silicon Valley's leading philanthropists, including Jeff Skoll, the fund was launched in 1998, and spent ten years incubating as part of the Silicon Valley Community Foundation, after which it became an independent 501(c)(3) nonprofit organization. Today, the Silicon Valley Venture Fund has emerged as one of the "top venture philanthropy non-profits and foundations" in the United States, and it has been credited with helping to "inspire the venture philanthropy movement around the world."[17] In 2021, the website described SV2 as "a community of more than 200 individuals and families who have come together to learn about effective giving and pool our resources to support innovative social ventures . . . Our mission is to unleash the resources and talents of the Silicon Valley community to achieve meaningful social impact."[18]

As will be seen, the Silicon Valley Social Venture Fund speaks the language of "community," "mission," and "meaning," but it is also steeped in the language of business. In part, this is because both Hero and Arrillaga-Andreessen came to philanthropy with a background in business. Both were trained at Stanford Business School and were deeply committed to the idea that insights from the business world could render philanthropic giving more "impactful." However, Hero and Andreessen also deployed the language of business because very early on they realized that this was the language they would *need* to speak if they were going to convince the newly minted techno-elites to get involved with philanthropy. Hero himself noted that when he began his work, tech entrepreneurs were not particularly swayed by the notion "that giving is a moral obligation." "You're rich, they're poor; you have to give your money away – that doesn't fly out here," he told a reporter in 2000.[19] After reviewing the results of a survey conducted on the giving proclivities among young tech entrepreneurs, Hero discovered that "Fifty-six percent of respondents said they would give 'a great deal more' to charity if they knew that charities were effectively managed." He further remarked, "These *donors are focused investors*. They use the word *invest*, not *contribute*, and there is a world of difference in these terms" (Hero 2001: 50–1; italics in the original).

Indeed, it could be argued that one of the main functions of SV2 is to translate the world of financial investing into the world of philanthropy so that donors feel more comfortable and confident giving their money away. As Peter Elkind explains, "Under the 'venture philanthropy' model, the donors subject non-profits to the sort of scrutiny a venture capital firm would apply, then offer their expertise to maximize their 'investment.' It insists on establishing 'metrics' to measure returns and looks for 'scalability' and 'an exit strategy.'"[20]

In addition to providing a sense of familiarity by deploying the venture philanthropy model, SV2 also provides its donors with a sense of superiority and distinction. By encouraging donors to approach the redistribution of capital with the same kind of rational, data-driven, performance-oriented approach that they use in their efforts to accumulate it, the Silicon Valley Social Venture Fund reproduces the idea that expertise and success in business is *the most valuable* "resource" or "talent" that can be used to achieve "meaningful social impact."

Moreover, while the mission statement professes to "unleash the resources and talents of the Silicon Valley community to achieve meaningful social impact," it is also clear that "the community" they are referring to is comprised of very specific people. The Silicon Valley Social Venture Fund doesn't allow just anyone to join its club; it is "invitation only." Selected "partners" are required to contribute at least US$2,500 a year to maintain their membership, and if they want to join the "Visionary Leadership Circle," which was established in 2015, they need to contribute at least US$20,000 a year. There is also a concern with admitting the right kind of people. As one member explained in an interview, "One thing we are providing to our members is a safe place to be." Or as another member remarked, "the ideal people to become members of this group" are "the hot CEOs and the hot venture capitalists."[21]

And yet, while SV2 promotes the idea that expertise in business can play a leading role in achieving meaningful social impact, it also promotes the idea that by participating in the Silicon Valley Social Venture Fund, members can *achieve expertise* in a range of social issues and develop "skills as philanthropists" that will be transferable in the future. For example, describing the "classic grant round" process, the website explains:

> In a Classic Grant Round, participating Partners learn about one issue area – for example, Education, the Environment, International Development, or Economic Opportunity & Employment – and get to know several Bay Area non-profits working in that sector. After five to six months of learning, diligence and evaluation, we choose one to receive a three-year general operating support grant.
>
> In this collaborative, experiential grantmaking process, Partners learn about the sector and how to conduct diligence on nonprofit organizations, which helps them build skills as strategic philanthropists and community leaders. They also connect with others who share their interest in a particular issue area.[22]

Here again, we see how techno-philanthropy approaches the world as a constellation of concrete problems, but again, what is perhaps more interesting in this case, is the way SV2 provides its "partners" with opportunities to experience themselves as qualified experts. The implicit assumption here is that "five or six months of learning, diligence and evaluation" is adequate to prepare these donors for becoming "leaders" of the community. The kind of expertise that usually takes years and years of study and experience to acquire is promised here with relative ease. Moreover, for those donors who can't "afford" to invest this much time, SV2 provides accelerated opportunities to participate. "Lighting Grant Rounds," as described on the website, are "a condensed one-month process," in which "Partners review a small group of potential Grantees culled from the portfolios of SV2 funder allies and choose one nonprofit to fund."[23]

The Silicon Valley Venture Fund, and other organizations like it, do more than keep the wheels of philanthropy turning. They have also become key sites for the reproduction of class privilege and power. They provide opportunities for wealthy donors to extend their influence into new spheres but, equally important, they teach donors that they are the rightful people to lead the community and solve the world's biggest problems. As the sociologist Shamus Khan notes in his excellent ethnography, *Privilege: The Making of an Adolescent Elite at St Paul's School*, "if we want to understand the recent increases in American inequality we must know more about the wealthy, as well as the institutions that are important for their production and maintenance" (Khan 2011: 5). I contend that the Silicon Valley Venture Fund is such an institution.

One of the most effective ways the Silicon Valley Venture Fund works to produce and maintain class privilege and power is by constructing philanthropy as a family endeavor. Encouraging "family philanthropy" is one of the four main "components" of "their social impact model." As they advertise, "SV2 Partners engage their families through SV2's hands-on learning, service and giving opportunities to develop the next generation of givers."[24] They offer a special program for teens, as well as a "kids' program" for children ages 4–12. While some might propose these are just glorified community services programs or (even daycare services), it is clear that a main emphasis of these programs is to teach children how to give "effectively," thereby providing them with opportunities to develop and hone their skills as budding young philanthropists. As stated on the website:

> The SV2 Teen Philanthropy Program offers a comprehensive philan-thropy and community service experience for SV2 Partners' children who are in 7th–12th grade. Teens gain exposure to pressing local social issues, learn about nonprofit organizations and think together about giving money away effectively. Since the program's founding in 2009, SV2 Teens have made over a dozen grants together in the areas or Resilient Youth, Environment, Education, Workforce Development, Housing & Basic Needs in the Bay Area, and Criminal Justice Reform.[25]

The program consists of nine sessions that are sponsored from January through May. During the first half of the program, teens learn about pressing social problems in the community as well as about developing positive "solutions." They spend two sessions doing site visits where they meet with nonprofit organizations "to learn more about what they do firsthand and discuss how they might use grant funds from SV2 Teens." The subsequent session is devoted to "Grant Making and Allocation." In this meeting, teens "reflect about their site visits, and ultimately decide how they want to allocate their grant funds to the organizations where they did site visits." The following session is devoted to a "celebration ceremony" in which "families and nonprofit leaders join the Teens for a celebration and ceremony led by the SV2 Teens in which they present their learnings, future goals, and the grant checks to their nonprofit Grantees."[26] As a final wrap-up, the program culminates with a session in which teens are provided an opportunity to offer feedback and reflections on their experiences.

The SV2 Teen Philanthropy program may indeed provide a valuable opportunity for teens to become more socially engaged and aware of the manifold problems that exist in society. But the program also imparts lessons that actually undermine the organization's stated mission of creating "a more equitable and sustainable Bay Area and world where everyone thrives." For what is communicated through this program is that incredibly complicated social problems, whether they be criminal justice reform, the environment, or housing or workforce development, can be adequately addressed by a group of wealthy teenagers within the course of just a few weeks. Reminiscent of the adolescents who Shamus Khan studied, and who felt that the high school papers they wrote at their elite boarding school might actually revolutionize a particular field of study, these teens are also taught that their privilege and wealth makes them *worth listening to.* Those who cut and give the checks not only have the right to advise others on what to do (regardless of the fact that the grantees may be older and wiser), but they should also be celebrated with honors.[27] Moreover, it is not just the teens that are celebrated but philanthropy itself. In the SV2 Teen Program, philanthropy is presented as a solution to, rather than symptom of, radical inequality. The program is geared towards producing "the next generation of givers," not a future where philanthropy is no longer "needed" because the problem of inequality has been resolved.

Blurring the lines between purpose and profit: impact investing and social enterprise

In addition to providing its members with opportunities to participate in grant-making processes, learning programs, and programs devoted to "family philanthropy," the Silicon Valley Social Venture Fund also offers opportunities for donors to engage in "impact investing," which they define as "investing for the dual purpose of both social impact and financial return." SV2 instituted impact investing as part of their philanthropic strategy in 2015 but, as numerous scholars have noted, the embrace of "impact investing" developed with particular zeal after the financial meltdown and global recession of 2008, and since then it has grown into a major industry itself (Verkerk 2013; Chiapello and Knoll 2020; Hellman 2020). Proponents of impact investing claim that by keeping the profit motive in play, impact investing can solve and scale solutions to social problems much more effectively than distributing money in the form of grants. As Diamandis and Kotler write, "If they [the techno-philanthropists] can use their donations to create a profitable solution to a social problem, it will attract more capital, far faster, and thus have a far bigger impact, far sooner, than would a solution based entirely on giving the money away" (Diamandis and Kotler 2014: 136). However, while proponents of impact investing extol its efficiency and capacity to "leverage" resources, we might pause to ask what else does impact investing accomplish?

I propose that if venture philanthropy achieves an ideological coup by transposing "concepts and language from the world of business to the world of nonprofit organizations," impact investing achieves its ideological force by transposing concepts and language from the social world – with all the collective responsibilities and obligations that entails – onto the realm of business. As McGoey observes, "Today's philanthrocapitalists are remarkably fond of the word 'social.' They affix the word to an ecumenical bounty of commercial endeavors, implying that this renders their actions more socially progressive" (McGoey 2016: 21). This becomes readily apparent, for instance, when we begin to survey the way SV2 describes its impact-investing initiative:

> Throughout the year, Partners learn more about the field of impact investing and decide which for-profit *social enterprises* to fund. SV2 has added investing in for-profit *social impact companies* to our mix of approaches to addressing social and environmental challenges in pursuit of the greatest impact. SV2 defines "impact investing" as investing for the dual purpose of both *social* impact and financial return.[28] (my emphasis)

And yet, as is more generally the case, while SV2 encourages more rigorous means to calculate social impact, or SROI (social return on investment), and while the language of the social is readily deployed by SV2, it is also never precisely defined. There is incredible latitude for partners to decide which business ventures represent true "social enterprises" or promise to deliver real "social impact."[29] For example, explaining "How it Works," the website states:

> A group of SV2 Partners conducts diligence on prospective investments throughout the year. SV2 is open to a variety of industry focus areas based on the interests of Partners who are participating in this work. We are looking to make angel or seed-stage investments for companies seeking to raise ideally up to $1.5M, but we are open to those seeking up to $3M. The SV2 Impact Investing Working Group – comprised of a self-selected group of Partners interested in impact investing – meets monthly to review companies and move them along a continuum for both a "closer look" and when appropriate "deeper dive." The Impact Investment Working Group collaboratively selects one or more *social impact companies* to invest in. Investment levels vary and the timing is year-round, kicking off in the fall of each year. In addition, SV2 hosts learning sessions throughout the year on various aspects of Impact Investing which any Partner of SV2 Grantee can attend. Interested Partners can also audit the Working Group and refer companies for consideration that align with SV2's Impact Thesis, regardless of participation in the Working Group.[30] (my emphasis)

The semantic elasticity that terms like "social enterprise," "social entrepreneur," "social impact," and" social value" take on has led many scholars to conclude that impact investing is evidence of a potentially worrisome form of "sector blurring" (Eikenberry and Drapal Kluver 2004). For instance, one of the companies that has been identified as a "social enterprise" is Google. In 2004, just before the company went public, founders Larry Page and Sergey Brin announced that approximately 1 percent of the company's profits would be devoted to pursuing social good.[31] Established as the "philanthropic arm" of the corporation, to this day Google.org aims to "look for ideas with the potential to change the world." As it states on the website, "Through Google.org Impact Challenges, we award community-driven nonprofits and social enterprises with support to make their community – and beyond – a better place."[32] Investing in Google thus becomes synonymous with investing for social impact.[33]

Impact investing, therefore, should not be viewed merely as a philanthropic feat. It should also be viewed as an ideological one that aims to achieve "capitalist recuperation of criticism" (Chiapello and Knoll 2020: 17). By blurring the boundaries between commerce and care, impact investing ultimately gives rise to the idea that engaging in capitalist enterprise is itself a form of philanthropy, or *philanthrōpos* – one of the most effective ways of expressing a "love of mankind."[34] Indeed, by including impact investing as part of its giving model, the Silicon Valley Venture Fund perpetuates the idea that the line between philanthropy and capitalism is indeed very thin, and that poverty and other social problems can, as Coimbatore Prahalad proposed, be "eradicated" through profits.

The Giving Pledge: making moral agents

While impact investing achieves its ideological force in part by conflating the domains of commerce and care and suggesting that capital accumulation provides a means to express one's devotion to mankind, the Giving Pledge uses different strategies in order to portray capitalism and techno-philanthropists as a boon to humanity. Indeed, a chapter devoted to the ideological work of techno-philanthropy would be remiss without a discussion of the Giving Pledge. For in the "field" of techno-philanthropy, the Giving Pledge produces the ultimate distinction for its members while at the same time producing a justification for capitalism and capitalists to continue to dominate society (Bourdieu 1984). It celebrates the techno-elite not just as hyper-agents, who, as Linsey McGoey puts it, "get shit done" (McGoey 2016: 7) but as moral agents whose benevolence, generosity, and sense of social obligation are presented as a "true" gift to society.

Established in 2010 by Warren Buffett and Bill and Melinda Gates, the Giving Pledge calls upon the wealthiest people in the world to publicly commit to give away "the majority of their wealth" during their lifetimes or upon their deaths. As Raj Kumar notes, "The Giving Pledge is nonbinding, has no legal status, and there are no stipulations about where the money should go or how it should be deployed, but it is incredibly meaningful as a promise and commitment, a statement of values, and a challenge to others" (Kumar 2019: 26). Indeed, the fact that it is "a pledge" is crucial to the ideological work it performs, for it promotes the idea that the wealthiest people in the world can be *trusted* to produce public good by following their conscience and moral compass, rather than being *required* to recognize their debts to society because of legally binding contracts or redistributive tax policies.[35]

The pledge is also a privilege. In order to sign the Giving Pledge, one *must* be a billionaire. While the "signatories" have increased over the years, from 40 in 2010 to more than 200 in 2021, this stipulation does work to create a club that is very exclusive. And yet, while the

Giving Pledge keeps its circle tight, it also claims to be inspired by the generosity of people "at all income levels." As the website explains:

> The Giving Pledge is a simple concept: an open invitation for billionaires, or those who would be if not for their giving, to publicly commit to giving the majority of their wealth to philanthropy. It is inspired by the example set by millions of people at all income levels who give generously – and often at great personal sacrifice – to make the world better. Envisioned as a multi-generational effort, the Giving Pledge aims over time to help shift the social norms of philanthropy among the world's wealthiest people and inspire people to give more, establish their giving plans sooner, and give in smarter ways.[36]

Moreover, as Kumar rightfully notes, the Giving Pledge is a "challenge to others," akin to the potlatches anthropologists have traditionally studied, in which chiefs and big men win prestige by giving the most wealth away. As one of the signatories reflected:

> What the Giving Pledge has enabled me to do is quantify my plan. Through the example and leadership of Bill and Melinda Gates and Warren Buffett, the Giving Pledge is inspiring successful men and women to engage in what I would call "competitive" philanthropy. Directing the same competitive instincts that these driven people employed to achieve the pinnacle of financial and social success, the Giving Pledge is encouraging us to outdo one another in giving our wealth away. Brilliant![37]

Larry Ellison, the billionaire founder of Oracle, also commented on the way the Giving Pledge challenges others to follow the example. In his Giving Pledge letter, he wrote:

> To whom it may concern, Many years ago, I put virtually all of my assets into a trust with the intent of giving away at least 95% of my wealth to charitable causes. I have already given hundreds of millions of dollars to medical research and education, and I will give billions more over time. Until now, I have done this giving quietly – because I have long believed that charitable giving is a personal and private matter. So why am I going public now? Warren Buffett personally asked me to write this letter because he said I would be "setting an example" and "influencing others" to give. I hope he is right.[38]

In some ways, the Giving Pledge is also reminiscent of the liturgical system in ancient Greece "whereby wealthy citizens were expected to make voluntary contributions to various state projects that were of benefit to the entire citizenry, or *demos*. In the liturgy system, as Rob Reich notes, "private donations for the production of public benefits were routine" (Reich 2018: 29). "The liturgical system in Athens," he further explains:

> cannot be understood apart from deeply seated social norms in ancient Greece that prized competition, honor, and virtue. Wealthy citizens sometimes competed for the privilege of liturgical service, expecting in return for their donations both honor and gratitude for their status as a civic benefactor. Motive in providing the liturgy was important; to receive honor and gratitude, gifts had to be provided in the spirit of benefiting the body politic, or demos, rather than for personal gain or status maintenance. In the absence of appropriate civic spirit, benefactors could fail to receive favor from their fellow citizens and, more threateningly, by jurors in any court appearances. They could even be punished by the courts. In this respect, liturgies can be seen as an instance of what Mauss observed about gift giving: the gift represents and reflects norms of obligation and reciprocity. (Reich 2018: 30)

The Giving Pledge does not subject signatories to the potential judgment and punishment of courts. Indeed, if anything, the pledge promotes the idea that the rich are fully capable of governing and censuring themselves, of inspiring the right course of action through their moral fortitude and ability, as Warren Bufffet puts it, to "set the right example." However, like the liturgy system, the Giving Pledge does take the issue of "motive" very seriously. In fact, the letters that signatories are asked to write upon taking the pledge not only serve as a public challenge to others. They also provide a highly ritualized means for signatories to explain their motives to the public. As stated on the Giving Pledge website, "Those who join the Giving Pledge are encouraged to write a letter explaining their decision to engage deeply and publicly in philanthropy and describing the causes that motivate them."

These letters are posted on the Giving Pledge website for all to read. In many of them, the signatories explain how their philanthropy is motivated by a sense of duty, obligation, and appreciation for the importance of reciprocity. For instance, as one Giving Pledge member writes: "I believe that those fortunate to achieve great wealth should put it to work for the good of humanity. In spotlighting this responsibility, the Giving Pledge reminds us all that our net worth is ultimately not defined by dollars but by how well we serve others."[39] Or, as Mark Zuckerberg and Priscilla Chan wrote when they signed the pledge in 2015, "We've had so much opportunity in our lives, and we feel a deep responsibility to make the world a better place for future generations. We've benefited from good health, great education and support from committed families and communities."[40] Yet another example comes from Laura and John Arnold, who write:

> We are deeply indebted to our community and our country for the many opportunities granted to us, and for a social and economic environment in which we could make the most of those opportunities. We consider it our responsibility to ensure the same opportunities for others. We view our wealth in this light – not as an end in itself, but as an instrument to effect positive and transformative change.[41]

In their letters, signatories also frequently discuss the importance of managing wealth properly so that it will produce the greatest good. Indeed, in many of these narratives, billionaire donors present themselves not as the owners of inordinate wealth but as the "vessels," "stewards," or "channels" through which wealth will flow and be sagely redirected into society. For example, one signatory writes:

> With the unwavering support of my wonderful daughters, I now feel a tremendous and growing responsibility to be a good steward of my resources. I have always believed that those who have the abilities and opportunities to accumulate wealth should utilize their skills, in addition to their wealth, to solve the world's problems. My objective is to apply the skills and knowledge that I utilized throughout my business career in the philanthropic realm. I will focus on the key issues, do my homework, partner with those who are the best at what they do, and try to seek long term solutions rather than "short-term fixes."[42]

In a similar vein, in their Giving Pledge letter, Marcel Arsenault and his wife Cynda Collins Arsenault observe: "Most people believe that money has an innate power to solve problems. Money is only an accelerant, which in the right hands can supercharge high performance. In the wrong hands money can lead to destructive ends. We view our money as an obligation and a tool to accelerate a more peaceful world for humanity."[43]

The language in these letters bears some interesting resemblance to the language Andrew Carnegie used in his 1889 essay *The Gospel of Wealth*, which remains an inspirational text for many of today's philanthropists. Warren Buffett reportedly gifted Bill Gates a copy of the essay, and they both claim to be big admirers of the text.[44] In a masterful display of "symbolic inversion" (Lincoln 1989) that framed elite philanthropists as the true providers of wealth, rather than expropriators of it, Carnegie wrote that the "the man of Wealth" has a "duty" to become the "agent and trustee for his poorer brethren, bringing to their service his superior wisdom, experience and ability to administer, doing for them better than they would or could for themselves" (Carnegie 1889: 8). Indeed, Carnegie went as far as to argue that because the poor lacked wisdom, they would benefit more from money begotten through his properly administered, charitable donations than through an increase to their wages. While the letters above are less openly disparaging than what Carnegie penned, they do reflect a very similar sentiment. By taking the Giving Pledge, the wealthiest people in the world once again propose that they are the rightful people to run it.

Finally, the ideological force of the Giving Pledge also stems from its recurring emphasis on "giving while living" (Callahan 2017: 118). As Callahan observes, "the apostles of giving while living" maintain that they shouldn't wait until they are dead to begin their philanthropic endeavors: by giving "earlier" and in "smarter" ways, philanthropists can significantly multiply their impact. This may in fact be the case, but the emphasis on giving while living also works to promote the idea that the world's richest people are not really in the business of accumulating capital but rather that accumulation is merely the means or a "tool" that enables them to pursue moral obligations and ends. The Giving Pledge thus affords distinction to its members and legitimates capitalist enterprise by "encompassing" (Dumont 1970) all of the rational, calculative logics of capital accumulation within a moral framework.

Conclusion: the power of the gift

In the era of digital capitalism, wherein lies the power of the gift? How does techno-philanthropy provide a means by which the techno-elite are able to extend their influence, justify their inordinate wealth, and promote capitalism as the best of all possible economic orders? Throughout this chapter, I have sought to demonstrate that "the captains of the digital age" achieve their power not only through their purse strings and their abilities to control and allocate vast resources, but also through their persuasiveness. The work of techno-philanthropy is as much ideological as it is economic. In their various attempts to take on the world's greatest problems, techno-philanthropists present themselves as being deeply committed to social uplift even as their techno-solutionist ideology precludes deeper considerations of the social relations that contribute to these problems in the first place. In the hands, or rather mouths, of techno-philanthropists, the spirit of digital capitalism not only speaks the language of "personal emancipation," as Eran Fisher proposes (Fisher 2010: 11), but also the language of social salvation. Indeed, techno-philanthropists justify the accumulation of wealth into the hands of a few by promoting themselves as the best-equipped people to serve the needs and interests of "humanity." Techno-philanthropists are heralded as hyper-agents whose unencumbered power and influence are paving the road to progress. This progress, moreover, does not require radical or systemic change but instead "innovation" – a term that is much beloved in the universe of techno-philanthropy. Techno-philanthropists reassure us that the capitalist system is working just fine. In fact, they propose that by transposing the logics and methods used to accumulate capital into the world of philanthropy, the power of the gift can be amplified immensely. The rationalizing and dehumanizing "iron cage" that caused Max Weber so much consternation can be transformed into a benevolent and enchanted society of compassion: indeed, for many techno-philanthropists, humanism and techno-solutionism, rather than Protestantism, provides them with their calling.

In the world of techno-philanthropy, therefore, the spirit of the gift is *not* cast as antithetical to the workings of capitalism, as Marcel Mauss famously proposed when he used his study of "primitive" gift-based societies to consider more humane alternatives to capitalism. Rather, the gift provides an opportunity to reproduce a capitalist orientation to the world. Even if the pursuit of M–C–M' is disrupted for the purposes of charitable redistribution, the *habitus* of the capitalist lives on! Moreover, as we have seen, in the world of techno-philanthropy there is more than enough room for "the givers" to have their charitable cake *and* profit, too. By integrating impact investing and social enterprise into their giving initiatives, techno-philanthropists propose that the line between capitalism and philanthropy is indeed very thin, if not ultimately indiscernible.

And yet, because the world and work of techno-philanthropy are also about reproducing class privilege and distinction, there is also a mechanism for ensuring that some techno-philanthropists stand out from all the rest. The Giving Pledge perpetuates the idea that certain philanthropists are not just hyper-agents but *moral* agents. It suggests that the most powerful and prestigious gifts do ultimately represent an inversion of the logic of capitalism. While the world's wealthiest people might deploy capitalist *means* to increase the impact of their gifts, their activities are ultimately "encompassed" in an undeniably moral framework: purpose, not profit, ultimately rules the day. The signatories of the pledge do truly recognize their obligations and debts to society, and agree, as Carnegie put it, that "to die rich is a disgrace." Techno-philanthropists promise, with the ultimate sincerity and spirit of generosity, to gift away "the majority" of the billions they have accumulated during their brief but world-changing lives.[45] By all of these means, techno-philanthropy works to invert the incredibly insightful epigraph with which this chapter began. Instead of proposing "that philanthropy is a problem posing as a solution," which I contend it is, techno-philanthropists present it as the solution to the world's most pressing problems.

Conclusion: The Spirit and Contradictions of Digital Capitalism

I wrote this book because I believe we should live in a world where the economy is designed to serve the needs of human beings, rather than live in a world where humans beings are used as fodder for the continual accumulation of capital. I wrote this book because I worry that the era of digital capitalism is making this alternative world even more difficult to envision and actualize. In the preceding chapters, I have explored how digital technologies are making possible new forms of capital accumulation, domination, and extraction, while also giving rise to novel forms of ideological justification that work to promote capitalism as the "only" or even "best possible" economic system. In this concluding chapter, I want to offer some reflections on where this book has taken us and where we might be going in the future. More specifically, I want to use this chapter to address three issues. First, by synthesizing data and arguments from the previous chapters, I want to explain how the spirit of digital capitalism both resembles and differs from the "spirits" that have come before, especially focusing on what makes it different than the "new" or neoliberal spirit of capitalism that Boltanski and Chiapello analyzed over twenty years ago.

Second, I want to argue that one of the defining features of the spirit of digital capitalism is that it is Janus-faced and it reveals a new set of contradictions at the heart of American society. I will discuss what these contradictions are, and I will propose that, although they can be ideologically smoothed over, they cannot be resolved because they ultimately inhere from the logic of digital capitalism itself. An economic system that increasingly utilizes digital technologies to perpetuate the relentless pursuit of M–C–M', and that systemically produces wealth in the hands of the few, *can only come into contradiction* with the values of freedom, autonomy, democracy, equality, generosity, creativity, and social responsibility that it claims to promote. Indeed, this may be why the proponents of digital capitalism work so hard to convince us otherwise. Going forward, digital capitalism may not require an ideology to keep the wheels of profit spinning but, as we have seen throughout this book, at present one is being produced; the captains of the digital age are working very hard to promote the idea that digital capitalism is the only, if not best, economic system. By examining this ideology, as well as considering some of the ways it is being challenged, we stand to gain a deeper understanding of our current historical and cultural moment.

Lastly, this book draws upon case studies of crowdsourcing, smartphone gaming apps, the pitch for greater convenience, and the rising influence of techno-philanthropy to illuminate the cultural contradictions of digital capitalism. However, the contradictions that emerge from these data can be gleaned in many domains of social life, as well as in the research of others who are working to understand how digital capitalism is transforming society. Given their pervasiveness, therefore, I want to ask, what are the consequences of living with these contradictions? How might they be giving rise to not only new forms of society but new kinds of human beings? Will Americans accept these contradictions with relative ease and indifference, or will they increasingly critique and resist the changes that digital capitalism is ushering forth? If postmodernism represented "the cultural logic of late capitalism" (Harvey 1990; Jameson 1991), what might be said of the cultural logic of digital capitalism today? Has the postmodern emphasis on pastiche, playfulness, the transient, and the ephemeral given way to a more serious, if not suspicious, structure of feeling where we are haunted by the knowledge that much of what we do will never be deleted (Mayer-Schönberger 2009), that our "algorithm identities" (Cheney-Lippold 2017) will stalk us like shadow puppets, and that digital technologies are not just rendering our lives more "flexible" but also more scrutable and controllable? Might all of this give rise to a cultural ethos that is not so much playful as it is anxious and, at times, even paranoid (Chun 2008)?

The spirit of digital capitalism

As the preceding chapters have demonstrated, the spirit of digital capitalism reinscribes many of the features that Boltanski and

Chiapello associated with the new spirit of capitalism more than twenty years ago. The outsourcing of labor, the reliance on leaner and more flexible production models, the dismantling of corporate hierarchy, the loss of secure and stable career tracks, the heightened competition brought forth by the globalization of capital have all, one could argue, become even more intensified in the years since they issued their analysis. Moreover, many of the ideas Boltanski and Chiapello associated with the new spirit of capitalism continue to resonate today. Committed engagement in the process of accumulation is still fostered through the idea that one's work is an opportunity to exercise creativity, ingenuity, and vision, rather than subordinate one's self to the hierarchy and domination of the firm manager. Stability and the desire for a lifelong career are rejected in favor of participating in projects and "networks" that enable one to continually develop one's knowledge and skills and enhance one's "employability" rather than move up a preordained corporate ladder. And capitalist firms like Amazon continue to justify their existence in terms of serving the ever-shifting desires and demands of consumers.

And yet, while there are continuities between the new spirit of capitalism and the spirit of digital capitalism analyzed in this book, there are also important differences. These differences, moreover, largely inhere in the way the spirit of digital capitalism attempts "to assuage the anxiety provoked by the following three questions":

- How is committed engagement in the processes of accumulation a source of enthusiasm, even for those who will not necessarily be the main beneficiaries of the profits that are made?
- To what extent can those involved in the capitalist universe be assured of a minimum security for themselves and their children?
- How can participation in a capitalist firm be justified in terms of the common good, and how, confronted with accusations of injustice, can the way that it is conducted and managed be defended? (Boltanski and Chiapello 2007: 16)

As I will detail below, the spirit of digital capitalism provides new ways of answering these questions.

While the spirit of digital capitalism still assures people that work is an opportunity to exercise creativity, vision, and ingenuity, it also arouses enthusiasm by promising workers, or rather "makers," that their labor gains them access to a *community* of like-minded others. Indeed, when we consider the fact that digital capitalism has in large part been shaped by the countercultural turned cyberculture pioneers of Silicon Valley, this is perhaps not so surprising. As Fred Turner has documented, long before Stewart Brand went on to revolutionize the use of the personal computer, spread the seeds of digital utopianism, and become a founding member of the Global Business Network, he was publishing the Whole Earth Catalog and teaching people how to live communal existences off the grid (Turner 2006). While some may propose that the value placed on community is little more than shallow lip service, it does mark a departure from the celebration of "the network" as the only frame of sociality in the era of late capitalism. The language of community is not just about celebrating shared connections; it is about celebrating shared passions and interests. The spirit of digital capitalism proposes that networks, on their own, are not enough. Digital capitalism requires shared commitments.

The spirit of digital capitalism also engenders excitement for participation in processes of capital accumulation by returning to the nineteenth-century celebration of the entrepreneur as hero. As we have seen, in the era of digital capitalism, it is proposed that an entrepreneur can go from a zero to a hero overnight, as one crazy idea from the crowd can be turned into a million- or even billion-dollar innovation. Indeed, the rise of crowdsourcing as a mainstream business practice again suggests that in the digital age networks are no longer enough; in many instances, the path to progress and profit requires the willingness to go out of network and seize upon the wisdom of strangers.

Another feature that makes the spirit of digital capitalism different from early ones is that it also arouses enthusiasm for participating in processes of capital accumulation by casting capitalist enterprise as part of a larger mission of techno-salvation. As Boltanski and Chiapello note, technological progress has long been part of the spirit of capitalism. In the late nineteenth century, it was entwined with notions of a technologically enhanced future made better by the benefits of industry. In the mid-twentieth century, the promise of science and technology was viewed as key to expanding the size and productivity of the capitalist firm. In the late twentieth century, technology was being deployed to dismantle the giantism of the firm, streamline production, and boost profit margins through outsourcing and increased efficiency.

However, while technology has long been central to capitalist dreams of prosperity, for today's digital capitalists technology is not just a *means* of enhancing corporate profits, it is also an *end*. Today's digital capitalists speak a much "bolder" and more ambitious language of techno-solutionism. The heroes of digital capitalism stand strident in their belief of measurable progress and the idea that technology can save the day. Instead of staring anxiously at the heavens above, wondering if they will be "saved," as Weber's industrial capitalists did, and instead of trying to read financial tea leaves in their attempts to turn derivatives into profits, the titans of tech cast their gaze across the globe and operate with a supreme confidence that they *are* the ones *doing the saving*, or rather, *doing the solving*, of the world's biggest problems. In other words, in the digital age, the "curious transformation of salvational uncertainty into capitalist methodicality – the core of Weber's insight" (Appadurai 2016: 6) – has been replaced by a *techno-solutionist certainty* that fuels "bold" and aggressive capitalist expansion. If we now live in a world that is disproportionately controlled by a small but extremely powerful group of tech-savvy elites, this is not because of their divinatory prowess, nor even because of their technological prowess. Rather, it is because of their power and determination to remake the world in their techno-solutionist image. Indeed, this, it might be argued, is their true "calling."

Thus, when it comes to arousing enthusiasm for participation in processes of capital accumulation, the spirit of digital capitalism is very persuasive. However, it is less so when it comes to assuring people that they will be able to carve out an existence for themselves. Indeed, this may end up being one of the greatest vulnerabilities of this ideology. The spirit of digital capitalism makes no pretense to fight for workers' rights or secure a fairer balance between the interests of capital and the interests of labor, as was the case during Fordism, and in this regard it does little to "assure a minimum security" for participants and "their children" (Boltanski and Chiapello 2007: 16). However, the spirit of digital capitalism also doesn't speak in such bald-faced terms about the neoliberal importance of individual responsibility, going it alone, or "pulling oneself up by one's bootstraps." In contrast to Margaret Thatcher's infamous phrase, society *does* exist in the spirit of digital capitalism, but it is a society of a peculiar kind – one that replaces a commitment to class struggle, with a commitment to planetary consciousness. It seeks to assure the existence of the "world," rather than dwell on ensuring the existence of its workers, who are increasingly offered recognition or "decimal dust" prizes, rather than life-sustaining forms of compensation for their labor.

The spirit of digital capitalism has also found new ways of portraying capital accumulation, and even the extreme inequality that digital capitalism engenders, in terms of the common good. While it continues to reproduce the neoliberal idea that a free-market system is crucial to the maintenance of a "free society," the spirit of digital capitalism also recuperates a justification from the late nineteenth century. Charity, as we have seen, and as I will discuss further below, is back with a vengeance. By becoming "another growth industry" in Silicon Valley, it provides the techno-elite with a pivotal means to justify their inordinate wealth. Moreover, the spirit of digital capitalism further presents itself as contributing to the common good by actively blurring the lines between commerce and care. As we saw in chapter 5, impact investing is framed as a philan-thropic activity. The pursuit of profit and the love of humankind are presented as complementary rather that contradictory ends.

And yet, despite its attempts to assuage the anxiety aroused by the three questions stated above, the spirit of digital capitalism also brings together its own "amalgam of very different, even incom-patible propensities and values" (Boltanski and Chiapello 2007: 17) and it announces itself in a language that can only be described as doublespeak. When we listen to this doublespeak, what we discover is a new set cultural contradictions at the heart of American society. It is to these contradictions that I now turn.

Competition and collaboration

The doublespeak of digital capitalism can be readily gleaned in the way that crowdsourcing is promoted as a solution to contem-porary business challenges. As we saw in chapters 1 and 2, in one breath business experts and entrepreneurs tell us that crowdsourcing achieves its efficacy by tapping into human beings' innate spirit of competition. In the next breath, they argue that it works by harnessing our social instincts for collaboration and cooperation. The suggestion that human nature is divided between these two opposing propensities is not, in itself, a contradiction. Nor is the suggestion that capitalism requires both propensities to keep the wheels of profit turning, as Richard Sennett has proposed (Sennett 2012). Rather, the key contradiction emerges from the disparity between what crowdsourcing promises and what it often delivers. Whether it takes the competitive or collaborative form, proponents of crowd-sourcing happily report that crowdsourcing levels the playing field, "democratizes innovation," and even safeguards free-market compe-tition. However, as we have seen in earlier chapters, crowdsourcing also reproduces social and economic hierarchies, contributes to the precarity of labor, takes advantage of and exacerbates structural inequalities, and assists corporations in their efforts to enhance their profits and monopoly power.[1]

Whether promoted by Peter Diamandis, Peter Thiel, or a vast array of others, incentive competitions provide a key means through which various forms of social and intellectual capital are captured and corralled into the hands of a networked few. At the same time that they claim to "democratize innovation," and thumb their noses at formal credentials, incentive competitions arouse enthusiasm by promising "solvers" an opportunity to join the ranks of an elite group of intellectual giants whose "smartness" marks them as "natural" leaders. Incentive competitions present innovation as a race that reproduces hierarchy in an even more damning form as it divides the population into unequivocal camps of winners and losers. Moreover, as Peter Diamandis and Karim Lakhani frequently proclaim, "the great thing" about incentive competitions is that you "pay only the winner," even while benefiting from the unremunerated labor of thousands of solvers who produce enough value to revolutionize an industry! Indeed, by replacing the dispensation of wages with the dispensation of a singular prize, incentive competitions naturalize, normalize, and even celebrate negative reciprocity as a key means of enhancing corporate efficiency and increasing profit margins by cutting labor costs. In this regard, Jathan Sadowski is correct in arguing that the era of digital capitalism does not represent an epochal shift. Rather, "the operations of capital," as he writes, "are adapting to the digital age, while also still maintaining the essential features of exclusion, extraction and exploitation" (Sadowski 2020: 50).

And yet, if all of this seems to fly in the face of promoting collaboration and looking out for one's "fellow man," promoters of incentive competitions attempt to smooth over this contradiction by presenting incentive competitions as part of a larger mission of social, if not species, salvation. Diamandis's XPRIZE calls on the "smartest and most passionate innovators" to "do good in the world" and take on the world's most pressing problems. By harnessing this "cognitive surplus," Diamandis proposes that incentive competitions can play a crucial role in accelerating progress. Moreover, in another classic example of doublespeak, proponents of incentive competitions celebrate the way it enables competition sponsors to outsource risk and expenses onto "solvers," but they also propose that online crowdsourcing platforms like HeroX are playing a pivotal role in addressing inequality by shifting the balance of power between employers and employees. As service representative, Kyla Jeffrey remarked:

> Part of our mission at HeroX is creating job liquidity, moving to an optimum we've already created with the Internet and the knowledge economy. We want to help make that global market. Once employers have to compete for talent rather than talent competing for jobs, we'll start to see balance in income disparity, which is a current existential threat to economies and politics.[2]

This, and many other examples discussed throughout this book, suggest that today, the spirit of digital capitalism does not simply legitimate "a new trade-off between social emancipation and personal emancipation" (Fisher 2010). In addition to responding to the humanist critique of capitalism, the spirit of digital capitalism also responds to the social critique. However, instead of posting a working alliance between capitalism and the state to respond to the social needs and problems of the world, as was the case during Fordism, in the era of digital capitalism these problems are purportedly remedied through market mechanisms like the one proposed above and, as will be discussed below, through the work of techno-philanthropy.

If proponents of incentive competitions smooth over contradictions by proposing that they can help bring about world-changing innovations and enable competition solvers to become heroes to humanity, proponents of collaborative crowdsourcing initiatives promise their participants the reward of unalienated labor and recognition from a community of like-minded peers. As we saw in chapter 2, the secret of community crowdsourcing initiatives very much lies in their ability to "harness" the desires for self-realization, personal expression, and meaningful connections to others in a mode of capital accumulation. It appropriates not just the cognitive surplus of crowdsourcing participants but the affective surplus that fuels the "passion economy" (Davidson 2020). Instead of explicitly celebrating negative reciprocity, and the financial perks that come with "paying only the winners," proponents of collaborative crowdsourcing "work to justify and normalize flexible and precarious work through an ambiguous association between capitalist exchange and altruistic social values" (Cockayne 2016: 73).

As we saw in chapter 2, corporations like GE are able to mask practices of extraction and exploitation and re-present them as benevolent forms of "investment" in an "innovation community" and a "sharing economy." By referring to their members as "makers" not workers, GE is able to defend deploying (again *not employing*) hundreds of designers and engineers to labor in their "microfactory" for free. The microfactory is presented as an enriching and collaborative "maker space," or "playground for adults," rather than a siphon which works to capture and expropriate various forms of social, intellectual, and emotional capital for the purposes of furthering corporate interests. Indeed, as I have argued throughout this book, it is precisely through such semantic sleights of hand that the pioneers of digital capitalism attempt to convince us that our current economic order is not just "the only possible order" but the "best of all possible orders." Moreover, it is precisely through such means that corporations like GE are able to appropriate "the wealth of networks" for their own ends (Benkler 2006). During the era of digital capitalism, we are not only witnessing the triumph of social networks and peer-to-peer production, as Yochai Benkler observes, but also the steadfast ability of corporate entities to co-opt social production for the purposes of capital accumulation. "Digital technology," as Robert McChesney reminds us, does not have "superpowers over political economy": "The democratization of the Internet is integrally related to the democratization of the political economy. They rise and fall together" (McChesney 2013: 15, 22).

Creativity and automation, liberation and surveillance

The spirit of digital capitalism arouses enthusiasm for engagement in processes of capital accumulation by promising us that in our lives as producers digital technologies, and the new forms of networking they facilitate, will liberate us from the shackles of stultifying "bullshit jobs" (Graeber 2018) and help us unleash our creativity. This promise is thoroughly contradicted by the experiences of workers who labor all day on platforms like MTurk to try and eke out enough income doing piecemeal tasks to support themselves (Gray and Suri 2019). But it is also contradicted when we consider the various ways surveillance capitalists attempt to track and influence our behavior for the purposes of pursuing commercial ends. In the realm of production, creativity is preached and promised but, in the sphere of consumption, automation and "rendering downtime productive" have become the end. The captains of the digital age do not want us to use our "free time" for imaginative play, or anything else that might interfere with their ceaseless pursuit of data extraction and profiteering. As we saw in the discussion of smartphone gaming apps, they want to further extend their digital tentacles into the nooks and crannies of our daily lives, so we are always working at the behest of capital. *And work it is.* What is taken from us by smartphone gaming apps "on our ride home from work," or "standing in line waiting for a latte," or "in between TV commercial breaks" may be described by the titans of tech as a form of play or, as Benkler puts it, "excess capacity," but in reality it is an expropriation of surplus labor. Moments, as Marx observed long ago, are still the elements of profit, and digital capitalists have become increasingly savvy at using technology to get labor power for free.

Moreover, as many of these chapters have illustrated, one of the key commodities that labor produces in the era of digital capitalism is data. As we saw in chapter 4, and as Shoshana Zuboff persuasively argues, the technologies and infrastructures of "Big Other" are animated by "the prediction imperative" and their ultimate goal is to automate us (Zuboff 2019). Technologies are increasingly deployed to collect data that can be sold for profit or used to further understand our behaviors, but they are also used to "herd" and "nudge" us into forms of behavior that "reliably" and "definitively" lead to "desired commercial results" (ibid.: 201). Thus, in the era of digital capitalism, the extraction of data, as Zuboff and others have argued, has become central to processes of capital accumulation. As we saw in chapter 4, Amazon Go is but one of the latest examples where we see this on display.

And yet, while Zuboff is correct in noting that surveillance capitalists increasingly use technologies to nudge and herd consumers to achieve commercial ends, I have also sought to demonstrate that corporate executives, from Jeff Bezos on down, still spend quite a lot of time and energy trying to persuade customers that all of this is being done in their best interests. According to people like Gianna Puerini and Dillip Kumar, the surveillance technologies deployed in Amazon Go stores are not about automating customers, but rather gifting them with the ultimate convenient, hassle-free shopping experience. Indeed, I have proposed that, in the era of digital capitalism, convenience itself has emerged as an ideology that is used to discursively justify a new set of extractive technologies and practices that serve the interests of capital. One might go as far as to suggest that the contradictions between creativity and automation, and liberation and surveillance, are ideologically reconciled through promises of providing customers more convenient lifestyles.

Techno-solutionism and social salvation

The Amazon Go case study also illustrates how the ideology of "solutionism" has come to permeate problem solving, or perhaps more aptly, problem making in the era of digital capitalism. As Evgeny Morozov astutely observes:

> solutionism presumes rather than investigates the problems that it is trying to solve, reaching "for the answer before the questions have been fully asked" . . . Solutionism, thus, is not just a fancy way of saying that for someone with a hammer, everything looks like a nail . . . It's also that what many solutionists presume to be "problems" in need of solving are not problems at all; a deeper investigation into the very nature of these "problems" would reveal that the inefficiency, ambiguity, and opacity – whether in politics or everyday life – that the newly empowered geeks and solutionists are rallying for are not in any sense problematic. Quite the opposite: these vices are often virtues in disguise. (Morozov 2014: 6)

Moreover, it is not just that these problems are "not problems at all" as Morozov suggests, but that they are also promoted in the service of pursuing other ends. The very problems and solutions that Amazon Go is bent on solving also provide an alibi for the technogentsia to become ever more implicated in the machinations of surveillance capitalism and expand their technological control over society. As Dillip Kumar intimated, the problems he has to solve for Amazon Go are part and parcel of a larger attempt to unlock "the holy grail of computer vision." Amazon Go customers thus become fodder for advancing the technological frontier. Moreover, the very desire to create a no-checkout shopping experience bespeaks yet another contradiction in contemporary society. For in one breath we are told that the promise of digital technologies lies in their ability to render human beings more socially connected, and in the next breath we find that if and when human sociality is perceived as enhancing "friction" and slowing down the process of capital accumulation, it is discouraged.

Indeed, as I suggested above, part of what makes the spirit of digital capitalism different from earlier "spirits" is precisely the way it simultaneously mobilizes and yet evades commitments to the social. On the one hand, as we saw in chapter 5, the captains of the digital age present themselves as being profoundly committed to social uplift. Through their various philanthropic world-saving initiatives, and through their attempts to cast their market endeavors as being oriented to the production of public not just private good, they pronounce a commitment to the social that is far more robust than what the earlier apologists of neoliberalism ever expressed. As Linsey McGoey puts it, "Today's philanthrocapitalists are remarkably fond of the word 'social.' They affix the word to an ecumenical bounty of commercial endeavors, implying that this renders their actions more socially progressive" (McGoey 2016: 21).

At the same time, however, the techno-solutionist ideology that animates so much of techno-philanthropic discourse also works to de-socialize the very world it purportedly aims to save. As I discussed in chapter 5, if the poor in the Third World can be saved with mosquito nets, toilets, and even sanitary pads, then there is little need to consider how the machinations of digital capitalism might contribute to their poverty and suffering in the first place. As Žižek observes, today's techno-philanthropists, or as he calls them "liberal communists," "hate a doctrinaire approach. There is no exploited working class today, only concrete problems to be solved" (Žižek 2006: 2). Ameliorating class struggle is thus displaced by projects aimed at pushing the technological frontier and securing planetary and species survival.

Charity and avarice

The spirit of digital capitalism also proposes that the people best suited to solve such problems, and to save the world from the myriad challenges it currently confronts, are the rich. As was the case in the era of the robber barons, in the age of digital capitalism, charity is back, as well as avarice. Cast as "hyper-agents" whose inordinate wealth enables them to "do some essentials things far better than anyone else" (Bishop and Green 2009: 12), techno-philanthropists use their gifts to legitimate and justify unprecedented levels of capital accumulation into the hands of the few. Despite what its proponents might say, the work of techno-philanthropy is not just about changing the world. Rather, techno-philanthropy has emerged as one of the central vehicles through which the logics of capitalism are valorized and reinscribed. As we saw in chapter 5, through their embrace of "venture philanthropy," "impact investing," and "social entrepreneurship," techno-philanthropists blur the boundaries between commerce and care and cast their philanthropic gifts, not as the antithesis to the logic of capital accumulation, but as an extension of it. By transmuting giving into a form of investing, techno-philanthropists are able to spread an essential element of the spirit of capitalism, even as some of the initiatives they promote defy the economic imperatives of M–C–M'. By moving concepts and language from the world of business to the world of nonprofit organizations, techno-philanthropy thus achieves an ideological coup as it once again presents and promotes capitalism as the best of all economic systems, and as it portrays techno-philanthropy as a *solution to* rather than *symptom of* radical inequality. As we have seen, proponents of techno-philanthropy, or as Bishop and Green refer to it, "philanthrocapitalism," cast radical inequality as a force for the common good. Whether this occurs through celebrations of billionaire "hyper-agents" or through hopeful projections about "the rising billions" of destitute masses whose consumer potential has yet to be tapped (Prahalad 2004), the message is the same: don't mess with the economic pyramid. Inequality is not a problem. It is an opportunity.

At the risk of sounding cynical, I want to suggest that perhaps one of the reasons this idea is so palatable among techno-philanthropists is because techno-philanthropists also *require* radical inequality to prove themselves as not only "hyper-agents" but as *moral* agents. The work of techno-philanthropy, I have argued, is also about reproducing class privilege, power, and distinction. Organizations like the Silicon Valley Social Venture Fund are geared towards producing "the next generation of givers," not the next generation of equal opportunity for all. Institutions such as the Giving Pledge, which is reserved for billionaires only, attempt to convince us that "the word" of the super-rich is indeed gold; they are to be trusted, rather than required by tax policies or other mechanisms for redistributing wealth, to fulfill their obligations to society.

The consequences of the cultural contradictions of digital capitalism

While this book may be unique in using a series of case studies drawn from the business world to bring the cultural contradictions of digital capitalism to light, I am certainly not the first person to emphasize that we live in a moment of profound contradiction. Indeed, this may be one of the most salient features of the "cultural logic" of digital capitalism, and it can be gleaned from a wide body of research. Mark Andrejevic, for instance, writes of the tension between participation and interactivity in the digital age. He notes that whereas internet technologies are frequently celebrated for enhancing consumer participation in a wide range of communicative contexts, they are simultaneously designed to gather as much data about consumers as possible, which in turn is used to better control them. In an essay entitled "The Pacification of Interactivity," he explores how interaction on the internet is structure by "coded protocols" that significantly constrain the information that internet users provide, and that render their "participation" more a form of programmed feedback than active collaboration. He observes, "The recurring ideological move of the interactive economy is to bulldoze this distinction, equating the provision of feedback with participation" (Andrejevic 2016: 188–9).

In a different vein, Nicholas John explores how "the metaphor of sharing" has been mobilized to construct a wide range of social practices that simultaneously can be co-opted to further capital accumulation, as well as used to resist it (John 2017). In their timely and important book, *The Costs of Connection*, Nick Couldry and Ulises Mejias provide a piercing critique of the way digital technologies are mobilized to not only facilitate new forms of convenience, but also to colonize our lives. The cost of connection and convenience, in their assessment, is the loss of privacy and freedom. Viktor Mayer-Schönberger points to another contradiction of the digital age. He argues that although digital technologies are frequently cast as an empowering tool of human communication, they also hinder our abilities to make choices unencumbered by the past. Instead of offering us freedom, the internet chains us to a past that may never be deleted. He argues that we must reclaim "the virtue of forgetting" (Mayer-Schönberger 2009). Psychiatrist Mark Rego proposes that the continuous surround of digital technologies designed to improve our lives is also exacerbating mental illness and generating a new condition of "frontal fatigue" (Rego 2021).

Nor is it only academics who are discussing these contradictions and calling attention to their potentially harmful consequences. For instance, Joe Toscano, a former design consultant for Google, quit his job after becoming disillusioned with the false promises of the tech industry and how it claims to be ushering in a new world of freedom. In an exposé book entitled *Automating Humanity,* he writes: "*Automating Humanity* is an insider's perspective on everything Big Tech doesn't want you thinking about – from how addictions have been installed at a global scale, to how profits are driven by fake news and disinformation, to how and why artificial intelligence will take jobs at an unimaginable pace. Welcome to the future. You're late!" (Toscano 2018: i).

Similarly, ex-Facebook vice president of user growth, Chamath Palihapitiya has also openly discussed the way Facebook seeks to stimulate user activity by creating technologies that activate dopamine feedback loops, thereby rendering social media technologies more addictive.[3] While Facebook claims it is in the business of connecting and empowering people around the world, he suggests that it is equally in the business of controlling them and rendering them more dependent on their technologies.

What then are the consequences of living with these contradictions? How do we navigate a world that presents us with a constant stream of doublespeak, in one breath, making us so many promises and in the next, suggesting that serious problems stir below the surface? How do we find our way out of the contradictions that animate life in the age of digital capitalism? Is it even possible? Will people quietly accept these contradictions as part of the new normal and modify their social and inner lives accordingly? Or, will the cultural contradictions of digital capitalism be critiqued and resisted as their weight becomes too heavy to bear?

The methodological approach I have taken in this book makes it very difficult for me to answer these questions. Much more research, preferably of an intensive, immersive, ethnographic kind, needs to be done to understand how the era of digital capitalism is being lived, experienced, and hopefully even resisted by subjects who are differentially positioned within its ambit. The case studies presented in this book, however, do suggest a number of ethnographic entry points that might help scholars further explore these issues in the future. For instance, if I had a cadre of anthropology students that I could dispatch to carry out research on capitalism in the digital age, I would encourage them to immerse themselves in Silicon Valley's venture philanthropy "community" to gain a better understanding of the ways the techno-elite use philanthropy to translate privilege into power. I would send them to take classes at the Harvard Business School's Digital Initiative and MIT's Media Lab, where many of the movers, shakers, and proponents of digital capitalism lecture about the "transformative" possibilities that digital technologies hold for the future of business. I would urge them to find ways of scaling the incredibly expensive and exclusive walls of Singularity University (a feat I unsuccessfully attempted) as it is playing a pivotal role in translating technological innovation into capitalist enterprise and vice versa. But, most of all, I would encourage them to pay close and careful ethnographic attention to the ways people are relating to new forms of digital technology in their everyday lives. How are these technologies changing the warp and woof of being human in the twenty-first century? How is digital capitalism fundamentally altering conceptions of time, space, labor, leisure, and identity? How is it generating not just a greater sense of convenience, but also frustration and "rage" as more and more of our lives are subsumed by "roboprocesses" (Gusterson 2019)? All of this, I suspect, might help us better diagnose and understand the cultural logic of digital capitalism, and in so doing it might help us better discern the prevailing "condition" of our time (Harvey 1990). My hope, therefore, is that this book might provide a departure point for such research in the future. However, even though I am limited by the methodological approach I have taken in this book, I do want to conclude this chapter by offering a few reflections of my own, for the cultural contradictions of digital capitalism make life challenging. I see my students, my sons, and even myself caught in their grasp and I wonder and worry what the future will hold for us.

One of the consequences, I propose, is that the cultural contradictions of digital capitalism are generating a profound sense of anxiety. As a college student coming of age in the 1990s, anxiety was not a term or experience that I often heard my peers discuss. My fellow students would complain about being exhausted, disillusioned, bored, angry, or even depressed, but anxiety didn't seem to be on their radar. By contrast, if there is a singular term and a feeling that seems to perpetually plague the students I teach today, it is anxiety. My students openly share their panic attacks, they exchange and compare their senses of worry and the chronic dis-ease that keeps them up at night. They give each other tips on which medications are most effective at "taking the edge off." They recognize and claim anxiety as one of the defining experiential realities of their generation. As one student playfully remarked when I asked my class what the future might hold for them after graduation, "Who the hell knows! I mean c'mon, is there anyone in this room who isn't taking anxiety medication right now?"

The uncertainty created by our flexible economy is, as Richard Sennett observes, creating a personal crisis for many who find themselves trying to make it in "the culture of the new capitalism." We continue to struggle with how to sustain a self and carve out a life in a world that chooses as its "ideal . . . an unusual sort of human being" (Sennett 2006: 5). As Sennett proposes, "the culture of the new capitalism," searches for a person who is oriented towards "the short term," who emphasizes future potential over previous accomplishments, and who is willing to abandon past experiences in order to maintain a competitive foothold in the present. All of this, he argues, promotes a "cultural ideal" that "damages many of the people" who are subjected to it (Sennett 2006: 5).

Though more than a decade has passed since Sennett issued his diagnosis, I believe it is still apt, if not even more compelling, today. Yet I want to propose that at the subjective level the cultural contradictions of digital capitalism also create a bewildering state of cognitive dissonance. It is not just that we have difficulty forging a coherent narrative for our lives or securing durable connections to others. The challenge also stems from the fact that in the era of digital capitalism we are constantly bombarded with conflicting messages and doublespeak, as the chapters in this book have tried to make clear. We are barraged with claims about the promise of the future as well as the peril it may hold. We are told that technology can set us free; at the same time we surrender our privacy and data to our smartphones and Alexas. We are encouraged to unleash our creativity and even gift it to others, yet we also suspect that, with each ping of our cell phones or advertisement on our Facebook pages, people with far more power than ourselves are attempting to control us so that they can ultimately profit from our behaviors. We are invited to continually reinvent ourselves so we can survive in the flexible economy, and yet in our social lives we are chained to a communicative infrastructure that tracks our digital footsteps and refuses to forget, thereby imbuing us with the fear that the past may indeed come back to haunt us at any time. This double bind, for lack of a better term, does something to a psyche. It inspires hope and dread, it produces a subject or "character" who is not so much "corroded," as Sennett proposes (Sennett 2011). Nor even alienated or anomic as Marx or Durkheim proposed in their critiques of capitalism. It produces, I believe, a subject who embraces "apathy as a cultural affect to defend the self" against the anxiety and contradictions of everyday living.[4] As my students all too frequently exclaim in a spirit of resignation, "Why bother? We're fucked!"

The consequences of the cultural contradictions of digital capitalism also play out in the realm of values and beliefs. Indeed, in American society they seem to be prompting a revision or at least reconsideration of what our most cherished values are. Do we value freedom and privacy more than convenience and connection? Do we value democracy and equal representation more than the unencumbered efficiency of "hyper-agents" who appear to be more effective at solving social problems than the government officials we elect to service in public office? Do we feel that their wealth should come with legal strings attached to ensure that it is redistributed throughout society, or do we put our faith in the good word of the billionaire elite who "pledge" to take care of us? Do we celebrate their inordinate wealth as a sign of the fruits and flourishing of our capitalist economy, or do we pause and ask on whose backs were their fortunes made, and in what universe should they command so much more power and resources than the rest of us?

All of these questions are inspired by an economic order that is systematically designed to put wealth and power in the hands of the few. For when maximizing profit is the ultimate rationale and measure of an economy, all the other values that we pay lip service to are bound to become subordinated to this end. The technologies too. The enthusiasts of the digital age are correct in proposing that we now have the technological capacity to unleash an unprecedented wave of human potential; digital technologies and communications *can* be used to create novel social formations that do truly rest upon relations of cooperation, reciprocity, sharing, and community. We are indeed at a moment when technologies can help set us free, as Marx himself proposed over a century and half ago. This is not just fanciful thinking. However, as we have seen throughout this book, the logics and interests of capital accumulation continually disrupt and thwart the emancipatory potential of "the wealth of networks." Thus, at the most fundamental level, the problem, as the saying goes, "is the economy, stupid."

Which brings me full circle to where this book began. In *The New Spirit of Capitalism*, Boltanski and Chiapello concede that capitalism is an economic system that benefits comparatively few and injures and dehumanizes many. As they write:

> In many respects, capitalism is an absurd system: in it, wage-earners have lost ownership of the fruits of their labor and the possibility of pursuing a working life free of subordination. As for capitalists, they find themselves yoked to an interminable, insatiable process, which is utterly abstract and dissociated from the satisfaction of consumption needs, even of a luxury kind. For two such protagonists, integration into the capitalist order is singularly lacking in justifications. (Boltanski and Chiapello 2007: 7)[5]

They further propose that if "capitalism has not only survived, but ceaselessly extended its empire, it is because it could rely upon a number of shared representations . . . and justifications, which present it as an acceptable and even desirable order of things: the only possible order, or the best of all possible orders" (ibid.: 10). Thus, although the problem is the economy, the solution to fixing the problem also involves interrogating and critiquing the ideologies that work to present capitalism as "the only possible" or even "best of all possible orders." It has been with this goal in mind that I have explored how the spirit of digital capitalism works to naturalize, normalize, and even valorize an economic system devoted to the perpetual pursuit of M–C–M'. For as long as this is the only economic system we can imagine, and as long as this remains the economic "bottom line," the potentials we develop, whether they be technological or social, will be limited in their capacities to make "the world," as the techno-philanthropists like to refer to it, a better place.

Glimmers of hope

Digital capitalism may seek to "control our lives" and "take over the world," as Jathan Sadowski aptly puts it, but it hasn't totally succeeded yet. There are glimmers of hope on many fronts that point to attempts to critique and resist the imperatives of this social and economic system. Although the doublespeak of digital capitalism looms large, a growing number of voices are talking back and exposing and challenging its claims. For instance, the idea that our data can and should be expropriated by corporate interests is now at least up for debate as an increasing number of critics propose that data mining is akin to a form of theft, rather than merely the "price we pay" for free internet services. The monopoly power of giant tech is finally stirring enough interest and concern for government officials to take notice. The effort to develop platform cooperatives, rather than platforms run by giant corporations, is well underway (Scholz and Schneider 2017). The appeals to embrace a "tactics for a dumber world" (Sadowski 2020) and challenge the intrusion of smart tech into our lives and cities is being taken up by protesters around the world who fear that these surveillance technologies will spell the demise of privacy and freedom.[6] Companies like Facebook are facing fines for violating users' privacy and they are increasingly lambasted for skewing democratic elections (Madrigal 2017; Snider and Baig 2019). Groups such as the Make Amazon Pay coalition are actively protesting the forms of technological surveillance and anti-union labor policies of "the most convenient company on earth" (Hyken 2018).[7]

On other fronts, the fight to establish healthcare as a basic human right rather than something that is purchased through the market or gifted to us by billionaire philanthropists has at least become a talking point in American politics. The waves of "hacktivism" that are challenging information politics in the digital age are becoming more common (Jordan 2015). The growing tide of young people who do not want to exist on the hamster wheel of capitalism – who are "lying flat," opting for tiny houses, and deciding that they might live more quality lives with less – all offer hope that people are still capable of imagining different kinds of lives and worlds that are not subordinated to the continuous pursuit of profit.[8] As it stands now, the spirit of digital capitalism has not achieved complete hegemony over our lives. Thus, while I wrote this book out of a sense of frustration, anger, and despair, there is also a small part of me that is hopeful. Perhaps the future is not as dark as it seems right now. Perhaps if we keep reminding each other that there are alternatives, things could be different. As science fiction writer Ursula Le Guin remarked in a 2014 literary award acceptance speech, "We live in capitalism. Its power seems inescapable. So did the divine right of kings. Any human power can be resisted and changed by human beings."[9] Hopefully, digital capitalism will not prove to be more impervious to change than monarchical rule.

Notes

Introduction: The Digital Age and the Spirits of Capitalism

1 As economist and sociologist Juliet Schor notes in her book, *After the Gig: How the Sharing Economy Got Hijacked and How to Win It Back*:

> In 2017 the three richest Americans (Warren Buffett, Jeff Bezos and Bill Gates) had more wealth than the bottom half of the population. The top four hundred from *Forbes*'s list of the richest Americans have nearly as much as two-thirds of the population. In addition, the share of the top 1 percent has grown substantially, and their assets now exceed those of the entire bottom 95 percent. Income has followed a similar trend. Between 1993 and 2017 the top 1 percent of households roughly doubled their incomes, taking home more than half of all the gains in income, compared to a mere 15.5 percentage increase for the bottom 99 percent. (Schor 2020: 95)

2 Following Marx, Heilbroner, Wallerstein, and Boltanski and Chiapello, I take this to be the defining logic of a capitalist economy and society.

3 For a fascinating discussion of the evolution of the term "business guru," see Orta 2019: 84.

4 Thus, while Dan Schiller coined the term "digital capitalism" in 1999, in this book I follow the lead of Jathan Sadowski who writes, "I call it *digital capitalism* merely to mean capitalism with digital technologies" (Sadowski 2020: 49).

5 Of course, as Christian Fuchs observes, digital capitalism is "not the only dimension of capitalism" today. Finance capitalism, hyper-capitalism, neoliberal capitalism, global capitalism also shape forms and processes of capital accumulation (Fuchs 2019: 30).

6 See also Roderick 2014.

7 This argument has largely been promoted by scholars working to develop a political economy of the media. For various takes on this position, see Smythe 1981; Terranova 2004, 2013; Andrejevic 2009,

2013; Hesmondhalgh 2010; Ross 2013; Scholz 2013; Fisher 2017; Wittel 2017.

8 As Christian Fuchs observes, "digitisation can turn knowledge into a gift that is distributed online. But in a capitalist society, people depend on wages for survival so that the online gift economy under capitalist class relations does not bring about a democratic communism, but rather . . . [i]t enforces the precarisation of digital and cultural labor in capitalism" (Fuchs 2019: 27).

9 A notable exception can be found in Jathan Sadowski's work. In his analysis of the techno-politics that animate digital capitalism, he points out that "the most insidious product of Silicon Valley is not a technology but an ideology . . . At the core of the technocratic ideology is a deeply held "solutionism": the belief that all the world's problems, even those that should not be thought of as problems in the first place, can be solved technologically" (Sadowski 2020: 66–7). Another exception includes van Dijck's attempt to "deconstruct the ideological grounds of datafication" (van Dijck 2014: 198).

10 Ever since Marx, the ideological underpinnings or, rather, "superstructures" of capitalism have attracted considerable scholarly attention, and a plentiful literature exists detailing how capitalist ideologies have mutated over time; see, for example, Laclau 1977; Hirschman 1997 (1977); Althusser 1994; Balibar 1994; Jameson 1991; Žižek 1994; Fisher 2009. However, in this study I follow the methodological lead of Boltanski and Chiapello in attempting to trace the ideologies that have developed in the era of digital capitalism, and I use their study as a basis for comparing and contrasting the ideologies of digital capitalism with those that accompanied early periods in the twentieth century.

11 They write:

> The spirit of capitalism is precisely the set of beliefs associated with the capitalist order that helps to justify this order and, by legitimating them, to sustain the forms of action and predispositions compatible with it. These justifications, whether general or practical, local or global, expressed in terms of virtue or justice, support the performance of more or less unpleasant tasks and, more generally, adhesion to a lifestyle conducive to the capitalist order. (Boltanski and Chiapello 2007: 10)

12 As they describe it:

> bourgeois morality affords elements of security in an original combination, combining novel economic propensities (avarice or parsimony, the spirit of saving, a tendency to rationalize daily life in all its aspects, development of capacities for book-keeping, calculation, prediction) with traditional domestic predispositions: the importance attached to the family, lineage, inheritance, the chastity of daughters in order to avoid misalliances and the squandering of capital; the familial or patriarchal nature of relations with employees – what will subsequently be denounced as paternalism – whose forms of

subordination remained largely personal in firms that were generally small in size; the role accorded charity in relieving the suffering of the poor. (Boltanski and Chiapello 2007: 17)

13 As Boltanski and Chiapello observe:

> To the themes of utility, general well-being and progress, which have been available for mobilization in virtually unchanged fashion for over two centuries, and to the justification in terms of incomparable efficiency when it comes to supplying goods and services, we must obviously add the reference to the emancipatory power of capitalism and political freedom as collateral of economic freedom. (Boltanski and Chiapello 2007: 13)

14 For instance, in 2019 it was estimated that the internet sector contributed US$2.1 trillion to the US economy, or approximately 10% of the US GDP. See: https://www.reuters.com/article/us-usa-internet-economy/internet-sector-contributes-2-1-trillion-to-u-s-economy-industry-group-idUSKBN1WB2QB

15 Business analysts Andrew McAfee and Erik Brynjolfsson refer to this as "phase two" of "the second machine age." They propose that phase one of the second machine age began in the middle of the 1990s and "describes a time when digital technologies demonstrably had an impact on the business world by taking over large amounts of routine work." "Phase two," which they propose we are in now, emerged in the beginning of the second decade of the twenty-first century and marks a time "when technologies are demonstrating that they can do work that we've never thought of as preprogrammed or routine" (McAfee and Brynjolfsson 2017: 16–17). Business professor and economist Arun Sundararajan also argues that the pervasive use of digital technologies began to radically transform economic activity in the second decade of the twenty-first century. He argues that what he calls "crowd-based capitalism" or "the sharing economy" emerged at scale around 2010. See Sundararajan 2016.

16 They write:

> management literature cannot be exclusively oriented towards the pursuit of profit. It must also justify the way profit is obtained . . . Management literature must therefore demonstrate how the prescribed way of making profit might be desirable, interesting, exciting, innovative or commendable. It cannot stop at economic motives and incentives. It must also be based on normative aims, taking into account not only personal aspirations to security and autonomy, but also the way these aspirations can be attached to a more general orientation to the common good. (Boltanski and Chiapello 2007: 58)

This is also a method followed by Gabriel Abend, in his book, *The Moral Background: An Inquiry into the History of Business Ethics* (Abend 2014).

17 https://en.wikipedia.org/wiki/Impact_investing

18 In his book, *Digital Disconnect: How Capitalism is Turning the Internet Against Democracy*, Robert McChesney provides a persuasive analysis of just this phenomenon. He observers that the scholarly literature on the internet can be broken down into two camps: the celebrants, who extol its revolutionary and democratic potentials, and the skeptics, who emphasize the various ways the internet is corroding human intelligence, freedom, and sociality. He proposes that:

> both camps . . . have a single, deep, and often fatal flaw that severely compromises the value of their work. That flaw, simply put, is ignorance about really existing capitalism and an underappreciation of how capitalism dominates social life. Celebrants and skeptics lack a political economic context. The work tends to take capitalism for granted as part of the background scenery and elevate technology to ride roughshod over history. Both camps miss the way capitalism defines our times and sets the terms for understanding not only the Internet, but most everything else of a social nature, including politics, in our society. (McChesney 2013: 13)

McChesney concludes that "The tremendous promise of the digital revolution has been compromised by capitalist appropriation and development of the Internet" (ibid.: 97).

Chapter 1 The Spirit of Competition: Crowdsourcing through Incentive Competitions

1 Retrieved from: https://www.youtube.com/watch?v=n7FM2T4Z9sg
2 The embrace of crowdsourcing points to a significant paradigm shift in both the organization of the corporation and in the realm of economic theory. Though the actual term "crowdsourcing" was first deployed by tech writer Jeff Howe in a 2006 article he published in *Wired* magazine, in academic circles the concept largely derives from the work of economist Eric Von Hippel, who also happened to serve as the chair of Lakhani's PhD committee. As far back as 1976, but more recently in his 2006 book, *Democratizing Innovation*, Von Hippel proposed a radical reformulation of Schumpeter's theory of innovation which "put at its core the profit-seeking incentives of either large manufacturing firms with market power or start-up entrepreneurial firms as the drivers of technical change." As Lakhani himself notes, Schumpeter's "view of the incentives of formal economic organization to innovate" became "the dominant scientific paradigm for economists, management scholars, businesspeople and policy makers," and it continues to form "the core intellectual foundation of innovation and entrepreneurial studies in many business schools and economics departments today" (Harhoff and Lakhani 2016: 1). Von Hippel, by contrast, developed a very different view of innovation, arguing that "*users* are as important or more important than producers

as sources of innovation in modern societies" (quoted in Harhoff and Lakhani 2016). This initial insight came from studying several decades of scientific innovations. Von Hippel found that 77 percent of the most important innovations had been developed "by scientists who had a direct need" of the product, rather than by "companies who had somehow figured out the market need and then innovated" (ibid.: 2). In his subsequent writings, he has discussed the role that community-user innovation has played in the development of the open-software movement. Indeed, both Von Hippel and Lakhani argue that the increased developments in digital technologies have played a pivotal role in enhancing the potential of user/crowdsourcing innovation.

3 Retrieved from: https://www.youtube.com/watch?v=n7FM2T4Z9sg
4 For some interesting treatments on the way competition and capitalism have been naturalized and configured within economic thought and theory, see Carlton 1949; McNulty 1968; Sahlins 2008.
5 Marx critiqued this idea on several grounds. First, although some disagree (Geras 1983), I would argue that while Marx certainly operates with a notion of what constitutes an authentic human existence, and authentic human needs, Marx's theory of historical materialism is predicated upon the idea that human beings are not imbued with an innate, universal nature. Rather for Marx, human beings are the kinds of creatures who produce their own natures through their particular modes of production. Competitiveness, greed, and the desire for perpetual accumulation are products of a capitalist system of production rather than panhuman universals. Second, as he elaborated in the *Economic and Philosophic Manuscripts*, and specifically in his critique of political economy, for Marx, capitalism is an economic system that leads not to progress or enrichment but denial and dehumanization. As he wrote:

> Political economy, this science of *wealth*, is therefore simultaneously the science of denial, of want, of *thrift*, of saving – and it actually reaches the point where it *spares* man the *need* of either fresh *air* or physical *exercise*. This science of marvelous industry is simultaneously the science of *asceticism*, and its true ideal is the *ascetic* but *extortionate* miser and the *ascetic* but productive *slave* . . . Thus political economy – despite its worldly and wanton appearance – is a true moral science, the most moral of all the sciences. Self-denial, the denial of life and of all human needs, is its cardinal doctrine. (Marx 1978 [1844]: 95)

6 His books, co-authored with Steven Kotler, include *Abundance: The Future is Better Than You Think* and *Bold: How to Go Big, Create Wealth, and Impact the World.*
7 Retrieved   from: http://fortune.com/2014/03/20/worlds-50-greatest-leaders
8 Retrieved from: https://www.forbes.com/sites/peterdiamandis/2014/07/07/solving-your-challenge-with-incentive-competitions/#403d579371d5
9 For instance, in the 2015 *New York Times* bestseller, *Bold: How to Go*

Big, Create Wealth, and Impact the World (co-written with Steven Kotler), Diamandis and Kotler write:

> The greatest tool we have for tackling our grand challenge is the passionate and dedicated human mind . . . ideas we've never before had access to will result in new discoveries, products, and inventions that will benefit us all . . . *Equally important is the entrepreneurial possibility hidden amongst these challenges. One idea that will become clearer as we go along is the notion that the world's biggest problems are also the world's biggest business opportunities.* Along exactly these lines, at Singularity University – the Silicon Valley-based university Peter co-founded with inventor, author, and futurist Ray Kurzweil – students study the use of exponential technology to address the world's grandest challenges. At SU, we believe that the best way to create billions of dollars' worth of value is to positively impact the lives of billions of people, thus our students are asked to create what are called ten to the ninth-plus companies – that is, companies that can have exactly this kind of billion-person impact. (Diamandis and Kotler 2015: xi; my emphasis)

10 Retrieved July 2019 from https://www.prnewswire.com/news-releases/nasa-and-herox-launch-lunar-loo-challenge-to-find-way-for-astronauts-to-poop-on-the-moon-301083564.html

11 As Fisher astutely observes:

> According to the digital discourse, digerati entrepreneurs are different from industrial-age capitalists because for the digerati, business does not all revolve around profit but on contributing to technological progress; their success is measured not only in terms of material gains but also in terms of their techno-logical skill, or how "techie," "geek," and "nerd" they are . . . In the digital discourse, reverence is directed toward the entrepreneur-cum-technological nerd. The real incentive for the new informational entrepreneur to engage in business, according to the digital discourse, is not making more money but making a real social contribution: discovering new opportunities for network technology and opening up new frontiers for the network society. (Fisher 2010: 90)

12 Retrieved   from: https://www.xprize.org/articles/xprize-turns-to-the-crowd-to-design-its-next-xprize

13 Incentive competitions can arguably be described as a form of peer-to-peer production. Michel Bauwens argues that peer-to-peer production is defined by its "equipotentiality" or "anti-credentialism." Anyone, rather than a permissioned few, can participate. Bauwens further argues that peer-to-peer production stands to usher in a "third mode of production, a third mode of governance, and a third mode of property, it is poised to overhaul our political economy in unprecedented ways" (Bauwens 2005: 499). However, the examples in this chapter suggest that peer-to-peer production has yet to overhaul our political economy, and instead is being co-opted by capitalist entrepreneurs like Peter Diamandis to further the accumulation of capital.

14 Retrieved from: https://thielfellowship.org/
15 Retrieved from: https://thielfellowship.org/
16 For instance, although Peter Thiel casts his Fellowship program as an "investment" in young and promising minds that enables them to avoid being saddled with staggering student debt, we might ask how the Fellowship program also exploits the young. After all, earning US$100,000 over a two-year period for coming up with a "genius" idea or product is far below the market value of such work. Furthermore, participants in the Fellowship are forced to drop out of college, thereby foreclosing another avenue to accrue cultural and social capital.
17 Retrieved from: https://www.forbes.com/sites/peterdiamandis/2014/07/07/solving-your-challenge-with-incentive-competitions/#403d579371d5
18 Retrieved from: https://news.trust.org/item/20140820032027-2s9zm
19 In his excellent book, *Winners Take All: The Elite Charade of Changing the World*, Anand Giridharadas explores how this winner-takes-all mentality and ethos permeate the techno-elites' efforts to cast themselves as social reformers and saviors of society, while nonetheless maintaining and reproducing the status quo of inequality. See Giridharadas 2019.
20 Indeed, it is interesting to note that whereas Le Bon proposed that the best way to influence the crowd was to appeal to their unconscious, Lakhani and Boudreau propose that the best way to influence the crowd is to appeal to the spirit of competition.
21 Retrieved March 2019 from: https://www.nasa.gov/content/iss-longeron-challenge-0
22 Retrieved March 2019 from: https://www.youtube.com/watch?v=sn44vNdstGc
23 Retrieved from: https://hbr.org/2013/04/using-the-crowd-as-an-innovation-partner
24 There are, of course, different intellectual property agreements that can be used in incentive competitions. The most stringent require the participant or "solver" to relinquish all property rights to the sponsor. In other cases, the solver may retain property rights over the innovation but grant the competition sponsor free access to the innovation.
25 For instance, in addition to the platforms Lakhani cites, companies can turn to Medallia Crowdicity, QMarkets Collective Intelligence Solutions, Planview Spigit, Ideanco, and Votigo, to name but a few.
26 As Srnicek writes:

> data have come to serve a number of key capitalist functions: they educate and give competitive advantage to algorithms; they enable the coordination and outsourcing of workers; they allow for the optimization and flexibility of productive process; they make possible the transformation of low-margin goods into high-margin services; and data analysis is itself generative of data, in a virtuous cycle. (Srnicek 2017: 41–2)

27 Retrieved from: https://www.herox.com/about

28 See: https://www.herox.com/blog/10-herox-a-platform-for-emergent-heroes

29 Retrieved from: https://www.therobotreport.com/alphapilot-ai-drone-competition-uses-herox-crowdsource-talent/

30 As Chiapello and Knoll note, the development of "social finance" and "impact investing," which is predicated upon the idea that financial ventures can be used to promote social good, began in the late 1990s but was reinvigorated in the wake of the 2008 financial crisis. They write:

> Surging after the 2008 financial crisis, when global finance lost societal legitimation and failed to prove its positive contribution to the common good, Impact Investing provided a new example of capitalist recuperation of criticism (Boltanski and Chiapello 2007; Chiapello 2013). Financial markets that were held responsible for economic recession, job losses, growing homelessness, and the emergence of anti-globalization and right wing movements and governments in the aftermath of the financial crisis (Tooze 2018) are now presented as part of the solution rather than the problem. Here, financiers are not the greedy irresponsible people causing the crisis, but responsible people who are potentially dedicating their talent, knowledge, and financial power to serve the common good. (Chiapello and Knoll 2020: 17)

31 Retrieved from: https://www.forbes.com/sites/peterdiamandis/2014/07/07/solving-your-challenge-with-incentive-competitions/#2709caf571d5

32 "The NASA Tournament Lab (NTL) is an online, virtual facility that facilitates the use of crowdsourcing to tackle NASA challenges." Retrieved March 2019 from: https://www.globenewswire.com/news-release/2017/02/15/1181973/0/en/NASA-s-Space-Poop-HeroX-Challenge-Breaks-Crowdsourcing-Competition-Records.html

33 Retrieved from: https://news.trust.org/item/20140820032027-2s9zm

34 Retrieved from: https://www.therobotreport.com/alphapilot-ai-drone-competition-uses-herox-crowdsource-talent/

35 Retrieved March 2019 from: https://www.prnewswire.com/news-releases/herox-helps-nasa-advance-moon-exploration-with-miniaturized-payload-design-competition-301038032.html

36 Retrieved March 2019 from: https://www.bizjournals.com/bizjournals/news/2015/03/16/xprize-spinoff-lets-amateurs-compete-as-equals.html

37 As Ryan Calo and Alex Rosenblat point out in their article, "The Taking Economy: Uber, Information, and Power," this tendency to promote incentive competitions as a means of bolstering competition and thereby disrupting "legacy markets" is a feature of the more persuasive rhetoric that presents "the sharing economy" as a new improved path to ushering in economic and social progress. See Calo and Rosenblat 2017.

38 Retrieved from: https://crowdsourcingweek.com/blog/herox-prize-challenges-social-network/

39 Retrieved from: https://www.therobotreport.com/alphapilot-ai-drone-competition-uses-herox-crowdsource-talent/

40 Retrieved from: https://www.herox.com/privacy-policy
41 Retrieved from: https://www.herox.com/partnerships
42 For example, Investopedia defines network effect as follows:

> The network effect is a phenomenon whereby increased numbers of people or participants improve the value of a good or service. The Internet is an example of the network effect. Initially, there were few users on the Internet since it was of little value to anyone outside of the military and some research scientists. However, as more users gained access to the Internet, they produced more content, information, and services. The development and improvement of websites attracted more users to connect and do business with each other. As the Internet experienced increases in traffic, it offered more value, leading to a network effect. (Retrieved from: https://www.investopedia.com/terms/n/network-effect.asp)

43 Retrieved from: https://irishtechnews.ie/rewards-problem-solving-christian-cotichini-herox/?__cf_chl_jschl_tk__=a0593ad8a4e1cfe
897327fdaea8304926d0ae105-1595695094-0-AdpLWh3fPhzZqzgCY
CUTNQRQ6qyrPtYuX7hfhtUUzx07Ez3B60ARc-nEXvdzF9OvlRpd
dqobnLMth7BGxrbxzdTKa8A_97NbACk-6BEusihviknrJGPHvuQpZ
TwPlqnZg_3JCw6TQTswiZzgwvip9GzpYn8FVCvenCmiOzxVPDllY
nrS6VnHr0HKhTdDleL6mdziY5ZJLjP6kT3rT6LwAcocBQrV1vwX-
yr-nAnGS7JCKdPEJOjiqkLYYf9rDfakRulqCOXTFAu-hNi8cCYME
xeHpcrRnZEBihwrhAVKPzuyFhemIfOhAZ64h3epAoVyjzjdbeAjSL-
Q0TQbSPu-ydtAAxD23g_p8BnAhAYMd0OWzYeob5J3Kkntk2ZNY
NsHTWlzAQKp6bZ3v0bC4lwWhRI
44 For a delightful discussion of the relevance of Marx's insight that competition leads to the restoration of monopoly, and the way this insight has been disregarded in "economic ideology," see Perelman 2011.
45 Indeed, the rhetoric deployed by Diamandis and others is reminiscent of the rhetoric deployed by business leaders and economists in the 1920s, who proposed that "the capitalist revolution in America" was turning laborers and the "every man" into capitalists. For a fascinating discussion of this, see Roberto 2018's chapter, "Every Man a Capitalist? Fascist Ideology of Businessmen in 1920s America."
46 This resonates with Koula Mellos's observation that "The transition to advanced capitalism facilitates the portrayal of bourgeoise class interests as universalistic" (Mellos 1978: 7). As Mellos writes: "The ideology operates such that it explicitly promotes not class interests, that is, interests of the bourgeois class, but universal interests. In this way, it aims at concealing the fundamental contradiction in the private appropriation of socially produced surplus value" (ibid.: 3).
47 Indeed, this chapter suggests the need to revisit Fisher's observation that "the central mode of social action in the discourse on networks is that of cooperation rather than struggle or competition, which characterizes the discourse on class." He continues: "Hence, the notion of network

work and its grounding in a technological reality allow for the substitution of a hierarchical, competitive, and antagonistic model of class by a dehierarchized, cooperative, aggregable, and inherently inclusive model of networks (at least in the long run, once the digital divide is bridged)" (Fisher 2010: 6).

    Fisher is correct in noting that the spirit of digital capitalism downplays class antagonisms and purports to usher in a more inclusive model of networks. However, competition is still very much a key value. It is regarded as an innate human characteristic, as something that inspires creativity and innovation, and as the guarantor of a well-functioning market.

48 See 2014 Technical Report, "Smart Factories: Crowdsourced Manufacturing" by Diederik Verzijl, Kristina Dervojeda, Fabian Nagtegaal and Jorn Sjaauw-Koen-Fa, PwC Netherlands, and Laurent Probst and Laurent Frideres, PwC Luxembourg.

49 Indeed, in a 2017 article published in the Harvard Business Review, Karim Lakhani and his colleague Marco Iansiti warn:

> The global economy is coalescing around a few digital superpowers. We see unmistakable evidence that a winner-take-all world is emerging in which a small number of "hub firms" – including Alibaba, Alphabet/Google, Amazon, Apple, Baidu, Facebook, Microsoft, and Tencent – occupy central positions. While creating real value for users, these companies are also capturing a disproportionate and expanding share of the value, and that's shaping the collective economic future. The very same technologies that promised to democratize business are now threatening to make it more monopolistic. (Iansiti and Lakhani 2017)

Chapter 2 The Spirit of Collaboration: Crowdsourcing through Communities

1 For a useful overview of "internet-mediated mutual cooperation practices," see Cammaerts 2016.

2 Two points should be noted here. First, as Pitirim Sorokin points out, Tönnies was certainly not the first to posit the differences between the *Gemeinschaft* and *Gesellschaft* mentality. He writes, "In its essentials the theory did not originate with Tönnies. Like many fundamental categories of social thought, it is in a sense eternal, appearing long before Tönnies and reiterated after him" (Sorokin 2017: ix). Second, the failure to invoke Tönnies in current writings on community crowdsourcing is probably not just the by-product of an ignorance of sociology. It also has to do with the fact that business entrepreneurs and experts tend to define community in quite different terms. While they agree that communities are bound together by shared sentiments and interests, and demonstrate loyalty to each other, they also emphasize that the

real bond that unites members of a community is their shared use of or interest in a specific technology or problem.

As Lakhani explains:

> in the case of innovation, it is useful to consider communities as groups of individuals, affiliated through a common technology or use condition, who connect with each other (regardless of the medium: online and/or face-to-face), and willingly and freely share with each other their problems and solutions to the various use conditions of that technology.

In many cases, especially in information goods like software, the community will not only enable sharing but often will take responsibility for a collective output in the form of a working solution (Boudreau and Lakhani 2013; Lakhani 2016: 111).

3   Given some of the ideas we have encountered from business leaders thus far, Tönnies is interesting in part because he casts competitiveness and self-interest *not* as innate propensities but, rather, as social products that are produced and exacerbated by the organizational forms of modern life. Indeed, Tönnies proposed that with the onset of modernity and collapse of the feudal world, the affective bonds of communities were largely being displaced by the instrumental relationships of societies. He viewed these two forms of sociality as antithetical to each other and anticipated that in the years going forward, the logics of society would prevail.

4   Retrieved   from: https://hbr.org/2013/04/using-the-crowd-as-an-innovation-partner

5   Retrieved from: https://www.cio.com/article/2442417/eric-von-hippel-and-karim-lakhani--open-source-means-something-for-nothing.html

6   Retrieved   from: https://hbr.org/2013/04/using-the-crowd-as-an-innovation-partner

7   Clay Shirky makes a similar observation in his discussion of the way "mass amateurization" breaks down professional categories and encourages people to pursue activities that were once the domain of professional specialists. See Shirky 2008.

8   Retrieved   from: https://irishtechnews.ie/rewards-problem-solving-christian-cotichini-herox/?__cf_chl_jschl_tk__=35c061d90026ef7650c
58c9f06db74e48a42daf9-1594490674-0-Ab81sO0kiLVNWh4x5lUw
Q3R6BKHcVi470d3S4o51qi7RxGeP3zIt0PmCDyJ4pRh9ux1I7Fi05
f0IF79NuACu2iWZaIQD7RSelxnQr4RKPEvHwRPSfh-FA-S8t876
lbYwCOt5p1fjE9fhHlQNN_9J98jyW21BwVHUg1f4wyPomNdRjzg
Atfx5hC_kkr_G1J-onzBkliD42JLrl-Nyru2t0cfIUEkiBmi8c4dQOAU-
-SxO55fEO-Bzejka5tQ6DN_95kpb4Wmz-1WSpZWTfy
RsyqttXpkO5eQDu2x-jbWHMnMunO0pBnpxb_UW282JNdViqYG9
C2dAhEOQAF4_3f5Kwq1TRPjHmvzczs2AlyRxxgWeDu7j4BiMoL1i
sY8li0gXUP9b7lpf4GH55lGcQfUmky0

9   For an excellent critique of the way "the sharing economy" operates as

a neoliberal discursive formation that works to "justify and normalize flexible and precarious work through an ambiguous association between capitalist exchange and altruistic social values," see Cockayne 2016 and Calo and Rosenblat 2017. See also Robert Reich's 2015 article, "The Share-the-Scraps Economy," in which he posits, "Customers and workers are matched online. Workers are rated on quality and reliability. The big money goes to the corporation that owns the software. The scraps go to the on-demand workers." Retrieved from: https://robertreich.org/post/109894095095

10 Howe himself notes that Threadless was one of the first companies to put the crowdsourcing model to work. In discussing how he first developed the concept of crowdsourcing, he reflects upon changes he was witnessing in the early 2000s and writes:

> What previous generations of humans called the hobby was achieving ascendancy over what said predecessors called work. Weird. Scary. And what does one call that? I called it crowdsourcing and wrote about the phenomenon first in *Wired* magazine in June 2006, and then in a book that followed a few years later. But the word is less interesting than the thing it attempts to name.
>
> And now here's where Threadless comes in, because Jake, and Jake, and Jeffrey were hip to this historical realignment eons ago, and they built a company that would be all about taking the wonderful, crazy, hysterically funny, bizarre, offensive, eccentric stuff that people make, and pulling it out of the garage, and the hut, and the upstairs shelf, and introducing it to anyone with an Internet connection. (Howe 2010: 115)

11 Tracy Robey reports that, by mid-2007, the cash prize had gone from US$750 to US$2500. However, in 2014, Threadless changed this policy and now artists retain their copyright and earn profits "beyond base cost on all printed items" (Robey 2017).

12 Retrieved from: https://www.threadless.com/forum/post/1011039/what_is_happening/

13 Titan of tech and venture capitalist Marc Andreessen also proposes that digital technologies are "revolutionizing" the way products come to market and enhancing the means by which social capital can be converted into financial capital. Commenting on the success of Teespring, another online T-shirt company that was founded in 2011 by Walter Williams and Evan Stites-Clayton, Andreessen observes:

> Teespring is the modern method to convert social capital into financial capital. It's one of those things where it first will strike you as absurd, and then if you swallow the red pill, you'll realize what is happening. It's a way for a Facebook group or a YouTube star on Instagram to start to be able to sell T-Shirts. At first you're, like, whatever, merchandise – big deal. But it actually turns out that what happens is that you have these Facebook groups or YouTube stars that have a million followers . . . [and] social capital is real. Your followers or

your fans are people who value you and they want to support you . . . Now what we would argue is that T-Shirts are just the beginning. It could just be anything; it just has to be something. It's memorabilia, and you care about it and you're passionate and you're indicating something about yourself . . . It's like a totem; it's a psychological anchor into something that you care about. (Quoted in McAfee and Brynjolfsson 2017: 264)

14 Retrieved from: https://www.threadless.com/forum/post/1011039/what_ is_happening/
15 This recalls an observation made by Lawrence Lessig in his 2008 book, *Remix: Making Art and Commerce Thrive in the Hybrid Economy*. Lessig argues that today goods are produced not just through "the commercial economy, which meters access on the simple metric of price," but also through a "sharing economy, where access to culture is regulated not by price but by a complex set of social relations." In sharing economies, he further contends one of the most important things that circulate are "good feelings" (Lessig 2008: 145–6).
16 In his book, *Cognitive Surplus: How Technologies Make Consumers into Collaborators*, Clay Shirky also deploys the term "cognitive surplus" in his exploration of the way digital technologies are making it possible to tap into and harness the ideas and abilities of the "crowd." See Shirky 2011.
17 In 1956, GE established its Crotonville campus in upstate New York with the aim of providing a facility to train its management employees and become the "best-managed company" in the world. The campus continues to operate and offers management courses as well as yearly "Global Customer Summits" which provide "an opportunity to learn and network, understand what's worked and what hasn't," as GE Regional Customer Manager Dimitri Leimonitis explains. Retrieved from: https://www.ge.com/news/reports/inside-crotonville-ges-corporate-vault-unlocked
18 Ries explains that much of the inspiration for *The Lean Startup* came from his studying of lean manufacturing, a process that originated in Japan with the Toyota company. He notes that they developed a "completely new way of thinking about the manufacturing of physical goods" (Ries 2014: 6). "Among its tenets are drawing on knowledge and creativity of individual workers, the shrinking of batch sizes, just-in-time production and inventory control, and an acceleration of cycle times." Ries has been instrumental in implementing these tenets at GE, particularly in helping them develop their Fastworks initiative. Fastworks is premised upon the idea that customers and customer feedback should be central to the design process of the product. Design teams create a prototype of a product and then actively solicit feedback from customers, and then adapt the prototype to cater to customers' needs and desires. See https://academy.nobl.io/how-ge-implemented-fastworks-to-act-more-like-a-startup/

19 See Liz Stinson's article, "How GE Plans to Act Like a Startup and Crowdsource Breakthrough Ideas." Retrieved from: https://www.wired.com/2014/04/how-ge-plans-to-act-like-a-startup-and-crowdsource-great-ideas/

20 GE began experimenting with crowdsourcing earlier than this. For instance, in 2010, it partnered with several venture capital firms and announced the US$200 million GE Ecoimagination Challenge: Powering the Grid. As reported by Katherine Tweed, a journalist for *Wired* magazine, the challenge was "an open call for ideas to update the electrical grid." Retrieved from: https://www.wired.com/2010/07/ge-announces-200-million-power-grid-challenge/

21 Retrieved from: https://www.wired.com/2014/04/how-ge-plans-to-act-like-a-startup-and-crowdsource-great-ideas/

22 Retrieved from: https://www.techrepublic.com/article/ge-launches-microfactory-to-co-create-the-future-of-manufacturing/

23 Retrieved from: https://firstbuild.com/about/

24 Retrieved from: https://firstbuild.com/about/how-firstbuild-works/

25 As Lindsey Gilpin reported in her 2014 article, "GE Launches Microfactory to Co-create the Future of Manufacturing," GE has subsequently opened microfactories in Chandler, Arizona, Knoxville, Tennessee, Las Vegas, and Germany, with plans to open up to 100 more around the world in the coming years. In 2016, GE also launched another open crowdsourcing platform connected to a network of microfactories that are capable of rapid design and prototyping called Fuse. Indeed, if, as Boltanski and Chiapello propose, the large bureaucratic firm stood at the center of the spirit of capitalism during the period of Fordist production, it could be argued that the microfactory stands at the center of spirit of capitalism in the digital age. The proliferation of the microfactory as a new model of manufacturing at GE and in other corporations embodies many of the principles of the Lean Startup movement and it graphically displays how digital technologies are not only becoming increasingly integrated into the production process, but are also animating the spirit of digital capitalism. As tech writer Ben Schrauwen observes in his 2019 article "Microfactories Move to Full Production," microfactories are celebrated for their abilities to integrate digital technologies into manufacturing platforms such that "companies can review data and analytics in real time and pivot based on information anytime, anywhere." In addition to increasing flexibility in the manufacturing process, the digitization of the manufacturing process fosters greater opportunities for customization. Schrauwen writes:

> As manufacturing shifts from mass commoditization to dynamic mass customization, factories must demonstrate the ability to adapt production on a moment-by-moment basis in order to compete. This level of customization is also heavily dependent on data and AI at each step, from demand to

anticipation, to helping customers shape the product via a consumer website, to the real-time manufacturing process.

Highly digitized and automated, with a small footprint allowing them to be located close to the customer, microfactories are right-sized to support mass customization and these "markets of one." The use of technologies such as additive manufacturing provides the opportunity to quickly adapt products at the digital level and output batch sizes of one without the cost and lead time of previous manual customization. (Schrauwen 2019)

26 The factory consists of brainstorming rooms where attendees can work on concept development. There is a lab where community members can gain access to makerbots, electronic benches, and universal laser printers, there is a shop floor or fabrication center, that houses more complicated machines and requires a "craftsman's badge" for entry, and there is the microfactory itself, where assembly of products is conducted.

27 Retrieved from: https://firstbuild.com/microfactory/

28 As stated on the website: "Intellectual property is very important to us. Contributions on the site are protected under a Creative Commons License. Therefore, even though work presented on this site is available for anyone to use at FirstBuild, attribution will be given to you as the initial author." Retrieved from: https://firstbuild.com/about/how-firstbuild-works/

29 Retrieved from: https://firstbuild.com/about/how-firstbuild-works/

30 For an in-depth exploration of the growing "precariat class," see Guy Standing 2011, 2017.

31 Moreover, as Maurice Godelier reminds us in *The Enigma of the Gift*, "the mark of the gift between close friends and relatives . . . is not the absence of obligations, it is the absence of 'calculation'" (Godelier 1999: 109). Thus, by framing the relationship between the corporation and "makers" as one of gift exchange, corporations are able to offer nominal incentive prizes or access to the means of production as a gesture of reciprocity while bypassing the thorny and potentially costly matter of "calculating" what a fair compensation might be. In this regard, the language of the gift serves to further legitimate practices of extraction.

32 This is also the point Tim Jordan raises in his book, *Information Politics: Liberation and Exploitation in the Digital Society*. He argues that although we need to work towards a society where information is free to be used by all, and not regarded as proprietary, he also points out that "a challenge of information as simultaneous complete use is to continue developing new means of support producers of information and to radically critique all those industries who seek their own survival and profit ahead of the benefit information can bring to all" (Jordan 2015: 24–5).

Chapter 3 The Spirit of the Game: Smartphone Apps and the Digital Extraction of Surplus Value

1 For an in-depth discussion of the precariat class, see Standing 2011.
2 For another interesting discussion of the exploitative dynamics and "information politics" of digital capitalism, see Tim Jordan's essays on the iPad and death and gaming in Jordan 2015.
3 Appadurai and Alexander note that for a growing number of low-income Americans, who cannot afford home access to the internet, the smartphone has become their primary means of accessing it (Appadurai and Alexander 2020).
4 This quote comes from Matt Bencke, the former CEO of Mighty AI, which is the company that took over Spare5. Retrieved from: https://www.pymnts.com/news/artificial-intelligence/2017/mighty-ai-startup-investment-spare5/. In this article, Bencke further explains:

> There will always be data challenges that businesses can't solve with computer power alone . . . We're using technology to scale the unique capabilities of the human mind. For our customers, it's a fast and cost-effective way to achieve results that would otherwise be impossible. Whether you're selling online, publishing rich content, or training a machine learning engine, you need to know what people think. We deliver that knowledge with game-changing quality and value.

In an article entitled, "Spare5: Humans Helping Machines Become Intelligent," a reviewer also describes Spare5's business model: "Spare5's business model involves a two-sided marketing proposition. On the one hand, the company creates groups, even virtual armies, of people with skills to help filter, clean and organize massive amounts of unstructured data. On the other hand, it attracts commercial clients who rely on using various types of unstructured data and are often overwhelmed by it." Retrieved from: https://mobilecloudera.com/spare5-humans-helping-machines-become-intelligent/

5 Retrieved from: https://smarts.co/apps-that-pay/
6 Retrieved from: https://techcrunch.com/2015/08/25/spare5-raises-10m-series-a-round-for-its-mobile-mechanical-turk-service/
7 When speaking of why the capitalist enters into this exchange with wage labor, Marx writes, "what really influenced him was the specific use-value which this commodity possesses of being a *source not only of value, but of more value than it has itself.* This is the special service that the capitalist expects from labor-power . . ." (Marx 1978 [1867]: 357).
8 See Jason Wuerch 2021, "Spare5 App Review: Scam or Legit Money Making App 2021?" *Frugalforless.* Retrieved from: https://www/frugalforless.com/spare5-review

9 Retrieved from: https://www.geekwire.com/2014/make-money-free-time-spare5-raises-3-25m-madrona-foundry-demand-work-platform/

10 Retrieved from: https://www.geekwire.com/2014/make-money-free-time-spare5-3-25m-madrona-foundry-demand-work-platform

11 Marx would likely find all of this disturbing yet unsurprising. While Marx worried that factory workers in the industrial age were being reduced to unskilled appendages of the machine, in the digital age, taskers become fodder for machines that are designed to become ever more intelligent so that they can more effectively control human beings and behaviors.

12 For more on the way algorithms are used to discipline and assess workers and consumers, see O'Neil 2016; Cheney-Lippold 2017; Eubanks 2017; Rosenblat 2018; Besterman and Gusterson 2019.

13 See Soper 2014.

14 Retrieved from: https://mobilecloudera.com/spare5-humans-helping-machines-become-intelligent

15 See "InboxDollars Review: Is it a Scam, or Legit?" (January 2021). Retrieved from: https://www.surveycool.com/inboxdollars-review

16 See "InboxDollars Review: Earn Money Completing Online Tasks At Home" by Robert Farrington, who helps millennials get out of or deal with student loan debt. Posted on The College Investor: Investing and Personal Finance for Millennials. Retrieved from: https://thecollegeinvestor.com/19965/inbox-dollars-review

17 Some of the gaming apps give "rewards" instead of paying out cash. They allow users to accumulate points or digital currency that can then be put towards Amazon, Xbox, or other gift cards. Indeed, more consideration should be given to how this platform/app economy is facilitating new forms of currency that are instrumental in redirecting people's labor to further forms of capitalist appropriation. By mandating that points are put towards Amazon, Xbox, or PlayStation gift cards, these companies basically play a role in facilitating the capture of this "earned income." For instance, "the rewards" earned cannot be spent on medical bills or rent. The very form of compensation ensures that this "income" will be redirected to further augment corporate profits.

18 See https://andatisiro.medium.com/earn-cash-for-your-everyday-online-activities-22474a302110

19 Retrieved from: https://play.google.com/store/apps/details?id=com.tetherstudios.solitaire.practice&hl=en_US&gl=US

20 See https://medium.com/@zMikeySlice/solitaire-cube-tournament-options-87b3cd96cd83

21 See https://play.google.com/store/apps/details?id=com.mistplay.mistplay&hl=en_US&gl=US

22 See https://www.mistplay.com/. Moreover, in order to redeem their points and be able to put them towards rewards, players are required

to provide their opinion of the game and answer a survey about their experience playing it. See https://moneytamer.com/mistplay-app-review/

23 See https://moneytamer.com/mistplay-app-review/

24 https://sitn.hms.harvard.edu/flash/2018/dopamine-smartphones-battle-time/

25 This is a point also made by Reith 2002 and Raymen and Smith 2017. Raymen and Smith, moreover, examine the ways that gambling has become integrated into "everyday life," in part through the emergence of online gambling platforms and smartphone apps that enable people to place and win bets from their living rooms. In a slightly different vein, Martin Young argues that in the era of late capitalism, gaming and gambling provide a "controllable" and "bounded" space for players to "consume risk," while at the same time deferring "the broad global anxieties associated with the risk society" (Young 2010: 269).

26 For language on how these apps kill time, see https://thesmartwallet.com/solitaire-cube-review/?articleid=9268

27 See https://www.owler.com/company/mty; https://www.zdnet.com/article/crowdsourced-ai-training-platform-mighty-ai-raises-14m-from-intel-google-accenture

28 There is, of course, a difference between revenues and profits. However, while companies are forthcoming in their revenue disclosures, the actual amount of profit grossed is difficult to get access to.

29 All of these reviews were taken from: https://play.google.com/store/apps/details?id=com.mentormate.android.inboxdollars&hl=en_US&gl=US&showAllReviews=true

30 See, for instance, McChesney 2013; LaGrandeur and Hughes 2017; Sadowski 2020; Zuboff 2019; Huberman 2021.

31 See "InboxDollars Review: Get Paid for Random Online Tasks" by Robert Farrington, who helps "millennials get out of or deal with student loan debt." Posted on The College Investor: Investing and Personal Finance for Millennials. Retrieved from: https://thecollegeinvestor.com/19965/inbox-dollars-review

32 See https://thecollegeinvestor.com/19965/inbox-dollars-review

33 See https://www.geekwire.com/2014/make-money-free-time-spare5-raises-3-25m-madrona-foundry-demand-work-platform/

34 As Nick Srnicek observes, "The problem for old capitalist firms that continues to the present day is that old business models were not particularly well designed to extract and use data" (Srnicek 2017: 42).

35 See https://www.geekwire.com/2014/make-money-free-time-spare5-raises-3-25m-madrona-foundry-demand-work-platform/

36 Indeed, as Sullivan and Gershuny point out, in our "liberal-market economy," it is increasingly the case that those with the most resources to consume various leisure goods and activities are also those with the least amount of free time (Sullivan and Gershuny 2004). Free time, in this sense, is no longer a sign of class privilege and "conspicuous leisure," as Veblen (1967 [1912]) observed at the turn of the twentieth

century, but rather it is increasingly becoming a sign of an economically precarious existence.

Chapter 4 In the Spirit of Convenience: Amazon Go and Surveillance Capitalism

1 See "Amazon Just Became the Second Company to Reach $1 Trillion. Here's How Much Jeff Bezos is Worth Now," by Brad Tuttle. https://money.com/amazon-1-trillion-jeff-bezos-net-worth/

2 For another discussion of the way convenience operates as a "dominant ideology," see Appadurai and Alexander 2020. For a discussion of how convenience has emerged as a central "value" of modern society, see Tierney 1993.

3 Taken from Amazon Go webpage, https://www.amazon.com/b?ie= UTF8&node=16008589011

4 See "Amazon Opens Its Largest Convenience Store Yet," by Kate Clark. Retrieved from: https://techcrunch.com/2018/09/04/amazon-opens-its-largest-amazon-go-convenience-store-yet/

5 See "List of Amazon Go Locations on Amazon.com." *GeekWire*, July 2019. Retrieved February 8, 2020 from: https://www.geekwire.com/tag/amazon-go/

6 See "Amazon Go Store Brings in 50% More Revenue Than Typical C-Stores." Retrieved February 8, 2020 from: https://csnews.com/analysts-amazon-go-stores-bring-50-more-revenue-typical-c-stores. And see https://www.supermarketnews.com/retail-financial/report-amazon-has-28-more-amazon-fresh-stores-works

7 Zuboff provides the following definition of surveillance capitalism:

> Surveillance capitalism unilaterally claims human experience as free raw material for translation into behavioral data. Although some of these data are applied to product or service improvement, the rest are declared as proprietary *behavioral surplus*, fed into advanced manufacturing processes known as "machine intelligence," and fabricated into *prediction products* that anticipate what you will do now, soon, and later. Finally, these prediction products are traded in a new kind of marketplace for behavioral predictions I call *behavioral futures markets*. (Zuboff 2019: 8)

8 Further describing the nature of instrumentarian power, Zuboff writes:

> Our conformity is irrelevant to instrumentarianism's success. There is no need for mass submission to social norms, no loss of self to the collective induced by terror and compulsion, no offers of acceptance and belonging as a reward for bending to the group. All of that is superseded by a digital order that thrives within things and bodies, transforming volition into reinforcement and action into conditioned response . . . In this way instrumentarian power produces

endlessly accruing knowledge for surveillance capitalism's domination of the division of learning in society. False consciousness is no longer produced by the hidden facts of class and their relation to production but rather by the hidden facts of instrumentarian power's command over the division of learning in society as it usurps the rights to answer essential questions. . . . Power was once identified with the ownership of the means of production, but it is now identified with ownership of the means of behavioral modification that is Big Other. (Zuboff 2019: 379)

9 Zuboff does speak about the way surveillance capitalism achieves its hold through "declarations." She argues that "six declarations laid the foundation for the wider project of surveillance capitalism," and she argues that "if one falls, they all fall" (Zuboff 2019: 178).

In addition to discussing these declarations, Zuboff does make brief mention of how the ideology of inevitablism provides surveillance capitalists with a means of legitimating their use of technocratic control. However, for the most part, her description of instrumentarian power leaves little space for the role that ideology plays in maintaining the extractive practices of surveillance capitalism.

10 For example, in *The Dominant Ideology Thesis* (1980), Abercrombie, Hill, and Turner argue that while dominant ideologies do exist, they no longer play a central role in lending cohesion to a society. Surveying their argument, Eagleton writes:

But in so far as the consent of the dominated to their masters is won at all, it is achieved much more by economic than by ideological means. What Marx once called "the dull compulsion of the economic" is enough to keep men and women in their places; and such strategies of reformism – the ability of the capitalist system to yield tangible benefits to some at least of its underlings – are more crucial in this respect than any ideological complicity between the workers and their bosses. (Eagleton 2007: 35)

Eagleton also notes that scholars such as Jürgen Habermas have argued that:

whereas rhetorical appeals to such public values played a central role in the "classical" phase of the system, they have now been effectively replaced by purely technocratic forms of management . . . On some such views, the system of late capitalism can be said to operate "all by itself", without any need to resort to *discursive* justification. It no longer, so to speak, has to pass through consciousness; instead, it simply secures its own reproduction by a manipulative, incorporative logic of which human subjects are the mere obedient effects. (Eagleton 2007: 37)

I suspect that Zuboff would be sympathetic to such arguments as she argues that Big Other ultimately comes to automate human beings, shaping our behavior, rather than attempting to "engineer our souls."

11 See "Amazon's Mission Statement." Retrieved from: https://www.thebalancesmb.com/amazon-mission-statement-4068548

12 Eagleton, for instance, identifies six dominant ideological strategies. He writes:

> The term ideology, in other words, would seem to make reference not only to belief systems, but to questions of *power*.
> What kind of reference, though? Perhaps the most common answer is to claim that ideology has to do with *legitimating* the power of a dominant social group or class. "To study ideology", writes John B. Thompson, "is to study the ways in which meaning (or signification) serves to sustain relations of domination." This is probably the single most widely accepted definition of ideology; and the process of legitimation would seem to involve at least six different strategies. A dominant power may legitimate itself by *promoting* beliefs and values congenial to it; *naturalizing* and *universalizing* such beliefs so as to render them self-evident and apparently inevitable; *denigrating* ideas which might challenge it; *excluding* rival forms of thought, perhaps by some unspoken but systematic logic; and *obscuring* social reality in ways convenient to itself. Such "mystification", as it is commonly known, frequently takes the form of masking or suppressing social conflicts, from which arises the conception of ideology as an imaginary resolution of real contradictions. In any actual ideological formation, all six of these strategies are likely to interact in complex ways (Eagleton 2007: 5–6).

13 See https://www.salesforce.com/blog/2013/06/jeff-bezos-lessons.html

14 One could, for instance, trace this insight back to John Kenneth Galbraith's critique of "Growthmanship" and "The Dependence Effect" (Galbraith 1987 [1958]), or Stuart Ewen's discussion of the ideological engineering that drove the creation of the twentieth-century's mass consumer society (Ewen 1976), or Baudrillard's classic essay on the ideological genesis of needs (1981), or even to Marx's writings in the *Economic and Philosophic Manuscripts* of 1844, when he described how the capitalist "puts himself at the service of the other's most depraved fancies, plays the pimp between him and his need, excites in him morbid appetites"(Marx 1844: 94).

15 https://www.youtube.com/watch?v=NrmMk1Myrxc

16 See https://www.youtube.com/watch?v=SeVfAV1-5GA

17 See https://www.newsbreak.com/pennsylvania/philadelphia/news/0KztFoJu/amazon-threatens-philadelphia-over-plan-to-ban-cashless-stores

18 See https://www.inquirer.com/business/amazon-go-accept-cash-ban-cashless-stores-philadelphia-new-jersey-20190410.html

19 See https://www.yelp.com/biz/amazon-go-seattle-4?hrid=Lvzp5LpWS2mS9B50VWYctw&rh_type=phrase&rh_ident=receipt

20 https://www.yelp.com/biz/amazon-go-seattle-4?hrid=Lvzp5LpWS2mS9B50VWYctw&rh_type=phrase&rh_ident=receipt

21 https://www.tomsguide.com/us/amazon-go-store,news-30035.html

22 See https://www.youtube.com/watch?v=SeVfAV1-5GA

23 See https://www.youtube.com/watch?v=SeVfAV1-5GA

24 See https://www.youtube.com/watch?v=SeVfAV1-5GA

25 See https://www.youtube.com/watch?v=SeVfAV1-5GA. Also, it could be argued that Kumar is deploying an ideological strategy of obfuscation in these remarks. For considering the power that Amazon wields in terms of shaping the retail landscape and structure, it seems a bit naive to suggest that the real deciders of the future will be the consumers rather than this trillion-dollar company.

26 See https://www.youtube.com/watch?v=SeVfAV1-5GA

27 See https://www.youtube.com/watch?v=SeVfAV1-5GA

28 The concept of friction is central to business management theory. Indeed, there is a wide literature that extols the way "reducing friction" lay at the heart of mastering the "art of business."

29 As Eve Chiapello reminds us in her essay, "Capitalism and Its Criticisms," "The interaction between capitalism on one side and criticisms of capitalism on the other gives rise to the spirit of capitalism of a given period" (Chiapello 2013: 62).

30 In his essay "Technology and Science as 'Ideology,'" Jürgen Habermas explores the way technology and science emerge not just as forces of production in advanced capitalist economies but as ideologies. He proposes that in advanced capitalist societies, relations and decisions that are in fact political in essence, and that should be debated and discussed, are instead treated as technical problems and therefore depoliticized. For instance, instead of debating whether or not capitalism is a humane or good system to live with, we ask, how do we keep the system going? We buy into this vision of the "good life" in part because it offers us cheap creature comforts and convenience, but what we really need to do is pause and ask ourselves, is this the kind of world we want to live in? And whose interests exactly does such a system serve? Do we want to live like hamsters on a wheel and devote our existence to trying to figure out ways to keep the wheel spinning, or do we want to model our society around different values and ends? See Habermas 1970.

Chapter 5 The Spirit of the Gift: The Work of Techno-philanthropy

1 "[P]hilanthropy is a problem posing as a solution" – phosda (2018). Comment on the video "The Robber Barons vs the Technophilanthropists | ABUNDANCE," uploaded by XPRIZE, 27 July. See https://www. youtube.com/watch?v=fpTYk52jAhc

2 Certainly, the idea that philanthropy provides a justification for the inordinate accumulation of capital into the hands of an elite few is not a novel one. For other critiques of the way contemporary philanthropy serves such a justificatory function, enhances elite power, and erodes

democracy, see Callahan 2017; Giridharadas 2019; Reich 2018; Žižek 2006.

3 See, for instance, https://www.washingtonpost.com/technology/2020/04/27/big-tech-coronavirus-winners;https://abcnews.go.com/Business/winners-pandemic-economy-big-tech-lockdown-essentials-soar/story?id=72495436; https://www.vox.com/recode/2020/10/30/21541699/big-tech-google-facebook-amazon-apple-coronavirus-profits; https://www.economist.com/leaders/2020/04/04/big-techs-covid-19-opportunity; https://www.usatoday.com/story/money/2020/12/01/american-billionaires-that-got-richer-during-covid/43205617/

4 https://www.npr.org/2020/12/16/947189767/mackenzie-scott-has-donated-more-than-4-billion-in-last-4-months. Also, as Ursula Huws notes, "Research by the US Institute for Policy Studies and Americans for Tax Fairness reported in June 2020 that the wealth of the top five billionaires (Jeff Bezos, Bill Gates, Mark Zuckerberg, Warrant Buffett, and Larry Ellison) had seen their combined net worth grow by $584 billion during the first three months of 2020, in a period $56.5 trillion was wiped off the value of household wealth" (Huws 2020: 5–6).

5 In her book, *No Such Thing as a Free Gift*, Linsey McGoey notes the three main critiques of contemporary philanthropy, or "philanthro-capitalism." The first "centers on the accountability and transparency of private philanthropic donors . . . The second concern is that philanthropy, by channeling private funds towards public service, erodes support for governmental spending . . . The third major concern is that many philanthropists . . . earned their fortunes through business strategies that greatly exacerbate the same social and economic inequalities that philanthropists purport to remedy" (McGoey 2016: 8–9). However, she also concludes that the voices of the critics are usually "drowned out by the deafening chorus of philanthropy enthusiasts who I think of as 'Ted Heads' – amiable entrepreneurs and executives who congregate at exorbitantly priced TED events around the world" (ibid.: 14).

6 Margaret O'Mara, February 10, 2021. "How Bezos Can Transform His Public Image." *New York Times.*

7 As Linsey McGoey notes:

> During the mid-twentieth century, America's richest and poorest citizens grew more financially equal. The income share of the wealthiest 1 percent of Americans fell from nearly 16 percent in 1940 to 7 percent in the 1970s . . . Since the 1970s, we've seen the reverse situation: the income share of the 1 percent has been steadily increasing. In 2010 alone, 93 percent of additional income created in the previous year went to the top 1 percent of taxpayers. (McGoey 2016: 107–8)

8 Indeed, one might suggest that the celebration of techno-philanthropists as "hyper-agents" is but a contemporary permutation on Carnegie's

insistence that inequality and extreme disparities in wealth can be a force for "progress." As he wrote: "We accept and welcome therefore, as conditions to which we must accommodate ourselves, great inequality of environment, the concentration of business, industrial and commercial, in the hands of a few, and the law of competition between these as being not only beneficial, but essential for the future progress of the race" (Carnegie 1889: 2). Retrieved from: https://production-carnegie. s3.amazonaws.com/filer_public/ab/c9/abc9fb4b-dc86-4ce8-ae31-a983b9a326ed/ccny_essay_1889_thegospelofwealth.pdf

9 Taken from his YouTube talk "The Robber Barons vs the Technophilanthropists." Retrieved from: https://www.youtube.com/watch?v=fpTYk52jAhc

10 Given the evangelical zeal with which techno-solutionism is promoted by techno-philanthropists, it might be more apt to coin it techno-solvationism.

11 See https://www.youtube.com/watch?v=N8qA7rVcGUc

12 See https://www.youtube.com/watch?v=N8qA7rVcGUc

13 Žižek, for instance, argues, "liberal communists are the enemy of every true progressive struggle today . . . the direct embodiment of what is wrong with the system . . . They may fight subjective violence, but liberal communists are the agents of structural violence that creates the conditions for explosions of subjective violence" (Žižek 2006).

14 See, for instance, McChesney 2013; Robinson 2014; McGoey 2016; Birn and Richter 2018.

15 See https://www.sv2.org/who-we-are/our-story/

16 When Hero began his work with the foundation, it was called the Community Foundation of Santa Clara County, but in 2006 he oversaw its merger with the San Mateo County-based Peninsula Community Foundation, and the foundation was renamed the Silicon Valley Community Foundation. See https://www.paloaltoonline.com/news/2016/08/22/peter-decourcy-hero-who-transformed-silicon-valley-philanthropy-has-died

17 See https://better.net/chicago/philanthropy/the-best-venture-philanthropy-nonprofits-foundations

18 See https://www.sv2.org

19 https://money.cnn.com/magazines/fortune/fortune_archive/2000/11/27/292465

20 See https://money.cnn.com/magazines/fortune/fortune_archive/2000/11/27/292465

21 See https://money.cnn.com/magazines/fortune/fortune_archive/2000/11/27/292465

22 See https://www.sv2.org/what-we-do/grants-impact-investments/classic-grant-rounds

23 See https://www.sv2.org/what-we-do/grants-impact-investments

24 See https://www.sv2.org/what-we-do/family-philanthropy

25 See https://www.sv2.org/what-we-do/family-philanthropy
26 See https://www.sv2.org/what-we-do/family-philanthropy
27 In his wonderful ethnography *Fresh Fruit, Broken Bodies*, Seth Holmes
    notes a similar phenomenon when writing about the affluent teenagers
    who worked alongside undocumented migrant workers from Mexico
    on the Tanaka Berry Farm in Washington. While the migrants were
    charged with doing the much more strenuous task of picking, the
    teenagers were the ones who weighed the berries they picked and
    determined if they were adequate. Their experience working summer
    jobs on the farm, Holmes notes, led them to believe that they really did
    understand the migrant experience, even though they occupied a much
    more privileged and less taxing position in the farm labor hierarchy. He
    also talks about how it naturalized the idea that it was totally appro-
    priate for white teenagers to be in charge of Mexican adults (Holmes
    2013).
28 See https://www.sv2.org/what-we-do/grants-impact-investments
29 In his article "Feeling Good and Financing Impact," Jacob Hellman
    makes a similar observation, arguing that although impact investors
    claim to promote more rigorous means for assessing social impact, their
    evaluations of what counts as real impact often come down to a set of
    more implicit "affective judgments" (Hellman 2020: 95).
30 See https://www.sv2.org/what-we-do/grants-impact-investments/impact-
    investments
31 See https://thenew.org/org-stories/google-org
32 See https://www.google.org/opportunities
33 For a brief but informative discussion of the history of social enterprise
    in Europe and the United States, see Defourny and Nyssens 2010.
34 Linsey McGoey is correct to note that many of today's philanthrocapi-
    talists no longer feel the need to "disguise" or "minimize self-interest"
    as a rationale for helping others. She writes: "The new philanthropists
    are increasingly proud, triumphant even, about the private economic
    fortunes to be made through embracing philanthrocapitalism. Not
    only is it no longer necessary to 'disguise' or minimize self-interest,
    self-interest is championed as the best rationale for helping others. It is
    seen not as coexisting in tension with altruism, but as a prerequisite *for*
    altruism" (McGoey 2016: 20).
       But upon reading the giving testimonials of several of the SV2
    members, I have found that impact investors are not equally triumphant
    about making private fortunes through embracing philanthrocapitalism.
    What they openly declare and espouse to relish is the social impact they
    are having, rather than the personal financial enrichment it brings.
35 Linsey McGoey observes that the pledge has become quite pervasive
    in the world of philanthrocapitalism. For instance, she notes that at the
    Clinton Global Initiative annual event, "attendees vie to outspend each
    other on the philanthropic pledges they make in the future." She also

points out that pledges do not always translate into actualized commitments. She writes, "The Clinton Global Initiative is a clearing house. Its annual extravaganza permitting donors to announce vast donations secure in the knowledge that a promise is not exactly a binding commitment. There is no global cabal of philanthropic bounty hunters, making sure CGI attendees make good on their pledges" (McGoey 2016: 31).

36 See https://givingpledge.org/About.aspx
37 See https://givingpledge.org/Pledger.aspx?id=158
38 See https://givingpledge.org/Pledger.aspx?id=192
39 See https://givingpledge.org/Pledger.aspx?id=160
40 See https://givingpledge.org/Pledger.aspx?id=314
41 See https://givingpledge.org/Pledger.aspx?id=163
42 See https://givingpledge.org/Pledger.aspx?id=162
43 See https://givingpledge.org/Pledger.aspx?id=395
44 See https://economistsview.typepad.com/economistsview/2006/07/the_gospel_acco.html
45 As Bill and Melinda Gates stated in an interview, "We agree with Andrew Carnegie's wisdom that 'The man who dies rich, dies disgraced,' and we also believe 'he who gives while he lives also knows where it goes.'" See   https://www.reuters.com/article/us-philanthropy-buffett-gates/warren-buffett-bill-gates-ask-billionaires-to-give-away-wealth-idUSTRE65F5CC20100616

Conclusion: The Spirit and Contradictions of Digital Capitalism

1   In his book *Digital Disconnect: How Capitalism is Turning the Internet Against Democracy*, Robert McChesney provides a wonderful example of this kind of doublespeak. He writes:

> As PayPal founder and billionaire Peter Thiel now tells students attending his lectures at Stanford, the moral of the story is that it is time to grow up and accept the new monopoly system. Competition is overrated, even destructive, and capitalism works better with a handful of monopolists "doing something so creative that you establish a market, niche and identity. You've established a creative monopoly and everybody has to come to you if they want that service." (McChesney 2013: 142)

In this view, it is the entrepreneurs behind the handful of monopolies who are the progressive force in society.

2 See: https://www.herox.com/partnerships
3 See: "Facebook Encourages Short-Term, Dopamine-Driven Feedback Loops that are Destroying Society: Ex-Facebook VP of User Growth," Technology News, *Firstpost*. https://www.firstpost.com/tech/news-analysis/facebook-encourages-short-term-dopamine-driven-feedback-

loops-that-are-destroying-society-ex-facebook-vp-of-user-growth-
4254243.html

4 I am grateful to Jathan Sadowski for this insight, which he shared with
me in a podcast interview in 2021. See https://podcast.econanthro.
org/2022/02/15/how-digital-capitalism-is-taking-over-our-lives-a-
conversation-with-jathan-sadowski/

5 This point was also made by Immanuel Wallerstein. He wrote:

> On the face of it, far from being a "natural" system, as some apologists have
> tried to argue, historical capitalism is a patently absurd one. One accumulates
> capital in order to accumulate more capital. Capitalists are like white mice on
> a treadmill, running ever faster in order to run still faster. In the process, no
> doubt, some people live well, but others live miserably; and how well, and for
> how long, do those who live well live? (Wallerstein 1983: 40)

6 See, for instance, Birch 2019; Cook 2019; Fussell 2019.
7 See: https://www.bbc.com/news/technology-59419572
8 See: https://www.brookings.edu/techstream/the-lying-flat-movement-
standing-in-the-way-of-chinas-innovation-drive
9 Quoted in Sadowski 2020: 163.

References

Abend, Gabriel. 2014. *The Moral Background: An Inquiry into the History of Business Ethics*. Princeton: Princeton University Press.

Abercrombie, Nicholas, Hill, Stephen, and Turner, Bryan S. 1980. *The Dominant Ideology Thesis*. London: George Allen & Unwin.

Adorno, Theodor. 2007 (1977). "Free Time," in Max Horkheimer and Theodor Adorno, *Dialectic of Enlightenment: Philosophical Fragments*, ed. Gunzelin Schmid Noerr, trans. Edmund Jephcott. Stanford, CA: Stanford University Press, pp. 162–70.

Althusser, Louis. 1994. "Ideology and Ideological State Apparatuses," in Slavoj Žižek (ed.), *Mapping Ideology*. London: Verso, pp. 100–40.

Andrejevic, Mark. 2009. "Exploiting YouTube: Contradictions of User-generated Labor," in Pelle Snickars and Patrick Vonderau (eds), *The YouTube Reader*. Stockholm: National Library of Sweden, pp. 406–23.

Andrejevic, Mark. 2013. "Estranged Free Labor," in Trebor Scholz (ed.), *Digital Labor: The Internet as Playground and Factory*. New York: Routledge, pp. 149–64.

Andrejevic, Mark. 2016. "The Pacification of Interactivity," in Darin Barney, Gabriella Coleman, Christine Ross, Jonathan Sterne, and Tamar Tembeck (eds), *The Participatory Condition in the Digital Age*. Minneapolis: University of Minnesota Press, pp. 187–205.

Appadurai, Arjun. 2012. "The Spirit of Calculation." *Cambridge Anthropology* 30(1): 3–17.

Appadurai, Arjun. 2016. *Banking on Words: The Failure of Language in the Age of Derivative Finance*. Chicago: University of Chicago Press.

Appadurai, Arjun and Alexander, Neta. 2020. *Failure*. Cambridge: Polity.

Aronowitz, Stanley. 1994. "Technology and the Future of Work," in Gretchen Bender and Timothy Druckery (eds), *Culture on the Brink: Ideologies of Technology*. Seattle: Bay Press, pp. 15–29.

Balibar, Étienne. 1994. *Masses, Classes, Ideas: Studies on Politics and Philosophy Before and After Marx*. London: Routledge.

Barbrook, Richard and Cameron, Andy. 1996. "The California Ideology." *Science as Culture* 26: 44–72.

Baudrillard, Jean. 1981. *For a Critique of the Political Economy of the Sign.* London: Telos.

Bauwens, Michel. 2005. "The Political Economy of Peer Production." *CTheory.* Retrieved from: http://www.ctheory.net/articles.aspx?id

Bell, Daniel. 1996 (1976). *The Cultural Contradictions of Capitalism*, 20th anniversary edn. New York: Basic Books.

Benkler, Yochai. 2004. "Sharing Nicely: On Shareable Goods and the Emergence of Sharing as a Modality of Economic Production." *Yale Law Journal* 114(2): 273–358.

Benkler, Yochai. 2006. *The Wealth of Networks: How Social Production Transforms Markets and Freedom.* New Haven: Yale University Press.

Benzon, Paul. 2020. "Work, Play, and the Banality of the Digital: Boredom as Form," in Shawna Ross and Andrew Pilsch (eds), *Humans at Work in the Digital Age.* London: Routledge, pp. 97–116.

Besterman, Catherine and Gusterson, Hugh (eds). 2019. *Life by Algorithms: How Roboprocesses are Remaking Our World.* Chicago: University of Chicago Press.

Bhattacharya, Sudip, Bashar, Abu, Srivastava, Abhay and Singh, Amarjeet. 2019. "NOMOPHOBIA: NO MObile PHone PhoBIA." *Journal of Family Medicine and Primary Care* 8(4): 1297–300.

Birch, Eugénie. 2019. "Why Is There a Backlash to Smart Cities? An Interview." 12/11. *Brink News* 12/11. Retrieved from: https://www.brinknews.com/why-is-there-a-backlash-to-smart-cities/

Birch, Kean. 2020. "Technoscientific Rent: Toward a Theory of Rentiership for Technoscientific Capitalism." *Science, Technology & Human Values* 45(1): 3–33.

Birn, Anne-Emanuelle and Richter, Judith. 2018. "US Philanthrocapitalism and the Global Health Agenda: The Rockefeller and Gates Foundations, Past and Present," in Howard Waitzkin and the Working Group for Health Beyond Capitalism (eds), *Health Care Under the Knife: Moving Beyond Capitalism for Our Health.* New York: Monthly Review Press.

Bishop, Matthew and Green, Michael. 2009. *Philanthrocapitalism: How Giving Can Save the World.* New York: Bloomsbury Press.

Boltanski, Luc and Chiapello, Eve. 2007. *The New Spirit of Capitalism*, 3rd edn, trans. Gregory Elliott. London: Verso.

Boudreau, Kevin and Lakhani, Karim. 2013. "Using the Crowd as an Innovation Partner." *Harvard Business Review.* Retrieved from: https://hbr.org/2013/04/using-the-crowd-as-an-innovation-partner.

Bourdieu, Pierre. 1984. *Distinction: A Social Critique of the Judgment of Taste*, trans. Richard Nice. Cambridge: Harvard University Press.

Callahan, David. 2017. *The Givers: Wealth, Power, and Philanthropy in a New Gilded Age.* New York: Alfred Knopf.

Calo, Ryan and Rosenblat, Alex. 2017. "The Taking Economy: Uber, Information, and Power." *Columbia Law Review* 117(6): 1623–90.

Cammaerts, Bart. 2016. "Internet-Mediated Mutual Cooperation Practices: The Sharing of Material and Immaterial Resources," in Darin Barney, Gabriella Coleman, Christine Ross, Jonathan Sterne, and Tamar Tembeck (eds), *The Participatory Condition in the Digital Age*. Minneapolis: University of Minnesota Press, pp. 145–66.

Carlton, Frank. 1949. "Competition and Capitalism." *American Journal of Economics and Sociology* 8(3): 251–7.

Carnegie, Andrew. 1889. "The Gospel of Wealth." Retrieved from: https://production-carnegie.s3.amazonaws.com/filer_public/ab/c9/abc9fb4b-dc86-4ce8-ae31-a983b9a326ed/ccny_essay_1889_thegospelofwealth.pdf

Chafkin, Max. 2021. *The Contrarian: Peter Thiel and Silicon Valley's Pursuit of Power*. New York: Penguin Press.

Cheney-Lippold, John. 2017. *We are Data: Algorithms and the Making of Our Digital Selves*. New York: New York University Press.

Chesbrough, Henry. 2006. *Open Innovation: The New Imperative for Creating and Profiting from Technology*. Cambridge: Harvard Business Review Press.

Chiapello, Eve. 2013. "Capitalism and Its Criticisms," in Paul Du Gay and Glenn Morgan (eds), *New Spirits of Capitalism? Crises, Justifications, and Dynamics*. Oxford: Oxford University Press, pp. 60–81.

Chiapello, Eve and Knoll, Lisa. 2020. "Social Finance and Impact Investing: Governing Welfare in the Era of Financialization." *Historical Social Research* 45(3): 7–30.

Chin, Monica. 2019. "My Trip to Amazon Go: The Surveillance State Sure is Convenient." *Tom's Guide* (May). Retrieved from: https://www.tomsguide.com/us/amazon-go-store,news-30035.html

Chun, Wendy. 2008. *Control and Freedom: Power and Paranoia in the Age of Fiber Optics*. Cambridge, MA: MIT Press.

Cockayne, Daniel G. 2016. "Sharing and Neoliberal Discourse: The Economic Function of Sharing in the Digital On-Demand Economy." *Geoforum* 77 (December): 73–82.

Cole, Ryan and Rosenblat, Alex. 2017. "The Taking Economy: Uber, Information, and Power." *Columbia Law Review* 117: 1623–90.

Cook, Morgan. 2019. "Protesters Call for San Diego to Suspend 'Smart Streetlight' Technology, Citing Privacy Concerns." *San Diego Union Tribune* 10/17. Retrieved from: https://www.sandiegouniontribune.com/news/watchdog/story/2019-09-17/protesters-call-for-san-diego-to-suspend-smart-streetlight-technology-ci-privacy-concerns

Couldry, Nick and Mejias, Ulises. 2019. *The Costs of Connection: How Data is Colonizing Human Life and Appropriating It for Capitalism*. Stanford: Stanford University Press.

Davidson, Adam. 2020. *The Passion Economy: The New Rules for Thriving in the Twenty-First Century*. New York: Alfred Knopf.

Defourny, Jacques and Nyssens, Marthe. 2010. "Social Enterprise," in Keith Hart, Jean-Louis Laville, and Antonio David Cattani (eds), *The Human Economy*. Cambridge: Polity, pp. 284–92.

Diamandis, Peter and Kotler, Steven. 2014. *Abundance: The Future is Better Than You Think*. New York: Free Press.

Diamandis, Peter and Kotler, Steven. 2015. *Bold: How to Go Big, Create Wealth, and Impact the World*. New York: Simon & Schuster.

Dumont, Louis. 1970. *Homo Hierarchicus: The Caste System and Its Implications*, 2nd edn. Chicago: University of Chicago Press.

Dyer-Witheford, Nick. 2015. *Cyber-Proletariat: Global Labor in the Digital Vortex*. Toronto: Pluto Press.

Eagleton, Terry. 2007. *Ideology: An Introduction*. London: Verso.

Eikenberry, Angela and Drapal Kluver, Jodie. 2004. "The Marketization of the Nonprofit Sector: Civil Society at Risk?" *Public Administration Review* 64(2): 132–40.

Elkind, Peter. 2000. "The Man who Sold Silicon Valley on Giving in the Land of the "Cyber-Stingy," Peter Hero Convinced High-Tech Millionaires that Charity Could be as Cutting-Edge as Any Startup." *Fortune*. Retrieved from: https://money.cnn.com/magazines/fortune/fortune_archive/2000/11/27/292465/

Eubanks, Virginia. 2017. *Automating Inequality: How High-Tech Tools Profile, Police, and Punish the Poor*. New York: St Martin's Press.

Ewen. Stuart. 1976. *Captains of Consciousness*. New York: McGraw-Hill.

Farman, Abou. 2020. *On Not Dying: Secular Immortality in the Age of Technoscience*. Minneapolis: University of Minnesota Press.

Farrington, Robert. 2021. "InboxDollars Review: Earn Money Completing Online Tasks at Home." *The College Investor* 9/16. Retrieved from: https://thecollegeinvestor.com/19965/inbox-dollars-review/.

Fisher, Adam. 2018. *Valley of Genius: The Uncensored History of Silicon Valley (as Told by the Hackers, Founders, and Freaks who Made It Boom)*. New York: Twelve Press.

Fisher, Eran. 2010. *Media and New Capitalism in the Digital Age: The Spirit of Networks*. New York: Palgrave Macmillan.

Fisher, Eran. 2017. "How Less Alienation Creates More Exploitation? Audience Labor on Social Network Sites," in Christian Fuchs and Vincent Mosco (eds), *Marx in the Age of Digital Capitalism*. Chicago: Haymarket Books, pp.180–203.

Fisher, Mark. 2009. *Capitalist Realism: Is There No Alternative?* Washington: Zero Books.

Foster, Robert. 2007. "The Work of the New Economy: Consumers, Brands, and Value Creation." *Cultural Anthropology* 22(4): 707–31.

Fourcade, Marion and Healy, Kieran. 2017. "Seeing Like a Market." *Socio-Economic Review* 15(1): 9–29.

Frumkin, Peter. 2003. "Inside Venture Philanthropy." *Society* 40: 7–15. https://doi.org/10.1007/s12115-003-1013-0

Fuchs, Christian. 2019. *Rereading Marx in the Age of Digital Capitalism*. Northampton: Pluto Press.

Fuchs, Christian and Fisher, Eran (eds). 2015. *Reconsidering Value and Labour in the Digital Age*. New York: Palgrave Macmillan.

Fussell, Sidney. 2019. "Why Hong Kongers are Toppling Lampposts." *The Atlantic*, August 30. Retrieved from: https://www.theatlantic.com/technology/archive/2019/08/why-hong-kong-protesters-are-cutting-down-lampposts/597145/

Galbraith, John Kenneth. 1987 (1958). *The Affluent Society*. Harmondsworth: Penguin Books.

Geras. Norman. 1983. *Marx and Human Nature: Refutation of a Legend*. London: Verso.

Ghosh, Ipshita. 2020. "Investment, Value, and the Making of Entrepreneurship in India." *Economic Anthropology* 7: 190–202.

Ghosh, Ipshita. 2021. "A Tale of Two Start-Up Fests: Imaginaries of Future Making in India." Paper presented at the 2021 AAA. Baltimore, MD.

Gilpin, Lindsey. 2014. "GE Launches Microfactory to Co-create the Future of Manufacturing." *Tech Republic*. Retrieved from: https://www.techrepublic.com/article/ge-launches-microfactory-to-co-create-the-future-of-manufacturing/

Giridharadas. Anand. 2019. *Winners Take All: The Elite Charade of Changing the World*. New York: Vintage Books.

Godelier, Maurice. 1999. *The Enigma of the Gift*. Chicago: University of Chicago Press.

Golumbia, David. 2009. "Games Without Play." *New Literary History* 40(1): 179–204.

Graeber, David. 2018. *Bullshit Jobs: A Theory*. New York: Simon & Schuster.

Gray, Mary L. and Suri, Siddharth. 2019. *Ghost Work: How to Stop Silicon Valley from Building a New Global Underclass*. Boston: Houghton Mifflin Harcourt.

Guilhot, Nicolas. 2007. "Reforming the World: George Soros, Global Capitalism and the Philanthropic Management of the Social Sciences." *Critical Sociology* 33: 447–77, 451.

Gusterson, Hugh. 2019. "Introduction: Robohumans," in Catherine Besteman and Hugh Gusterson (eds), *Life by Algorithms: How Roboprocesses are Remaking Our World*. Chicago: University of Chicago Press, pp. 1–27.

Habermas, Jürgen. 1970. "Technology and Science as 'Ideology,'" in *Toward a Rational Society: Student Protests, Science, and Politics*. Boston: Beacon Press, pp. 81–122.

Harhoff, Dietmar and Lakhani, Karim (eds). 2016. *Revolutionizing Innovation: Users, Communities and Open Innovation*. Cambridge, MA: MIT Press.

Hart, Keith, Laville, Jean-Louis, and Cattani, Antonio (eds). 2010. *The Human Economy*. Cambridge, UK: Polity Press.

Harvey, David. 1990. *The Condition of Postmodernity: An Enquiry into the Conditions of Cultural Change*. Cambridge: Blackwell Publishers.

Haven, Janet and boyd, danah. 2020. "Philanthropy's Techno-solutionism Problem." Data & Society Research Institute. Retrieved from: https://knightfoundation.org/philanthropys-techno-solutionism-problem/

Heilbroner, Robert. 1985. *The Nature and Logic of Capitalism*. New York: W. W. Norton.

Hellman, Jacob. 2020. "Feeling Good and Financing Impact." *Historical Social Research* 45(3): 95–116.

Hero, Peter. 2001. "Giving Back the Silicon Valley Way: Emerging Patterns of a New Philanthropy." *New Directions for Philanthropic Fundraising* 3: 47–57.

Hesmondhalgh, David. 2010. "User-Generated Content, Free Labour and the Cultural Industries." *Ephemera* 10 (3–4): 267–84.

Hirschman, Albert. 1997 (1977). *The Passions and the Interests: Political Arguments for Capitalism before Its Triumph*, 20th anniversary edn. Princeton: Princeton University Press.

Holmes, Seth. 2013. *Fresh Fruit, Broken Bodies: Migrant Farmworkers in the United States*. Berkeley: University of California Press.

Howe, Jeff. 2006. "The Rise of Crowdsourcing." *Wired* 6/01. Retrieved from: https://www.wired.com/2006/06/crowds

Howe, Jeff. 2008. *Crowdsourcing: Why the Power of the Crowd is Driving the Future of Business*. New York: Random House.

Howe, Jeff. 2010. "Actions and Inventions Come First," in Jake Nickell (ed.), *Threadless: Ten Years of T-shirts from the World's Most Inspiring Online Design Community*. New York: Abrams, pp. 114–15.

Huberman, Jenny. 2021. "Amazon Go, Surveillance Capitalism, and the Ideology of Convenience." *Economic Anthropology* 8(2): 337–49.

Huws, Ursula. 2020. "Reaping the Whirlwind: Digitalization, Restructuring, and Mobilization in the Covid Crisis," in Leo Panitch and Greg Albo (eds), *Beyond Digital Capitalism: New Ways of Living*. London: Merlin Press.

Hyken, Shep. 2018. *The Convenience Revolution: How to Deliver a Customer Service Experience that Disrupts the Competition and Creates Fierce Loyalty*. Shippensburg, PA: SOUND WISDOM.

Iansiti, Marco and Lakhani, Karim. 2017. "Managing our Hub Economy." *Harvard Business Review* September–October. Retrieved from: https://hbr.org/2017/09/managing-our-hub-economy

Jameson, Fredric. 1991. *Postmodernism: Or, the Cultural Logic of Late Capitalism*. Durham: Duke University Press.

Jeffrey, Craig. 2010. *Timepass: Youth, Class, and the Politics of Waiting in India*. Stanford: Stanford University Press.

John, Nicholas. 2017. *The Age of Sharing*. Cambridge: Polity Press.

Jordan, Tim. 2015. *Information Politics: Liberation and Exploitation in the Digital Society*. London: Pluto Press.

Kalleberg, Arne. 2009. "Precarious Work, Insecure Workers: Employment Relations in Transition." *American Sociological Review* 74(1): 1–22.

Kaplan, David. 1999. *The Silicon Valley Boys and Their Valley of Dreams*. New York: William Morrow and Company.

Khan, Shamus. 2011. *Privilege: The Making of an Adolescent Elite at St Paul's School*. Princeton: Princeton University Press.

Kumar. Raj. 2019. *The Business of Changing the World: How Billionaires, Tech Disrupters, and Social Entrepreneurs are Transforming the Global Aid Industry.* Boston: Beacon Press.

Kwet, Michael. 2019. "Digital Colonialism: US Empire and the New Imperialism in the Global South." *Race & Class* 60(4): 3–26.

Laclau, Ernesto. 1977. *Politics and Ideology.* London: Verso.

LaGrandeur, Kevin and Hughes, James. 2017. *Surviving the Machine Age: Intelligent Technology and the Transformation of Human Work.* New York: Palgrave Macmillan.

Lakhani, Karim. 2016. "Managing Communities and Contests to Innovate," in Dietmar Harhoff and Karim Lakhani (eds), *Revolutionizing Innovation: Users, Communities, and Open Innovation.* Cambridge, MA: MIT Press, pp. 109–35.

Le Bon, Gustave. 2002 (1895). *The Crowd: A Study of the Popular Mind.* New York: Dover Publications.

Lessig, Lawrence. 2008. *Remix: Making Art and Commerce Thrive in the Hybrid Economy.* New York: Penguin Books.

Letts, Christine, Ryan, William, and Grossman, Allen. 1997. "Virtuous Capital: What Foundations Can Learn from Venture Capitalists." *Harvard Business Review*, March–April, pp. 2–7.

Lincoln, Bruce. 1989. *Discourse and the Construction of Society.* New York: Oxford University Press.

MacKenzie, Donald. 2018. "Material Signals: A Historical Sociology of High-Frequency Trading." *American Journal of Sociology* 123(6): 1635–83.

Madianou, Mirca. 2019. "Technocolonialism: Digital Innovation and Data Practices in the Humanitarian Response to Refugee Crises." *Social Media + Society* 5(3): 1–13.

Madrigal, Alexis. 2017. "What Facebook Did to American Democracy and Why It was So Hard to See It Coming." *The Atlantic* 10(12). https://www. theatlantic.com/technology/archive/2017/10/what-facebook-did/542502/

Mandeville, Bernard. 1997. *The Fable of the Bees and Other Writings.* United States: Hackett Publishing Company.

Marcuse, Herbert. 1964. *One-Dimensional Man.* Boston: Beacon Press.

Marx, Karl. 1978 (1844). "Economic and Philosophic Manuscripts of 1844," in Robert Tucker (ed.), *The Marx–Engels Reader.* New York: W. W. Norton, pp. 66–125.

Marx, Karl. 1978 (1867). *Capital, Volume One*, in Robert Tucker (ed.), *The Marx–Engels Reader*, 2nd edn. New York: W. W. Norton.

Mauss, Marcel. 1925. *The Gift: The Form and Reason for Exchange.* London: W. W. Norton.

Mayer-Schönberger, Viktor. 2009. *Delete: The Virtue of Forgetting in the Digital Age.* Princeton: Princeton University.

McAfee, Andrew and Brynjolfsson, Erik. 2017. *Machine, Platform, Crowd: Harnessing Our Digital Future.* New York: W. W. Norton.

McChesney, Robert. 2013. *Digital Disconnect: How Capitalism is Turning the Internet Against Democracy.* New York: The New Press.

McGoey, Linsey. 2016. *No Such Thing as a Free Gift: The Gates Foundation and the Price of Philanthropy.* London: Verso.

McKenzie, Monique de Jong. 2020. "Micro-assets and Portfolio Management in the New Platform Economy." *Distinktion: Journal of Social Theory.* Retrieved from: https://www.tandfonline.com/doi/abs/10.1080/1600910 X.2020.1734847

McNulty, Paul. 1968. "Economic Theory and the Meaning of Competition." *Quarterly Journal of Economics* 82(4): 639–56.

Mellos, Koula. 1978. "Developments in Advanced Capitalist Ideology." *Canadian Journal of Political Science* 11(4): 829–61.

Morozov, Evgeny. 2014. *To Save Everything, Click Here: The Folly of Technological Solutionism.* New York: Public Affairs.

Mosco, Vincent. 2004. *The Digital Sublime: Myth, Power, and Cyberspace.* Cambridge, MA: MIT Press.

Nadeem, Shehzad. 2015. "On the Sharing Economy." *Contexts* 14(1): 12–14.

Nickell, Jake. 2010. *Threadless: Ten Years of T-shirts from the World's Most Inspiring Online Design Community.* New York: Abrams.

Noble, David. 1999. *The Religion of Technology: The Divinity of Man and the Spirit of Invention.* New York: Basic Books.

O'Neil, Cathy. 2016. *Weapons of Math Destruction: How Big Data Increases Inequality and Threatens Democracy.* New York: Random House.

O'Neill, Bruce. 2017. *The Space of Boredom: Homelessness in the Slowing Global Order.* Durham: Duke University Press.

Orta, Andrew. 2019. *Making Global MBAs: The Culture of Business and the Business of Culture.* Berkeley: University of California Press.

Palmer, Bryan. 2020. "The Time of Our Lives: Reflections on Work and Capitalist Temporality," in Leo Panitch and Greg Albo (eds), *Beyond Digital Capitalism: New Ways of Living.* London: Merlin Press.

Perelman, Michael. 2011. "Decoding Economic Ideology." *World Review of Political Economy* 2(1): 76–89.

Piketty, Thomas. 2020. *Capital and Ideology,* trans. Arthur Goldhammer. Cambridge: Belknap Press of Harvard University.

Prahalad, Coimbatore Krishnarao. 2004. *The Fortune at the Bottom of the Pyramid: Eradicating Poverty through Profits.* Upper Saddle River: Prentice Hall.

Rasiel, Ethan. 1999. *The McKinsey Way: Using Techniques of the World's Top Strategic Consultants to Help You and Your Business.* New York: McGraw-Hill.

Raymen, Thomas and Smith, Oliver. 2017. "Lifestyle Gambling, Indebtedness and Anxiety: A Deviant Leisure Perspective." *Journal of Consumer Culture* 20(4): 381–99.

Reffell, Clive. 2019. "HeroX: The Social Network of Prize Challenges." *Crowdsourcing Week* 7/2.

Rego, Mark. 2021. *Frontal Fatigue: The Impact of Modern Life and Technology on Mental Illness*. Austin: River Grove Books.

Reich, Robert. 2015. "The Share-the-Scraps Economy." Retrieved from: https://robertreich.org/post/109894095095

Reich, Rob. 2018. *Just Giving: Why Philanthropy is Failing Democracy and How It Can Do Better*. Princeton: Princeton University Press.

Reith, Gerda. 2002. *The Age of Chance: Gambling in Western Culture*. London: Routledge.

Ries, Eric. 2014. *The Lean Startup: How Today's Entrepreneurs Use Continuous Innovation to Create Radically Successful Businesses*. New York: Currency Press.

Roberto, Michael. 2018. *The Coming of the American Behemoth: The Origins of Fascism in the United States 1920–1940*. New York: Monthly Review Press.

Robey, Tracy. 2017. "What Happened to the Internet's Favorite T-Shirt Company?" *Racked* 6(11). Retrieved from: https://www.racked.com/2017/11/6/16551468/threadless-t-shirts-ecommerce

Robins, Kevin and Webster, Frank. 1999. *Times of Technoculture: From the Information Society to Virtual Life*. London: Routledge.

Robinson, William. 2014. *Global Capitalism and the Crisis of Humanity*. Cambridge: Cambridge University Press.

Roderick, Leanne. 2014. "Discipline and Power in the Digital Age: The Case of the US Consumer Data Broker Industry." *Critical Sociology* 40(5): 729–46.

Rosenblat, Alex. 2018. *Uberland: How Algorithms are Rewriting the Rules of Work*. Oakland: University of California Press.

Ross, Andrew. 2013. "In Search of the Lost Paycheck," in Trebor Scholz (ed.), *Digital Labor: The Internet as Playground and Factory*. New York: Routledge, pp. 13–32.

Sadowski, Jathan. 2019. "When Data is Capital: Datafication, Accumulation, and Extraction." *Big Data & Society* (January–June): 1–12.

Sadowski, Jathan. 2020. *Too Smart: How Digital Capitalism is Extracting Data, Controlling Our Lives, and Taking Over the World*. Cambridge, MA: MIT Press.

Sahlins, Marshall. 1972. *Stone Age Economics*. New York: Aldine de Gruyter.

Sahlins, Marshall. 2008. *The Western Illusion of Human Nature*. Chicago: Prickly Paradigm Press.

Schervish, Paul. 2003. "Hyperagency and High-Tech Donors: A New Theory of the New Philanthropists." Social Welfare Research Institute, Boston College. http://hdl.handle.net/2345/bc-ir:104107

Schiller, Dan. 1999. *Digital Capitalism: Networking the Global Market System*. Cambridge, MA: MIT Press.

Scholz, Trebor. 2013. "Why Does Digital Labor Matter Now?" in Trebor Scholz (ed.), *Digital Labor: The Internet as Playground and Factory*. New York: Routledge, pp. 1–10.

Scholz, Trebor and Schneider, Nathan (eds). 2017. *Ours to Hack and to Own: The Rise of Platform Cooperativism, a New Vision for the Future of Work and a Fairer Internet*. New York: OR Books.

Schor, Juliet. 2020. *After the Gig: How the Sharing Economy Got Hijacked and How to Win It Back*. Berkeley: University of California Press.

Schrauwen, Ben. 2019. "Microfactories Move to Full Production." *Industry Week*, Feb. 20. Retrieved from: https://www.industryweek.com/technology-and-iiot/article/22027187/microfactories-move-to-full-production

Schüll, Natasha Dow. 2012. *Addiction by Design: Machine Gambling in Las Vegas*. Princeton: Princeton University Press.

Scott, James. 1976. *The Moral Economy of the Peasant: Rebellion and Subsistence in Southeast Asia*. New Haven: Yale University Press.

Segal, Howard. 1985. *Technological Utopianism in American Culture*. Chicago, IL: University of Chicago Press.

Sennett, Richard. 2006. *The Culture of the New Capitalism*. New Haven: Yale University Press.

Sennett, Richard. 2011. *The Corrosion of Character: The Personal Consequences of Work in the New Capitalism*. New York: W. W. Norton.

Sennett, Richard. 2012. *Together: The Rituals, Pleasures, and Politics of Cooperation*. New Haven: Yale University Press.

Shirky, Clay. 2008. *Here Comes Everybody: The Power of Organizing Without Organizations*. New York: Penguin Books.

Shirky, Clay. 2011. *Cognitive Surplus: How Technology Makes Consumers into Collaborators*. New York: Penguin Books.

Smith, Adam. 1977. *An Inquiry into the Nature and Causes of the Wealth of Nations*. Chicago: University of Chicago Press.

Smythe, Dallas W. 1981. *Dependency Road*. Norwood, NJ: Ablex.

Snider, Mike and Baig, Edward. 2019. "Facebook Fined $5 Billion by FTC, Must Update and Adopt New Privacy, Security Measures." *USA Today* 7(24). Retrieved from: https://www.usatoday.com/story/tech/news/2019/07/24/facebook-pay-record-5-billion-fine-u-s-privacy-violations/1812499001/

Soper, Taylor. 2014. "Make Money in Your Free Time: Spare5 Raises $3.25m from Madrona, Foundry, NEA for On-Demand Work Platform." *GeekWire* 12(14). Retrieved from: https://www.geekwire.com/2014/make-money-free-time-spare5-raises-3-25m-madrona-foundry-demand-work-platform/

Sorokin, Pitirim. 2017. "Foreword," in Charles Loomis (ed. and trans.), *Community and Society* by Ferdinand Tönnies. Eastford: Martino Fine Books.

Srnicek, Nick. 2017. *Platform Capitalism*. Cambridge: Polity Press.

Standing, Guy. 2011. *The Precariat: The New Dangerous Class*. London: Bloomsbury Press.

Standing, Guy. 2017. *The Corruption of Capitalism: Why Rentiers Thrive and Work Does Not Pay*. London: Biteback Publishing.

Stephany, Alex. 2015. *The Business of Sharing: Making It in the New Sharing Economy*. Basingstoke: Palgrave Macmillan.

Stinson, Liz. 2014. "How GE Plans to Act like a Startup and Crowdsource Breakthrough Ideas." *Wired*. Retrieved from: https://www.wired.com/2014/04/how-ge-plans-to-act-like-a-startup-and-crowdsource-great-ideas/

Stout, Noelle. 2019. *Dispossessed: How Predatory Bureaucracy Foreclosed on the American Middle Class*. Oakland: University of California Press.

Sullivan, Oriel and Gershuny, Jonathan. 2004. "Inconspicuous Consumption: Work-Rich, Time-Poor in the Liberal Market Economy." *Journal of Consumer Culture* 4(1): 79–100.

Sundararajan, Arun. 2016. *The Sharing Economy: The End of Employment and the Rise of Crowd-Based Capitalism*. Cambridge: MIT Press.

Surowiecki, James. 2005. *The Wisdom of Crowds*. New York: Anchor Books.

Taylor, Linnet and Broeders, Dennis. 2015. "In the Name of Development: Power, Profit and the Datafication of the Global South." *Geoforum* 64: 229–37.

Terranova, Tiziana. 2004. *Network Culture: Politics for the Information Age*. London: Pluto Press.

Terranova, Tiziana. 2013. "Free Labor," in Trebor Scholz (ed.), *Digital Labor: The Internet as Playground and Factory*. New York: Routledge, pp. 33–57.

Thompson, John. 1990. *Ideology and Modern Culture*. Stanford: Stanford University Press.

Tierney, Thomas. 1993. *The Value of Convenience: A Genealogy of Technical Culture*. Albany: SUNY Press.

Tönnies, Ferdinand. 2017 (1887). *Community and Society*, trans. and ed. Charles Loomis. Eastford: Martino Fine Books.

Tooze, Adam. 2018. *Crashed: How a Decade of Financial Crisis Changed the World*. London: Penguin Books.

Toscano, Joe. 2018. *Automating Humanity*. Canada: Power House Books.

Turner, Fred. 2006. *From Counterculture to Cyberculture: Stewart Brand, the Whole Earth Network, and the Rise of Digital Utopianism*. Chicago: University of Chicago Press.

Turner, Fred. 2013. *The Democratic Surround: Multimedia and American Liberalism from World War II to the Psychedelic Sixties*. Chicago: University of Chicago Press.

Valentine, David. 2012. "Exit Strategy: Profit, Cosmology, and the Future of Humans in Space." *Anthropological Quarterly* 85: 1045–67.

van Dijck, José. 2014. "Datafication, Dataism and Dataveillance: Big Data between Scientific Paradigm and Ideology." *Surveillance & Society* 12(2): 197–208.

Veblen, Thorstein. 1967 (1912). *The Theory of the Leisure Class*. New York: Viking.

Verkerk, Maarten. 2013. "Social Entrepreneurship and Impact Investing." *Philosophia Reformata* 78(2): 209–21.

Verzijil, Diederik, Dervojeda, Kristina, Nagtegaal, Fabian, and Jorn Sjauw-Koen-Fa, PwC Netherlands, and Probst, Laurent and Frideres, Laurent, PwC Luxembourg. 2014. (Technical Report) *Smart Factories: Crowdsourced Manufacturing*. Business Innovation Observatory Contract No 190/PP/ENT/CIP/12/C/N03C01.

Von Hippel, Eric. 2006. *Democratizing Innovation*. Cambridge, MA: MIT Press.

Wallerstein, Immanuel. 1983. *Historical Capitalism with Capitalist Civilization*. London: Verso.

Wexler, Max. 2011. "Reconfiguring the Sociology of the Crowd: Exploring Crowdsourcing." *International Journal of Sociology and Social Policy* 3(1–2): 6–20.

Whyte, William. 2002 (1956). *The Organization Man*. Philadelphia: University of Pennsylvania Press.

Winsor, John, Paik, Jin, Tushman, Mike, and Lakhani, Karim. 2019. "Overcoming Cultural Resistance to Open Source Innovation." *Strategy & Leadership* 47(6): 28–33.

Wittel, Andreas. 2017. "Digital Marx: Toward a Political Economy of Distributed Media," in Christian Fuchs and Vincent Mosco (eds), *Marx in the Age of Digital Capitalism*. Chicago: Haymarket Books, pp. 68–104.

Wuerch, Jason. 2021. "Spare 5 App Review: Scam or Legit Money Making App 2021?" *Frugalforless*. Retrieved from: htpps://www/frugalgorless.com/spare5-review

Young, Martin. 2010. "Gambling, Capitalism and the State: Towards a New Dialectic of the Risk Society?" *Journal of Consumer Culture* 10(2): 254–73.

Zhao, Yuezhi and Schiller, Dan. 2001. "Dances with Wolves? China's Integration into Digital Capitalism." *Info* 3(2): 137–51.

Žižek, Slavoj. 1994. "The Specter of Ideology," in Slavoj Žižek (ed.), *Mapping Ideology*. London: Verso, pp. 1–33.

Žižek, Slavoj. 2006. "Nobody Has to be Vile." *London Review of Books* 28(7) (April). Retrieved from: https://www.lrb.co.uk/the-paper/v28/n07/slavoj-zizek/nobody-has-to-be-vile

Zuboff, Shoshana. 2019. *The Age of Surveillance Capitalism: The Fight for a Human Future at the New Frontier of Power*. London: Profile Books.

Zunz, Olivier. 2012. *Philanthropy in America: A History*. Princeton: Princeton University Press.

Index

Abercrombie, Nicholas, 166n10
Adorno, Theodor, 79
affective surplus, 134
aid industry, 103, 105
Alexa, 143
Alexander, Neta, 162n3
Alibaba, 156n49
Amazon
  advertising, 5, 39, 97
  Amazon Go, 17, 80, 81–3, 85, 86, 87–95, 97–8, 136–7
  data selling, 92
  hub firm, 156n49
  justifications, 129
  Make Amazon Pay, 145
  nudging, 86
  promises, 12
  stock value, 102
  success, 81
  surveillance capitalism, 84
American Dream, 23
Ancient Greece, 121–2
Andreessen, Marc, 158n13
Andrejevic, Mark, 139–40
anxiety, 142–3
Apache, 46
Appadurai, Arjun, 13–14, 15, 162n3
Apple, 12, 46, 81, 156n49
Arnold, Laura and John, 123
Arrillaga-Andreessen, Laura, 113–14
Arsenault, Marcel and Cynda Collins, 123

Baidu, 156n49
Barbrook, Richard, 27
Bauwens, Michel, 152n13
behavioral surplus, 5, 17, 82, 83–4, 85, 90–1, 97
Bell, Daniel, 3
Bencke, Matt, 70, 73, 76, 162n4
Benkler, Yochai, 18–19, 61–3, 135, 136
Benzon, Paul, 57, 78
Bernays, Edward, 72
Bezos, Jeff, 86, 87, 97, 102, 103, 136
Bhattacharya, Sudip, 79
big data, 6
Big Other, 69–70, 83, 84–5, 93, 97, 136
Bingo Box, 66
Bishop, Matthew, 103–4, 106, 138, 139
Boltanski, Luc
  American cultural contradictions, 16
  concept of ideology, 18
  justifying capitalism, 144–5
  methodology, 15
  new spirit of capitalism, 12, 128–9, 131, 132
  shared representations, 1
  spirits of capitalism, 7–11, 17, 35, 127, 130, 160n25
  techno-philanthropy and, 101
Boudreau, Kevin, 31–3
Bourdieu, Pierre, 28
bourgeois values, 8–9, 37

boyd, danah, 106
Brand, Stewart, 130
Brin, Sergey, 119
Buffet, Warren, 120, 122, 123

Callahan, David, 102, 124
Calo, Ryan, 154n37
Cameron, Andy, 27
Candy Jam, 71
capitalism
  aims, 4
  cultural contradictions, 3–4
  digital capitalism *see* digital
    capitalism
  Protestantism and, 3, 13
  reproduction, 2
  spirits *see* spirits of capitalism
  see also Boltanski, Luc; Chiapello,
    Eve; Marx, Karl
Carnegie, Andrew, 102, 104, 110,
  123–4, 126, 169n8
Cash Karma, 66
Chan, Priscilla, 122–3
charity *see* techno-philanthropy
Cheney-Lippold, John, 128
Chesbrough, Henry, 62
Chiapello, Eve
  American cultural contradictions, 16
  capitalist recuparation of criticism,
    119
  concept of ideology, 18
  impact investing, 36
  justifying capitalism, 144–5
  methodology, 15
  new spirit of capitalism, 12, 128–9,
    131, 132
  shared representations, 1
  spirits of capitalism, 7–11, 17, 35,
    127, 130, 160n25, 168n29
  techno-philanthropy and, 101
Chin, Monica, 90
China, 13
City Light Capital, 34–5
Cockayne, Daniel, 59, 134
cognitive surplus, 26, 41, 54, 59, 133,
  134
Cole, Ryan, 59
Colgate-Palmolive, 42
collaboration
  community in society, 43–7

crowdsourcing model, 22, 43–64
  accidental business, 50–5
  assessment, 59–64
  forms, 50–5
  going corporate, 55–9
  negative reciprocity, 49–50, 60, 134
  human nature, 47–50
  new forms, 4
colonialism, 6
community
  community crowdsourcing, 134
  discourse, 130
  role in society, 43–7
  Tönnies on, 44–5, 59–60
  see also collaboration
competition
  collaboration and, 132–5
  crowdsourcing, 20–42
    assessment, 41–2
    democratization of innovation,
      38–9, 41–2
    HeroX, 23, 25, 30–1, 34–41, 42,
      47–8, 133–4
    ideology, 22–7
    leveling playing field, 27–9
    model, 21–2
    negative reciprocity, 31, 33–4,
      133, 134
    networks, 39–41
    paying winners only, 29–34
    platform capitalism, 34–41
    unremunerated labor, 31–2
  Diamandis, 23–33
  globalization and, 10, 11, 12
  labor market, 47
  protecting, 37–41
  saving the world, 22–7
  smartness, 26–7
concept leaders, 58
convenience
  Amazon Go, 81–3, 86, 87–95,
    97–8, 136, 145
  assessment, 95–9
  creep factor, 90, 98
  friction reduction, 95, 97
  ideology, 17, 81–99
    naturalization, 87–90, 96
    obfuscation, 90–2
    promotion, 93–5
  see also surveillance capitalism

coral reefs, 26
Cotichini, Christian, 25, 34–5, 36–7, 40, 42, 47–8
Couldry, Nick, 140
COVID-19, 71
Creative Commons License, 57, 58
creativity, 11, 12, 37, 46, 55, 57, 135–6, 143
creep factor, 90, 98
Crocker, Betty, 95–6
crowds
    appeal to unconscious, 153n20
    Le Bon on, 20–1, 41, 153n20
    political resource, 41
    wisdom, 20–1, 43
crowdsourcing
    collaboration model, 22, 43–64
        accidental business, 50–5
        assessment, 59–64
        benefits, 43
        community, 44–7
        forms, 50–5
        going corporate, 55–9
        human nature, 47–50
    competition model
        assessment, 41–2
        HeroX, 23, 25, 30–1, 34–41, 42, 47–8, 133–4
        ideology, 22–7
        leveling playing field, 27–9
        meaning, 21–2
        minimizing risk, 31
        negative reciprocity, 31, 33–4, 133, 134
        networks, 39–41
        paying winners only, 29–34
        platform capitalism, 34–7
        protecting competition, 37–41
        unremunerated labor, 31–2
    competition vs collaboration, 132–5
    ghost workers, 6
    global recession (2008) and, 29–30
    meaning, 21
    models, 21–2
    rise, 130
    surplus value, 61, 66
cultural capital, 27
cultural relativism, x
cyber-proletariat, 6

data collection, uses, 6
Davidson, Adam, 134
DeHart, Jacob, 50–3
democracy
    capitalism and, 3
    democratization of innovation, 35, 37, 38–9, 41–2, 43, 132–3
    democratization of internet, 62, 135
    digital capitalism and, 4, 7, 12, 19, 26
    doublespeak, 4
    networks and, 61
    philanthropy and, 103, 104, 112
    social media and, 145
    surveillance capitalism and, 83, 91, 93
    value, 143–4
democratic socialism, 1, 2
Diamandis, Peter
    cheap labor, 94
    cognitive surplus, 133
    competitive crowdsourcing, 23–33, 34–5, 36, 40, 42, 52, 133
    emotional surplus, 54
    influences, 105
    market world, 105
    techno-philanthropy, 100, 104, 108, 118
digital capitalism
    cultural contradictions, 13, 127–46
        consequences, 139–45
    doublespeak, 132–3, 141, 143, 145
    glimmers of hope, 145–6
    heroes, 14, 131
    operation, 4–7
    Silicon Valley, 11–16
    spirit, 128–32
digital colonialism, 6
doublespeak, 4, 132, 133, 141, 143, 145
Drapal Kluver, Jodie, 119
Dumont, Louis, 18
Durkheim, Emile, 143
Dyer-Witheford, Nick, 6

Eagleton, Terry, 18, 82, 86, 87, 93, 97, 98, 166n10, 167n12
earthquakes, 26
eBay, 100

Efficiency Movement, 110
Eikenberry, Angela, 119
Elkind, Peter, 114
Ellison, Larry, 121
emancipation, 18–19, 25, 29–20, 61, 63, 93, 101, 125, 134, 144
emotional surplus, 54, 59
Ewen, Stuart, 167n14

Facebook
   addictive technology, 141
   advertising, 39, 143
   data selling, 92
   hub firm, 156n49
   mega corporation, 12
   privacy and, 145
   surveillance capitalism, 84
factory inspectors, 65–6
financial crisis (2008), 29, 74, 154
financial sector, 13–14
FirstBuild, 56–9
Fisher, Eran, 3, 25, 26, 48–9, 55, 94, 101, 125, 134, 156n47
flexibility
   current virtue, 30, 129
   flexible accumulation, 3, 10–11
   labor, 7, 12, 59
   social effect, 143
food security, 27
Fordism, 3, 9–10, 131, 134
Foster, Robert, 53–4
Fourcade, Marion, 6
Fowler, Emily, 30, 33, 34–5, 36
free market
   competition, 37–8
   ideology, 1, 2, 27
   political freedom and, 9
   techno-philanthropy and, 104–6, 132
freedom
   illusion, 140–1
   Marx on, 97
   surveillance capitalism and, 91–2
   value, 143
friction reduction, 95, 97
Frumkin, Peter, 111–12
Fuchs, Christian, 147n5, 148n8

Galbraith, John Kenneth, 167n14
gaming see smartphone gaming apps

Gates, Bill, 28, 105, 109, 120, 123, 172n45
Gates, Frederick T., 110
Gates, Melinda, 120, 172n45
Gates Foundation, 107–8
General Electric (GE), 42, 55–9, 60, 63, 134–5
General Mills, 51
Gershuny, Jonathan, 164n36
Ghosh, Ipshita, 13
ghost workers, 6, 85
gift
   business of giving, 110–12
   Giving Pledge, 120–4, 125–6
   power, 124–6
   techno-philanthropy, 101–2
Gilded Age, 102–3
Gilpin, Lindsey, 160n25
Giridharadas, Anand, 104–5, 153n19
Giving Pledge, 120–4, 125–6, 139
Global Business Network, 130
Global South, 6
globalization, 10, 11, 12, 102, 129
Godelier, Maurice, 161n31
Golumbia, David, 78–9
Google
   advertising, 5, 39, 100
   data selling, 92
   hub firm, 156n49
   promises, 12
   social enterprise, 119
   surveillance capitalism, 84
Google.org, 107, 119
Gottesman, Greg, 77, 79
GrabCAD, 56
Graeber, David, 47, 135
Gray, Mary, 6, 85
Great Depression, 103
Green, Michael, 103–4, 106, 138, 139
Grossman, Allen, 111
GSN Casino, 71
Guilhot, Nicolas, 110
Gusterson, Hugh, 75, 142

Habermas, Jürgen, 166n10, 168n30
hacktivism, 146
Harley Davidson, 42
Harvard Business School Digital Initiative, 50, 141

Harvey, David, 10, 128, 142
Haven, Janet, 106
Haynes, Trevor, 72
healthcare, 105, 106–7, 146
Healy, Kieran, 6
hedonism, 3
Heilbroner, Robert, 4
Hellman, Jacob, 171n29
herding, 5, 84, 136
Hero, Peter, 113–14
heroic players, 14, 131
HeroX, 23, 25, 30–1, 34–41, 42,
    47–8, 133–4
hierarchies, 10–11, 27, 28, 31, 79,
    129, 133
Hill, Stephen, 166n10
Holmes, Seth, 171n27
housing crisis, 74
Howe, Jeff, 21, 29, 47, 61, 150n2
hub firms, 156n49
humanitarianism, 13
hurricanes, 26
Hyken, Shep, 81, 95, 145

Iansiti, Marco, 156n49
IBM, 10, 46
ideology
    changing spirits of capitalism, 7–11
    concept, 18–19
    convenience see convenience
    crowdsourcing competition model,
        22–7
    end of ideology, 82, 86, 97
    free market, 1–2, 27
    MarketWorld, 104–6, 107
    transhumanism, 1–2
    see also specific ideologies
Immelt, Jeffrey, 55–6
impact investing, 4, 11, 17, 36, 109,
    117–20, 132, 138–9
InboxDollars, 66, 68, 69, 70–1, 74–5,
    76, 77
India, 13
individualism, 3
inequality, 2, 7, 18, 29–30, 34, 41–2,
    61, 101, 102–4, 106, 109, 117,
    131–4, 139
InnoCentre, 32, 33
International Space Station, 24, 32
International Space University, 24

Jeffrey, Kyla, 38, 134
Jobs, Steve, 28
John, Nicholas, 140
Jordan, Tim, 161n32

Kaggle, 32, 33
Kalleberg, Arne, 31
Khan, Shanus, 116, 117
Knoll, Lisa, 36, 119
Kotler, Steven, 24–30, 100, 104, 118
Kumar, Dillip, 93–5, 96, 97, 105,
    136, 137
Kumar, Raj, 120, 121
Kurzweil, Ray, 23, 28

labor see workers
Lakhani, Karim
    case study, 55
    communities and, 43, 45–6
    community crowdsourcing and,
        47
    competitive crowdsourcing, 21–2,
        23, 31–3, 34, 41, 42, 52, 133,
        150n2, 156n49
    crowdsourcing, 50
    influence, 49, 50
    open-source movement and, 46,
        48
    terminology, 43
Le Bon, Gustave, 20–1, 44, 153n20
Le Guin, Ursula, 146
Lessig, Lawrence, 159n15
Letts, Christine, 111
liberal communists, 109, 138
Lifepoints, 66
Lindbergh, Charles, 24
Linux, 46
Local Motors, 56
Longitude Prize, 24
L'Oréal, 42
Lyft, 6

M–C–M, 2, 109, 125, 127, 127–8,
    139, 145
McChesney, Robert, 62, 135,
    150n18, 172n1
McGoey, Linsey, 110, 118, 120,
    138, 169n5, 169n7, 171n34,
    171n35
machine learning, 82, 87

Mahjong Solitaire, 71
Make Amazon Pay, 145
Mandeville, Bernard, 9
Mantilla, Steffa, 71–2
Marcuse, Herbert, 91–2
MarketWorld, 104–6, 107
Marx, Karl
    alienation, 143
    depravity and capitalism, 167n14
    exploitation, 82, 98
    freedom ideology and, 97
    hidden abode of factory
        production, 69–70, 78
    hypocrisy of industrial capitalism,
        60
    ideology and, 18, 97
    justifications of capitalism and, 23
    M–C–M, 2, 109, 125, 127, 127–8,
        139, 145
    moments, 17, 66
    monopolies, 40–1, 42
    overaccumulation, 54
    surplus labor, 5
    on technology, 144
    time theft, 17, 65–6, 77, 80, 136
    values, 61
    see also surplus
Maus, Marcel, 60, 125
Mayer-Schönberger, Viktor, 140
Meiggs, Brian, 67
Mejias, Ulises, 140
Mellos, Koula, 155n46
methodology, 15–16
Microsoft, 156n49
Mighty AI, 73
Mistplay, 66, 71–2
MIT, 51, 141
Monkey Bubbler Shooter, 71
monopolies, 40–1, 42, 145
morality
    bourgeois morality, 9
    competition and, 31
    ideology and, 18
    making moral agents, 120–4, 125,
        139
    moral economy, 98
    moral judgment, 6
    moral missions, 25
    moral obligations, 114
    philanthropy, 126

Morozov, Evgeny, 137
Mozilla Voice Technology Challenge,
    37
MTurk, 6, 85
Mycoskie, Blake, 53
mystification, 90–2

Nadeem, Shezad, 50
Napoleon, 24
NASA, 25, 32, 36, 37, 61
naturalization, 87–90, 96
negative reciprocity, 31, 33–4, 49–50,
    60, 133, 134
neoliberalism, 7, 103, 127, 131–2,
    138
networks
    age of flexible accumulation, 11
    benefits, 61
    competition crowdsourcing, 39–41
    digital capitalism, 5, 129
    information economy, 19
    new forms, 135
    wealth of networks, 18–19, 135
New Deal, 103
New Democrats, 111
New Media Underground Festival,
    50–1
new oil, 6, 40, 75
New Space, 24, 25
Nickell, Jake, 50–3
nomophobia, 79
nudging, 5, 84, 85, 86, 97, 136

open-source movement, 46, 48
Oracle, 121
organization man, 9, 11
outsourcing, 10, 12, 21, 129, 130,
    133–4
Outspell, 71

Page, Larry, 119
Paik, Jin, 48–9
Palihapitiya, Chamath, 72, 141
passion economy, 134
PayPal, 28, 68, 75, 100, 172n1
peasantry, 98
personal expression, 3, 134
philanthrocapitalism, 139
philanthropy see techno-philanthropy
Piketty, Thomas, 34

Pitney Bowes, 51
platform capitalism, 6, 34–41, 70
postmodernism, 128
poverty reduction, 27, 103, 105–6, 120
power asymmetries, 90, 93
Prahalad, Coimbatore Krishnarao, 105–6, 139
privacy
    convenience and, 90, 98, 140
    regulation, 145
    surrendering, 143
PrizeRebel, 66
Protestantism, 3, 13, 125
Puerini, Gianna, 88, 91, 92, 97, 136

Rasiel, Ethan, 107
Raymen, Thomas, 164n25
Reffell, Clive, 37
Rego, Mark, 140
Reich, Rob, 122
Reith, Gerda, 164n25
Ries, Eric, 55–6
robber barons, 11, 102, 103
Roberts, Tracy, 158n11
roboprocesses, 142
Rockefeller, John D., 102, 110
Roosevelt, Theodore, 102–3
Rosenblat, Alex, 59, 154n37
Ryan, William, 111

Sadowski, Jathan, 5, 6, 14, 26, 42, 133, 145, 173n4
Schiller, Dan, 4–5
Schor, Juliet, 29, 147n1
Schrauwen, Ben, 160n25
Schüll, Natasha Dow, 72–3
Schumpeter, Joseph, 150n2
Scott, James, 98
Scott, Mackenzie, 102
Second Gilded Age, 102
self-interest, 45
self-realization, 3, 134
Sennett, Richard, 132, 142–3
sharing economy, 49–50, 59, 60, 60–1, 135
Shirky, Clay, 159n16
Siemens, 42
Silicon Valley
    genius elite, 26–7, 28, 29, 41

spirit of digital capitalism, 11–16
startup culture, 111–12
Silicon Valley Social Venture Fund, 112–20, 139
Singularity University, 23, 141
Skoll, Jeffrey, 28, 113
smart people, 26–7, 133
smart technologies, 5, 26–7, 145
smartphone gaming apps
    assessment, 77–80
    blurring boundaries of work and leisure, 67, 70–3, 136
    free time or free labor, 77–80
    earning with apps, 67–70
    explosion, 66–7
    free time, 66–7, 136
    micro-tasks, 68
    multiplying moments, 73–7
    surplus value, 17, 65–80
Smith, Adam, 9
Smith, Oliver, 164n25
social contract, 41
social entrepreneurs, 35–6, 105, 109, 110, 117–20, 138–9
social finance, 154n30
social justice, 10
social responsibility, 10, 123, 128, 131
solidarity, 10
Solitaire Cube, 66, 71
Soper, Taylor, 68–9
Sorokin, Pitirim, 156n2
Space Poop, 25
space tourism, 24
Spare5, 66, 67–8, 69, 70, 73, 75, 76, 77
spirits of capitalism
    age of flexible accumulation, 3, 10–11
    changes, 7–11, 13–14
    digital capitalism see digital capitalism
    end of nineteenth century, 8–9
    Fordist era, 9–10
Srnicek, Nick, 6, 34, 39–40, 70, 164n34
Stephany, Alex, 60, 61
Stinson, Liz, 56
Stites-Clayton, Evan, 158n13
Stout, Noelle, 74
Sullivan, Oriel, 164n36

Sundararajan, Arjun, 63
Suri, Siddharth, 6, 85
Surowiecki, James, 21
surplus
  affective surplus, 134
  behavioral surplus, 5, 17, 82, 83–4, 85, 90–1, 97
  cognitive surplus, 26, 41, 54, 59, 133, 134
  crowdsourcing and, 61, 66
  emotional surplus, 54, 59
  smartphone gaming apps, 17, 65–80
  surplus labor, 5, 64, 65–6, 77–8, 84, 136
  time theft, 17, 65–6, 77, 80, 136
surveillance capitalism
  Amazon Go, 82–95, 136–7
  assessment, 95–9
  China, 13
  digital colonialism, 6
  naturalization, 87–90
  obfuscation and, 90–2
  prediction imperative, 5
  promotion, 93–5
  terminology, 70
  Zuboff, 17, 83–6, 92, 93, 95, 96–7, 98, 136
Survey Junkie, 66
Swagbucks, 66

Taps for Money, 66
Taylorism, 110
techno-philanthropy
  agendas, 106–7
  business of giving, 110–12
  economic strategies, 11
  free society and, 104–6, 132
  Giving Pledge, 120–4, 125–6, 139
  hyper-agents, 102–4, 106, 138–9, 143–4, 146
  impact investing, 4, 11, 36, 109, 117–20, 125, 132, 138–9
  maintaining the status quo, 109
  MarketWorld, 104–6, 107
  power of gift, 124–6
  Silicon Valley Social Venture Fund, 112–20
  social enterprise, 35–6, 100, 105, 109, 117–20, 138–9

spirit of the gift, 17, 99, 100–26
  techno-solutionism, 106–9, 137–8
techno-solutions, 94, 130, 137–8
Teespring, 158n13
Tencent, 156n49
Tepper, Alex, 56
Thatcher, Margaret, 131
Thiel, Peter, 28, 29, 33, 133, 172n1
Thiel Foundation, 28–9, 39
Thompson, John, 18, 41
Threadless T-shirt, 50–4, 55, 57
Tierney, Thomas, 95
Tom Shoes, 53
Tönnies, Ferdinand, 44–5, 59–60
TopCoder, 32, 33
Toscano, Joe, 140–1
transhumanism, 1–2
TreasureTrooper, 66
Turner, Bryan, 166n10
Turner, Fred, 15, 130
Tushman, Mike, 48–9

Uber, 6, 31

Valentine, David, 25
Veblen, Thorstein, 164n36
venture capitalism, 23, 25, 29, 34–5, 100, 110–11, 115
venture philanthropy, 109, 110–114, 118, 138, 141
Von Hippel, Eric, 150n2

Wallerstein, Immanuel, 173n5
Weber, Max, 3, 8, 13, 14, 15, 125, 131
Wexler, Mark, 21
Whole Earth Catalog, 130
Whyte, William, 9, 11
Wikipedia, 26, 61
Williams, Walter, 158n13
Winsor, John, 48–9
Wittel, Andreas, 7, 53
workers
  blurring boundaries of work and leisure, 67, 70–3
  free time or free labor, 77–80
  Carnegie on, 124
  commodification, 7, 53
  crowdsourcing and, 47, 49
  digital nomads, 6–7

workers (*cont.*)
  exploitation, 7, 82, 98
  flexible labor, 7, 12, 59
  free labor, 31–2, 34, 42, 49, 50,
    58, 62–3, 75, 77–80, 133,
    135
  ghost workers, 6, 85
  Maus on, 60
  outsourcing, 10, 12, 21, 129, 130,
    133–4
  precarity, 7, 11, 31, 59, 62–3, 66,
    73, 133, 134
  rights, 10
  smartphone gaming apps, 70–80

  surplus labor, 5, 64, 65–6, 77–8,
    84, 136
  time theft, 17, 65–6, 77, 80, 136

XPRIZE competitions, 26, 35, 133
XPRIZE Foundation, 23

Zana Africa, 107
Žižek, Slavoj, 106, 108–9, 138,
  170n13
Zubhoff, Shoshana, 5, 17, 69–70,
  82–6, 92, 93, 95, 96–7, 98,
  136
Zuckerberg, Mark, 28, 122–3